Substance, Style, and Strategy

Substance, Style, and Strategy

LEE A. JACOBUS

New York Oxford
OXFORD UNIVERSITY PRESS
1998

Oxford University Press

Oxford New York
Athens Auckland Bangkok Bogota Bombay
Buenos Aires Calcutta Cape Town Dar es Salaam
Delhi Florence Hong Kong Instanbul Karachi
Kuala Lumpur Madras Madrid Melbourne
Mexico City Nairobi Paris Singapore
Taipei Tokyo Toronto Warsaw

and associated companies in
Berlin Ibadan

Published by Oxford University Press, Inc.,
198 Madison Avenue, New York, New York, 10016
http://www.oup-usa.org
1-800-334-4249

Library of Congress Cataloging-in-Publication Data
Jacobus, Lee A.
Substance, style, and strategy/Lee A. Jacobus.
p. cm.
ISBN 0-19-507837-3
1. English language—Rhetoric. 2. English language—Style.
3. Report writing. I. Title
PE1408.J265 1998
808'.042—dc21 97-23048
CIP

Printing (last digit): 9 8 7 6 5 4 3 2 1

Printed in the United States of America
on acid-free paper

Contents

Preface

This book has resulted from my years of teaching advanced composition to students who recognized in themselves a need and a desire for more opportunity to write. Some of the students had professional goals in writing, such as those who expected to find work in law, teaching, publishing, magazines, broadcast journalism, and other such callings. Others recognized that they would have a better chance at finding interesting work—and keeping it—if they could write better. I had sometimes said in class that if they were very lucky, in later life someone would ask them to write down their opinion on an important issue and that the training they had in writing would help them make their thoughts of value.

Of course there are other than professional goals to worry about when it comes to writing. For one thing, writing is generally a lonely experience, and its most important reward may be in the fact that it permits the individual to express ideas, feelings, connections, and thoughts that were, in advance of the writing, essentially vague and felt rather than explicit and examinable. My approach to teaching writing is less connected with the anticipated professional goals of my students than it is with their anticipated delight in being able to put thoughts and feelings into effective prose. In other words, I recognize all too well that most students are career-driven when they enter an advanced writing course, but I also recognize that what the course has to offer is an intellectual development that transcends career and profession. At best, an advanced writing course offers refinement of the mind.

The structure of this book follows to some extent the structure of the course I developed for my students. The first chapter, "Developing a Personal Style," discusses the primary issues of subject, audience, style, and the writing process. Some of the common difficulties in writing show up here, and I offer some tips that usually work to help smooth out the difficulties. This chapter emphasizes the fact that there are precious few rules in writing that good writers do not break some of the time. It also emphasizes the fact that any tips for writers will work most of the time, but that no tip can be treated as universally true. Style is treated on the levels of individual words, sentences, and paragraphs, and some of the discussion centers on the analysis of useful examples. In addition to matters of style, this chapter discusses organizing, drafting, revising, and polishing an essay.

The second chapter, "Writing the Personal Essay," gives writers a chance to reflect on their own experiences and to understand how that experience can be transformed into interesting writing. The chapter treats diaries and journals, emphasizing their importance to most writers. Examples of journals from writers as diverse as Edward Weston and Anne Frank help students see the range and scope possible in the form. An extensive analysis of the style and structure of Richard Ford's "Accommodations" illustrates the ways in which the principles of the chapter can be put into action by the writer.

"Writing the Biographical Essay," the third chapter, moves the writer from the personal toward the communal and social, with a shift in focus toward biography. Our natural fascination with other people leads to writing about them. It also leads to the use of secondary sources, which is discussed in this chapter for the first time. Students are encouraged to write about people they know as well as about people unknown to them, but potentially fascinating. This chapter also further develops the narrative skills introduced in the previous chapter, with a discussion of chronological structure and its usefulness for writing about others. Using Joan Didion's discussion of Georgia O'Keeffe, the chapter illustrates the difference between making judgments and careful observations about someone and creating an encyclopedia entry about the person.

"Writing the Argumentative Essay," chapter 4, attempts, in nontechnical terms, to clarify the ways in which a position can be defended by the writer. The emphasis is on reasoning and claims as well as on evidence and judgment. Evan Connell's selection, "Were Custer's Men Brave?," illustrates some of the principles of argument as inquiry, carefully balancing evidence, probability, and supposition. The distinction between kinds of arguments is important in this chapter, which ends with an examination of the materials of a journalistic debate, a specialized form of argument. The chapter treats argument as a source of information and a process of inquiry as well as a means of persuasion. The principles of argumentative structure end the chapter.

"Writing the Familiar Essay," chapter 5, concerns the kinds of essays popular in journals, magazines, and newspapers and on the radio. These are the essays that meditate on everyday life, on landscape and social issues, on conundrums, paradoxes, and ordinary wonders. These essays sometimes combine personal writing, biography, and argument and sometimes omit them altogether. The chapter emphasizes the movement from the abstract to the concrete as well as from the concrete to the abstract. Writers such as Cynthia Ozick, Regina Barreca, and E. M. Forster demonstrate the range possible in this mode of writing. The resources of metonymy, metaphor, and image figure prominently in this part of the book.

Chapter 6, "Writing the Critical Essay," focuses on the modes of thinking that center on examination and evaluation. This chapter emphasizes critical approaches to texts, although the concept of *text* is enlarged to include visual art and film. The examples in the chapter move from William Wordsworth in poetry to Francis Bacon in the essay and Niccolò Machiavelli in politics. Heinrich Boll's short story, "The Laugher," provides an extended opportunity for examing the issues of assumption and biases as well as the distinctions between fact and opinion. The focus on evaluation is one of the key points of this chapter, which continually demonstrates the ways in which texts can be submitted to analysis. The point of the chapter is to help students make a good beginning at addressing complex texts.

"Appendix: The Materials of Research" may be consulted at any time in the course of working with this book. It is chapter length and aims to supplement all of the book's chapters. It provides useful directions for consulting print sources as well as modern sources of online research, such as Lexis-Nexis, CD-ROM searches of ERIC, the MLA bibliography, and other sources available in most college libraries. The chapter covers CD-ROM online databases and services and the use of the World Wide Web, and it includes a Lexis-Nexis electronic search sample. In addition, the chapter provides a thumbnail description of the proper methods of citation for a research essay. Most students in an advanced writing course will be familiar with much of the material in this chapter.

This book owes a great deal to several generations of students in my Advanced Writing course at the University of Connecticut. I owe much to those students who maintain contact with me and who have returned to tell me how useful the course was to them. Naturally, I owe much also to colleagues who have shared ideas about the ways in which the course ought to be taught and who have participated with me in the expectation that this course would make a difference in students' abilities as thinkers and writers.

Substance, Style, and Strategy

1

Developing a Personal Style

> I'll tell you what I like about writing. When I'm doing it, there's only the doing, the movement of my pen across the paper, the shaping of rhythms as I go, myself the rhythm, the surprises that jump up out of the words, from heaven, and I *am* doing this, and I am this doing, there is no other "I am" except for this doing across the paper, and I never existed except in this doing.
> I'll tell you what I hate about writing. Finishing it. It comes to an end. You can't come forever. When I'm finished, I can't remember what it was like inside the doing. I can't remember. When I'm not writing, I want to become the man with the brutal face.
> A sentence, a sentence, my family for a sentence.
>
> FRANK LENTRICCHIA, *THE EDGE OF NIGHT: A CONFESSION* (NEW YORK: RANDOM HOUSE, 1994), P. 7

The Writing Process

Frank Lentricchia, a well-known literary critic, describes an experience that most writers have: giving themselves over to the process of writing, but having little or no conscious awareness of what the process is or how it works. All advanced writers go through some version of what Lentricchia describes. The man with the brutal face is a man of action, the apparent opposite of a writer, and perhaps Lentricchia at rest.

Writers write. Most do not study writing or worry about it until they come to a point of being blocked—something that happens rarely. Those who study it suggest writing is a process that is continuously recursive, which means that writers constantly review their work for subject, organization, audience, and style. The writing process involves both moments of conscious choice and patterns of habit. The more you write, the more you refine your habits and your choices.

Some of the concerns involved in the writing process are:

- Narrowing your subject
- Considering your audience
- Finding material about your subject
- Organizing your material
- Refining your style
- Writing a first draft
- Revising
- Polishing
- Proofreading

Throughout this book, the writing process will be considered from many different points of view, but our first consideration is understanding style and how to develop it.

Narrowing Your Subject

Inexperienced writers say they could write their entire life story on one side of a three-by-five inch card, but those who write frequently have little trouble finding something to write about. If you are in a college course reading this book, you will have the added incentive of an instructor who can guide you to a subject. The first problem for an experienced writer is how to narrow a subject to fit a reasonable number of pages. The least experienced writer may imagine it possible to write the history of the world in five pages, while the most experienced writer will find it difficult to write the history of the last ten minutes in five pages.

The act of writing actually helps you discover what aspect of your subject needs development. Once you get under way, ideas will occur to you that will help you decide what to keep, what to omit, and how to focus on the most important points. At that point, you have begun the process of narrowing your subject.

The later chapters in this book reflect different kinds of writing projects: autobiography, biography, persuasion, meditative or reflective writing, and criticism. The appendix offers suggestions for research. In each kind of writing, the challenge will not be finding a subject so much as refining it and focusing on the aspects of the subject that will be most useful to you.

Choosing Your Audience

Some writers try to define their audience by asking certain questions: Who is my audience? Will my audience listen? Will what I say help them? Will it change their thinking? Once you have established whom you write for, you can decide how to present yourself. It is something like deciding how to dress for any given situation.

Decisions regarding your audience and your presentation are in some ways ethical in that they imply a matter of choice. In terms of ethical behavior, one chooses to act well or ill. In terms of writing, one chooses to express an idea in one way or another. An ethical style of writing involves an awareness of how one projects oneself to an audience and an awareness of one's own ethical position on any given subject. Consider, for example, the ethics that are expressed in the following sentences:

1. The homeless will always be among us; compassion calls us to their aid.
2. Government giveaways sure as hell won't solve the homeless problem.
3. Homelessness is the simple result of politics, crass politics.
4. Who wants to be homeless? More important, who wants to help them?
5. Insular poverty produces a permanent underclass who, in turn, feed the legions of the homeless hovering over every steam grate in our shivering cities.
6. Like fallen angels, the homeless clutch themselves into cardboard communities beneath overpasses, near shopping malls, hibernating in snowy hutches, virtually invisible under the noses of the very people who abhor them.
7. If the homeless won't help themselves, why should I worry about them?

You may see in these sentences more than just a projection of a personal attitude. You may see that some of these sentences do not reflect the tradition of charity supposedly at the heart of those who fashioned our Constitution. The notion of an ethical style implies the kinds of stylistic choices that you make in an effort to give power to your writing. It implies the ways in which you present yourself to your audience, and to an important extent the way you imagine yourself in relation to your subject matter.

If you examine the sample sentences, you can see that each postulates a different audience and presents a different stand on the part of the writer. In each of the sentences we can gauge both the nature of the audience and the ethical stance of the writer:

1. The audience is charitable and concerned about the plight of the homeless. The writer projects a deep concern, a personal response to a painful situation.
2. The audience is hostile to taxation, welfare, and government action to help the homeless. The writer expresses annoyance, sharing the audience's hostility to government.
3. The audience sees the homeless as less responsible for their plight than the politics that created it. The writer's view centers on a resentment of politics.
4. The audience is curious, uncommitted to the question of responsibility for the homeless. The writer is exploratory, open.
5. The formality of language implies an audience that has studied the subject. The position of the writer is definitive, scholarly, and absolute.
6. The audience is neutral toward the homeless. The writer is literary, critical, and to an extent accusing: a fallen angel is, after all, a devil.
7. The audience is openly hostile to the homeless. The writer also expresses hostility on the basis of a judgment about the homeless.

A further analysis of these sentences would produce more information about audience and writer, and your own reading of the sentences may uncover slightly different attitudes and expectations. But you can see that if the last writer—hostile to the homeless—

were to address the first audience—which sees the homeless in a favorable light—the writing would fail. The audience would be turned off almost immediately.

Implied in this, too, is another ethical issue. If a writer is hostile about a topic and addresses an audience that is favorable about the topic with an essay that does not fully express hostility, is the writer then ethical? The price of being ethical in such a situation is probably not being read. Should the writer "fudge" an ethical position in order to be read? Writers handle this question in a variety of ways. Is it better not to write than to make a false appeal to an audience? Most writers would say yes.

Finding Material About Your Subject

Finding good material can involve research, recollection, and/or analysis. Research sources such as journals, magazines, books, lectures, and reference materials can provide a great deal of information. Your own memory can provide information. Friends can make useful suggestions. Information gathered from these sources can help you focus on the main ideas that you wish to develop about your subject. But in the final analysis you need to decide what points you can make on the basis of the material you have at your command, then get to work with each point until you are satisfied that it works the way you wish it to work.

SPECIAL TECHNIQUES

Some writers depend on special techniques to explore a subject. They make a grid, either imaginary or on paper, and fill it in. For example, here is a simple grid built on the journalist's famous who-where-when-why-how technique applied to the problem of the homeless.

Journalist's technique   Subject: The Homeless

Who: Men, women, old and young, some children

When: Now, constantly for the last twenty years

Where: All over America, big towns, small towns

Why: Poverty, lack of subsidized housing, loss of jobs; mental instability; closing of public institutions

How: Under bridges; over steam grates; in cardboard boxes; in public buildings

Using this technique, you could write a brief piece on the homeless by beginning with the first item, *Who*, and finding out just who the homeless are. What are their ages, their backgrounds, their outlooks? You would want to attack the second item, *When*, by checking through newspaper files and searching the term *homeless* until you noticed a change, a time when the citations grow larger. Are there more homeless today than twenty years ago? The third item, *Where*, can also be researched, and you may want to discover whether homelessness is more or less prevalent in urban settings or in rural regions of the country. The fourth item, *Why*, is much more difficult to answer. Research or questioning would certainly provide many opinions, all of which are worth examining. The last item, *How*, leads you to explore how the homeless live, why some prefer the street to shelters, and what the risks of homelessness might be. Another "how" might be how the homeless became destitute.

The journalist's technique has served some writers well, but it is only one way to begin to explore a subject. The classical technique, a much older method, is designed to explore a subject from different points of view:

Classical technique   Subject: The Homeless

Definition: Who or what is your subject?
Your subject is the urban homeless defined as those who live in the city without work or the support of family or social services.

Comparison: How can your subject be usefully compared with things like or unlike it?
The homeless sit or lie in the streets while purposeful, successful, and busy people walk past and around them on their way to work.

Circumstance: What are the circumstances surrounding your subject?
They are vulnerable and at risk. Their health is poor, their sanitation is poor, and their prospects are bleak.

Cause and effect: What has caused your subject to be as it is and what are its effects?

Many of the homeless are out of work, down on their luck, and faced with the high cost of housing. Others are long-term victims of drugs, alcoholism, or mental disease. The homeless are seen by some as nuisances in public parks, buildings, and rest areas.

Possibility: What is or has been possible for your subject?

In the United States, the homeless formed hobo camps during the Great Depression of the 1930s. In the 1950s and 1960s society seems to have been able to prevent homelessness. Since then society seems to be either unable or unwilling to solve the problem of homelessness.

Testimony: What has been said by or about your subject?

In a major article in the *Atlantic Monthly*, one writer suggested that the existence of a permanent underclass is one major factor in the presence of a large number of homeless in the United States today. In one sense that means that the homeless cannot solve their problems on their own.

Obviously, there are overlaps among these categories. But taken separately, *Definition* would demand that you explain who the homeless are and why they are considered homeless. *Comparison* would permit you to look at what distinguishes the homeless from other people, perhaps also poor, who have not become homeless. *Circumstance* gives you the chance to study the lifestyle of the homeless. What is their routine, their ordinary day? *Cause and Effect* asks you to explore what caused them to become homeless and discuss what the effect of a large number of homeless people is on a society. *Possibility* permits you to ask why some homeless will not accept public assistance, or how it is possible in the wealthiest nation for there to be so many poor. You may also wish to explore the possibility of ending homelessness—what would it take? Has it ever been possible to avoid homelessness? *Testimony* would permit you to listen to what the experts say about the homeless and what the homeless themselves say about their situation.

The classical technique is extremely powerful. With some subjects it encourages you to develop material through research, but with other subjects it encourages you to develop material through personal exploration and reflection. Both the journalist's technique and the classical technique are flexible. For example, you could combine them and in a short essay develop ideas from every one of the nine items. Or, you could write a short essay using only one item, for example, *Circumstance*, to examine the circumstances of the homeless with an eye toward explaining how they live, how they survive in a hostile environment.

These techniques help you work up material for your subject and provide you with useful approaches. Most writers rely on a variety of methods. They might initially veer toward definition or cause and effect without being aware that they are doing so. On the other hand, being conscious of the method permits the writer to cover all the bases, get all the important information into the essay. In the journalistic technique, for example, the point is to account for each of the five items in order to cover the subject fully. The classical technique is more forgiving. One may account for only some of the items and still do a good job.

Organizing Your Material

Once you have material in note form, as early drafts, and/or in annotated photocopies (for quotations) to work up in your essay, you will need to organize what you have to say. No matter what organizational method you use, you will find it best to begin by listing the segments that you think will appear in what you write. List them in the order they come to you, like a shopping list, with each item representing something you wish to write about. If you have control over your material at an early stage, you might begin with a simple outline. After you have your list or outline made, begin to think about the order of presentation. There are several possibilities.

CHRONOLOGICAL ORDER

Chronological order starts at the beginning and goes to the end. An alternative is to start in the middle of things, then go back to the beginning and follow with the ending. You may also use the method popularized in films: the flashback. The flashback involves interrupting your narrative to tell what happened earlier. As with most devices, it is best to use it sparingly. Playing with the organization of your material in terms of time has a great many possibilities, as you will see when you read Richard Ford's "Accommodations" in chapter 2. Straight chronology is always effective, but the flexibility of flashback and reorganization of events to increase suspense is also powerful.

Spatial order

Spatial organization is another powerful method. If you narrate events in different cities, different locales, different rooms—then using the cities, rooms, or locales to organize your thoughts and ideas can help your readers visualize your material. Associating certain specific ideas or conclusions with specific locales can make your writing memorable.

Order of importance

If you have five points that you wish to make about your subject, rank them in order of importance. Then decide which is to come first, second, and so on. Imagine, for example, that you have five important points to make regarding the homeless. Rank them 1 to 5 and begin with 1. Go right on to 2, then 3, then 4, then 5. Another way is to begin with 2, the second most important point; go to 3, 4, and 5; then end with 1, the most important point. This is called Nestorian order. Its rationale is that the second most important point gets your reader's attention, but when you get to the end, your most important point will stay in the reader's memory and act as a convincer.

An Overview of Your Style

A detailed discussion of style follows, but for the purposes of establishing an overview, certain important aspects of style need to be treated here. First, your tone and attitude toward your material need to reflect your decisions about your audience and your own values. Your decisions regarding audience naturally affect your decisions about style. Your choice of words, the length and character of your sentences, and the structure of your paragraphs not only *affect* your style, they *are* your style. More will be said about this. For the moment, however, we list ten tips that will help you produce a vigorous style.

TEN TIPS FOR A VIGOROUS STYLE

1. Get to the point quickly.
2. Use strong verbs and avoid the verb "to be" as much as possible.
3. Use concrete nouns and name things specifically.
4. Avoid chains of prepositional phrases (as in: "bundles of papers in bags of leather from contented cows in peaceful pastures with signatures of men in positions of power").
5. Use modifiers (adjectives and adverbs) sparingly.
6. Connect descriptive passages to specific sensory experiences, such as sight, sound, smell, taste, touch.
7. Use language that explains itself or that is appropriate for your audience. Think complexly, but write simply.
8. Keep your sentences short, but say what you mean.
9. "Listen" to your sentences and make their rhythms functional and interesting.
10. Focus your paragraphs on a central idea and make them short but complete.

Writing a First Draft

The beauty of the first draft is its impermanence. Writers using a computer or word processor have an advantage in being able to print out and examine various drafts as they work, and then easily make changes.

The first draft should be experimental. You may take your ideas and organize them in ways that please you at the moment. You can play with your tone, with your word choice, and with any aspect of your style. You want to make your first draft as good as possible, but knowing that you have a chance to review and change your draft takes a great deal of pressure off the whole process of writing. You will profit from asking a friend to read it for you and make comments. (It helps to make a collaborative arrangement so that you can return the favor).

The Perfectionist Syndrome

The quest for perfection can be a curse for a writer. If you are afflicted with this curse, make a sign stating "The first draft need not be perfect" large enough for you to read when you begin writing.

Once the first draft is finished, let it sit for a time. Then go back and see if it makes good sense. Letting time pass helps you recognize passages that may be confusing. You knew what you meant when you wrote it, but today it is not so clear. Letting a draft sit for a while also helps you discover if you have omitted something essential to your argument.

Revising

Revision means looking at things again. It also means seeing them differently, and in writing it means making changes. "Revisioning" your first draft will involve thinking about your overall organization and deciding how well you have covered your subject and how well you have presented it to your audience. You may find that you left things out and need to provide segments that were missing.

Creating an outline of your first draft helps you see what you have, how you have organized it, and what is missing. Outlining takes many forms. If you have learned a useful method, then stick with it. One particularly effective method of outlining is to write a list of sentences consisting mainly of strong verbs and specific nouns. The point is to make each sentence represent one writing focus. Here is a sample outline of a brief essay on the homeless using this method:

- The homeless need help.
- Help means training, jobs, opportunity.
- Society dehumanizes the homeless.
- Dehumanizing the homeless makes them worthless.
- Local towns must raise society's consciousness about the homeless.
- Programs must emphasize the humanity of the homeless.

An outline of this kind can give you a good sense of what you want to say, what you need to know to say it, and how you ought to organize it. Its simplicity makes it very flexible. It works best when you use strong verbs, avoiding the verb "to be." Outlining your early drafts will help you produce a better version of your essay.

If you work on a computer, remember that revision works best on hard copy. You can see a full page at a time, and you can compare pages quickly.

Polishing

The polishing stage permits you to correct nagging mechanical problems. When you polish your draft, you edit out incorrect spelling, weak or grammatically poor sentences, and mechanical errors.

TIPS ON POLISHING YOUR PROSE

1. Check for agreement of subjects and verbs.
2. Check for agreement of pronouns and their referents.
3. Edit out use of the passive voice.
4. Weed out the verb "to be" in all its forms.
5. Edit "down": avoid wordiness, repetition.
6. Edit out run-on sentences.
7. Check for sentence fragments.
8. Edit out faulty use of semicolons and colons.
9. Check for omission of the apostrophe in possessives.

All of the problems in the box will figure in our discussion from time to time. If you feel unsure about any of them, review them in a handbook of grammar and usage. As an advanced writer, it may be enough for you to have such a checklist to consult during revision.

Proofreading

Finally, the last go-through before you let your work out of your hands should involve a careful proofreading. Using the spell checker on a word processing program is not enough. The spell checker cannot tell the difference between "one" and "won," "your" and "you're," or "led" and "lead." Your eyes are the only reliable final judges of accuracy and clarity.

Some writers insist that they cannot adequately proof their own work. If this is the case with you, you may wish to make a collaborative arrangement with a friend for proofing each other's work, However you set things up, keep in mind that everything you write should be proofed before it leaves your hand. It is not just a courtesy; it is a responsibility.

Matters of Style

Whenever you write a sentence, you have many choices in shaping your thoughts. Each differs in significance and in effect. However mild an alteration of meaning, every choice you settle on contributes toward your style. Stylistic choices reveal your capacity for thought and feeling. Education, experience, reflection, and sensibility come into play with every conscious decision about how to say what you want to say. Be satisfied for the moment that your style reveals certain personal qualities, but that you control what is revealed in ways that help you achieve your goals as a writer. You are not a victim of your style, nor do you have only one style.

Audience

Every writer has a range of styles appropriate for differing audiences. Were you to write a letter to fourth graders on the subject of ecology, you would make some stylistic choices that might not work for an audience of college students. Fourth graders may not understand "ecology," and many other concepts and words your peers know and understand may be outside their experience. The more you know about your audience, the more careful and intelligent your stylistic choices. If you want to be informative, use language and ideas appropriate to your audience's background and interest in your subject.

When you want to stir your audience's emotions, your stylistic choices may become more poetic: you may use images, metaphors, careful and pointed description, all for effect. Certain kinds of language, including technical language, formal language, slang, and profanity, will affect the emotional responses of your audience. When arguing a position, you must decide whether it is necessary to excite a specific emotional response, and then make your stylistic choices accordingly.

Frankly, the degree to which you excite your audience's emotions is a touchy issue. On the one hand, writers may justifiably appeal to the emotions of an audience on behalf of a worthy cause:

helping famine victims, earthquake and flood victims, the homeless, battered wives, any group that suffers and is in pain. Appeals for money for such groups often include a "case history" of an individual, with all the details of that individual's pain and difficulties. It is a stylistic choice to describe the conditions of pain of an individual rather than to list statistics and columns of numbers that reveal the extent of a disaster or a situation that we could remedy with our contributions. Some writers have a gift that helps them make the desperate situation live in the reader's imagination, knowing that when the writing transcends the abstraction of statistics it will not only affect the emotions, but move the reader to respond appropriately.

James Baldwin: An Appeal to Emotion

James Baldwin gave vent to considerable anger in the following paragraph describing the construction of housing projects in Harlem. His description was so emotionally stirring that residents of Riverton protested loudly, claiming that he must be talking about another project nearby. His appeal to emotion was successful.

> The projects in Harlem are hated. They are hated almost as much as policemen, and this is saying a great deal. And they are hated for the same reason: both reveal, unbearably, the real attitude of the white world, no matter how many liberal speeches are made, no matter how many lofty editorials are written, no matter how many civil-rights commissions are set up.
>
> The projects are hideous, of course, there being a law, apparently respected throughout the world, that popular housing shall be as cheerless as a prison. They are lumped all over Harlem, colorless, bleak, high, and revolting. The wide windows look out on Harlem's invincible and indescribable squalor: the Park Avenue railroad tracks, around which, about forty years ago, the present dark community began; the unrehabilitated houses, bowed down, it would seem, under the great weight of frustrations and bitterness they contain; the dark, the ominous schoolhouses from which the child may emerge maimed, blinded, hooked, or enraged for life; and the churches, churches, block upon block of churches, niched in the walls like cannon in the walls of a fortress. Even if the administration of the projects were not so insanely humiliating (for example: one must report raises in salary to the management, which will then eat up the profit by raising one's rent; the management has the right to know who is staying in your apartment; the management can ask you to leave, at their discretion), the projects would still be hated because they are an insult to the meanest intelligence.
>
> Harlem got its first private project, Riverton—which is now, naturally, a slum—about twelve years ago because at that time Negroes were not al-

lowed to live in Stuyvesant Town. Harlem watched Riverton go up, therefore, in the most violent bitterness of spirit, and hated it long before the builders arrived. They began hating it at about the time people began moving out of their condemned houses to make room for this additional proof of how thoroughly the white world despised them. And they had scarcely moved in, naturally, before they began smashing windows, defacing walls, urinating in the elevators, and fornicating in the playgrounds. Liberals, both white and black, were appalled at the spectacle. I was appalled at the liberal innocence—or cynicism, which comes out in practice as much the same thing. Other people were delighted to be able to point to proof positive that nothing could be done to better the lot of the colored people. They were, and are, right in one respect: that nothing can be done as long as they are treated like colored people. The people in Harlem know they are living there because white people do not think they are good enough to live anywhere else. No amount of "improvement" can sweeten this fact. Whatever money is now being earmarked to improve this, or any other ghetto, might as well be burnt. A ghetto can be improved in one way only: out of existence.

Baldwin is known as a powerful stylist. His audience is largely white and liberal, although his early readers were African-American and in many cases residents of Harlem. His description of the hopelessness of the ghetto, the contempt of the society that could construct such a place, hit home for his audiences in 1960. Today, audiences will also react emotionally to this passage, and given the fact that almost forty years have passed without conditions changing substantially, the responses may be even more intense than they were when Baldwin wrote the piece.

Baldwin uses several forms of repetition at the beginning of this sample. He repeats "hated" three times as a means of emphasis. Hate is a powerful emotion. He also uses structural patterns, as in the three clauses beginning "no matter how many." This particular pattern, called parallel structure, repeats the same form (a qualifier, a subject, and a verb) for emphasis. Like most special stylistic devices, it must be used cautiously. Baldwin is careful not to overdo it.

ABRAHAM LINCOLN: A MAN OF MANY STYLES

Sometimes you will want to use a formal style, for example, in applying for a job. Sometimes you will need to be firm or even curt, as in replying to an insult or giving advice to someone you consider a pest. Sometimes you will want to be casual and relaxed, as when writing a humorous piece for a newspaper. Circumstances will dictate your stylistic choices more often than not.

The following three examples from the writings of Abraham Lincoln show that he thought carefully about how he expressed his ideas.

Brusque style

During the early phases of the Civil War, General McClellan complained to Lincoln that his horses were worn out. Since Lincoln had sent McClellan almost eight thousand fresh horses and McClellan's army had been out of contact with the enemy for six weeks, Lincoln lost his patience. He sent this telegram:

> Washington City, D. C. Oct. 24, 1862
>
> Majr. Genl. McClellan
>
> I have just read your despatch about sore tongued and fatigued horses.
>
> Will you pardon me for asking what the horses of your army have done since the battle of Antietam that fatigue anything?

After receiving McClellan's wounded reply, Lincoln apologized for being so curt, but he reminded McClellan that his original dispatch was deeply discouraging and that it had damaged Lincoln's hopes for a successful campaign.

Direct, forceful style

Long before he became president, Lincoln received a request from his stepbrother, John D. Johnston, for eighty dollars, a considerable sum in 1848. Johnston said the money would get him out of debt and help him get a fresh start. Lincoln, however, realized that giving him the money was not the answer. Lincoln managed to get the essence of his thought into the first paragraph of his letter:

> Your request for eighty dollars I do not think it best to comply with now. At the various times when I have helped you a little, you have said to me, "We can get along very well now" but in a very short time I find you in the same difficulty again. Now this can only happen by some defect in your *conduct*. What that defect is, I think I know. You are not *lazy*, and still you *are* an *idler*. I doubt whether since I saw you, you have done a good whole day's work, in any one day. You do not very much dislike to work; and still you

> do not work much, merely because it does not seem to you that you could get much for it. This habit of uselessly wasting time, is the whole difficulty; and it is vastly important to you, and still more so to your children that you should break this habit. It is more important to them, because they have longer to live, and can keep out of an idle habit before they are in it, easier than they can get out after they are in.

Here Lincoln is direct and forceful. He does not use imagery or metaphor, and he avoids ambiguity. Later in the letter, Lincoln urges Johnston to go to work for someone and begin saving his money. To show that he is willing to help, Lincoln offers to give Johnston one dollar to match each dollar Johnston earns by honest labor. This must have been a difficult letter to write.

Eloquent style

Lincoln also could be supremely eloquent. His "Address Delivered at the Dedication of the Cemetery at Gettysburg" is one of the most memorable of American speeches. Its brevity is owing in part to Lincoln's awareness that Edward Everett, who spoke before him, would hold forth for more than an hour.

> Four score and seven years ago our fathers brought forth on this continent, a new nation, conceived in Liberty, and dedicated to the proposition that all men are created equal.
>
> Now we are engaged in a great civil war, testing whether that nation, or any nation so conceived and so dedicated, can long endure. We are met on a great battle-field of that war. We have come to dedicate a portion of that field, as a final resting place for those who here gave their lives that that nation might live. It is altogether fitting and proper that we should do this.
>
> But, in a larger sense, we can not dedicate—we can not consecrate—we can not hallow—this ground. The brave men, living and dead, who struggled here, have consecrated it, far above our poor power to add or detract. The world will little note, nor long remember what we say here, but it can never forget what they did here. It is for us the living, rather, to be dedicated here to the unfinished work which they who fought here have thus far so nobly advanced. It is rather for us to be here dedicated to the great task remaining before us—that from these honored dead we take increased devotion to that cause for which they gave the last full measure of devotion—that we here highly resolve that these dead shall not have died in vain—that this nation, under God, shall have a new birth of freedom—and that government of the people, by the people, for the people, shall not perish from the earth.
>
> November 19, 1863

Commentators have noted how dull it would have been to say, "Eighty-seven years ago," as opposed to Lincoln's "Four score and seven years ago." Lincoln chose an indirect but interesting way of denoting the time. His choice echoes the Bible's "four score and ten," the normal life span of a man, an appropriate echo for an address at a cemetery. Lincoln, like Baldwin, also chose specific forms of repetition, such as in "we can not dedicate—we can not consecrate—we can not hallow—this ground"; the word "dedicate" used six times; "that" clauses used three times in the last few lines; and the memorable repetition of "people" in "government of the people, by the people, for the people" at the end.

Style: Words and Sentences

What you write about and what you think about your subject will definitely affect your style, but every decision about style will come down to your choice of words, sentence patterns, and later your paragraph structure. As you write and revise, you make many choices and many changes in each of these areas. Looking closely at how other writers make these choices can help you in your own decisions.

THREE CONSIDERATIONS FOR STYLE

1. Word choice—formal, casual, technical, or poetic
2. Sentence choice—short, long, loose, or tightly structured
3. Paragraph choice—short, long, loose, or tightly structured

Word Choices

Unusual word choices often delight us as readers. The great French writer Gustave Flaubert became famous for spending hours searching for the right word in a sentence. Most of us are not quite so compulsive, but choosing strong words will always make sentences more interesting to a reader. Yet, it is important not to hunt through the thesaurus or strain all morning to find a fancy word where a plain word will do. The point is to find a good word, and then put it to work.

In the following paragraph, by Wendy Wasserstein writing about her friendships with women, a number of words are italicized to isolate them for our examination.

> What I have constantly been afraid to acknowledge, however, is the difficulty of sustaining these friendships. Perhaps I never speak about *soured* female relationships because men are always so ready to portray women as competitive, jealous *felines*. Furthermore, men claim to have the joys of male bonding on canoe trips and hunting *sprees*, while women are relegated to gossiping in car pools. I have always felt I was betraying my sex by uttering even a passing thought of criticism. In my mind, if I can't maintain a female friendship, which should be warm and supportive, then I must be not only a competitive and jealous *wench*, but also politically incorrect.
>
> Wendy Wasserstein, "The Ties That Wound," from *Between Friends*, ed. Mickey Pearlman. Boston: Houghton Mifflin, 1994, p. 109.

The italicized words are interesting because they seem unexpected or colorful in context, but in looking at this selection we need to see that the uncommon words are effective only in contrast with the common words and expressions that surround them, for example, "male bonding," "warm and supportive," and "politically incorrect," all in very common use in the 1990s. The italicized words add a bit of spice by evoking powerful associations. For example, "soured" introduces our experience with soured milk. Milk, like friendship, is something essential to growth and life, but repugnant when it goes bad. "Felines" is a formal way of saying "cats," but it also includes tigers and lions, thereby intensifying the comparison with women. "Sprees" seems inappropriate for describing the activity of hunting; Wasserstein's implication is that hunting may be inappropriate. "Wench" is associated with an age in which women were sometimes spoken of with contempt by men.

Many other word choices in this paragraph are also effective, such as "sustaining," "portray," "relegated," "uttering," and "competitive." All these words are carefully thought out and all work together to make this a well-crafted and memorable paragraph.

Always look for opportunities to improve your word choices. Some simple rules are listed in the box text.

GENERAL RULES THAT SOMETIMES WORK FOR WORD CHOICE

1. Aim for direct, simple prose and choose everyday words.
2. When you choose an unusual or striking word, decide what effect you wish the word to have on your reader.
3. Look for opportunities to use strong verbs in place of actionless verbs or the verb "to be."
4. Use adjectives and adverbs lightly. Make them precise and descriptive.
5. If you rely on a thesaurus to help avoid repetition, look up the word you choose in a dictionary. Not all words in a thesaurus are interchangeable.
6. Examine the entire context in which your words reside; don't be fancy for no reason.

Keep in mind that simplicity is a virtue and that unusual words flavor your writing much as pepper flavors eggs. Consider the examples that follow. Each seems to illustrate the suggestions listed in the box.

> My first notebook was a Big Five tablet, given to me by my mother with the sensible suggestion that I stop whining and learn to amuse myself by writing down my thoughts.
>
> Joan Didion, "On Keeping a Notebook," from *Slouching Toward Bethlehem*. Copyright © 1965, Farrar, Straus, and Giroux. The Wallace Literary Agency.

Didion's choice of words is simple and direct. She refers to her "Big Five tablet" by its proper name. Even if we have never seen the precise product, we are familiar with similar ones. The expression "sensible suggestion" connects with a mother's role, and the reference to "whining" relates to a bored child. Didion's style is marked by a directness and honesty of expression. It is also marked by a large number of action words—"given," "stop," "learn," and "writing."

The following example, from a writer who spent his life as an academic and wrote numerous works on teaching, is a little more formal. Jacques Barzun's audience was likely to be more interested in arguing for or against him than Joan Didion's.

> The once proud and efficient public school system of the United States—especially its unique free high school for all—has turned into a wasteland where violence and vice share the time with ignorance and idleness, besides serving as battleground for vested interest, social, political, and economic.
>
> Jacques Barzun, "The Wasteland of American Education," page 1 of Preface, from *Teacher in America*, Liberty Press/Library Classics of Indianapolis. Copyright 1980 by Jacques Barzun.

Barzun chooses simple adjectives—"proud and efficient"—to describe what public schools once were. The important thing about the adjectives is that they are clear and direct. In describing public school as a "wasteland," Barzun uses a particularly strong metaphor derived from modern literature. It suggests hopelessness and despair. Terms such as "violence and vice" and "ignorance and idleness" rely on alliteration—the repetition of the same letter or sound in each word—for effect. The alliteration sets the words apart and helps emphasize their meaning. These words are nouns, the names of qualities, but Barzun puts a special spin on them because they actually stand for something else: people who are violent or vicious, people who are ignorant and idle. In this case, Barzun is simple on the surface, but somewhat more complex beneath the surface. Unlike Joan Didion, Barzun does not use many action words. Barzun's strength is in his nouns and descriptive words.

The difference in style between Joan Didion and Jacques Barzun in these excerpts must also be accounted for by the differences in their reasons for writing. Didion writes a memoir, which is personal, informal, and to an extent intimate. Barzun writes a public document, which is formal and academic. Our reaction to each will differ considerably.

This discussion of the use of words is meant to sensitize you to the issues of choice in your own writing. Observing other writers' choices is one small part of the study of writing.

Sentence Choices

Today's writers differ in one important way from those who were popular a hundred years ago: modern sentences are much shorter. Modern writing is also much more informal, and the reasons for that are probably evident in the way we now dress, the way we communicate by telephone, the way we relate to one another in increasingly casual fashion. In other words, our styles of writing are tied into our general styles of life.

Popular writers—in magazines and newspapers—almost always prefer to break up a long sentence into two or three short ones. Newspaper writers and editors, because of the newspaper's narrow columns, are especially concerned with avoiding lengthy sentences that make the writing look too dense and uninviting.

What we refer to when we mention a writer's style will always include the writer's approach to sentences. Writers who use long sentences much of the time, or short sentences most of the time, mark their style with these choices. Here are two examples.

> It is now theoretically possible to recreate an identical creature from any animal or plant, from the DNA contained in the nucleus of any somatic cell. A single plant root-tip cell can be teased and seduced into conceiving a perfect copy of the whole plant; a frog's intestinal epithelial cell possesses the complete instructions needed for a new, same frog. If the technology were further advanced, you could do this with a human being, and there are now startled predictions all over the place that this will in fact be done, someday, in order to provide a version of immortality for carefully selected, especially valuable people.
>
> Lewis Thomas, first paragraph from "On Cloning a Human Being," from *The Medusa and the Snail*. Copyright ©1974 etc. by Lewis Thomas. Viking Penguin, Inc.

This example is by a scientist famous for communicating with a general audience. Thomas understands his audience, respects its intelligence, and develops his thoughts in ways appropriate to the matter at hand. None of his sentences is so extensive as to produce unusual difficulties for those interested in his subject. You would expect this kind of writing in a popular scientific journal or in a book on scientific subjects. As a test of the effectiveness of the writing you might ask whether, after reading this opening paragraph, you would be interested in continuing. Lewis Thomas did not know that a sheep would be cloned in 1996, but he would not have been surprised if he were told about it.

The second example is the opening paragraph of an essay on writing by Annie Dillard, famous as a meditative essayist.

> It is early spring. I have a temporary office at a state university on the West Coast. The office is on the third floor. It looks down on the Square, the enor-

> mous open courtyard at the center of campus. From my desk I see hundreds of people moving between classes. There is a large circular fountain in the Square's center.
>
> Annie Dillard, first paragraph from "Singing with the Fundamentalists." Copyright ©1985 by Annie Dillard and Blanche C. Gregory, Inc.

Here the sentences are very short. Dillard's thoughts are clear, but from this very brief sample one cannot know how she will develop things. As it turned out, she observed a group of people singing near the fountain and went to hear them. But from this opening paragraph one gets only a sense of anticipation and perhaps a bit of restlessness. The brisk short sentences are like a prize fighter's light jabs. They set things up. They do not finish them off.

If a writer uses a complicated sentence structure—combining several independent clauses with various kinds of dependent clauses and various phrases—the choice to do so will qualify in part the style. Naturally, the subject of the essay will affect any decisions on sentence complexity. The same is true if a writer uses simple, relatively brief sentences. We may not always be conscious of what makes us feel that a style is recognizable or memorable, but it can often be the length and complexity of sentences as much as the choice of words.

Writers will sometimes veer toward longer sentences because their ideas take time to develop and complex structures match the complexity of their thought. On the other hand, many writers can think very subtly and still use surprisingly short sentences. They achieve such brevity by breaking the longer ideas into manageable parts. If writers consciously regard style on the level of the sentence (and not all writers do), they may aim not just to write long or short sentences, but to achieve balance by matching a short sentence with one or two longer sentences. Variety, not just for its own sake but for the sake of clarity and for the power of effect, can make most writing more interesting,

Three Writers and Their Sentence Choices

The following examples are the first three sentences from essays by very different modern writers. The sentences reflect a number of stylistic decisions—word choices, use of distinctive rhythms, and special descriptive ways of looking at the world of concrete things. For the moment, let us concentrate on the effect of the length and relative complexity of the sentences.

> I am listening to *The Doors' Greatest Hits*. It is Abby's album. She bought it last week, along with something called *Scary Monsters, Super Creeps* by David Bowie, and I was amused that she would spend her carefully hoarded babysitting money on the songs that she heard while she was cutting her teeth and tottering from couch to coffee table to chair and riding on her father's shoulders in peace marches on the commons of all the towns around Boston.
>
> Nancy Mairs, "Shape," in *Carnal Acts*, Harper & Row, 1991, p. 19

> I always expected to meet my father on the street, probably downtown, because I imagined him wandering lost in a daze for years across Europe, through Africa, up South America, across the States, and finally some day standing at a streetlight down at 10th and Magee wondering which way to go now. I knew we would stop and stare at each other, drawn by some deep instinct that was a father and his boy—no matter he'd only seen a picture of me one month old, and I a bunch of worn photographs of him taken before my lifetime. I knew he would be changed; the war and the years of wandering would have stolen his handsome youth.
>
> James Tate, "The Route as Briefed," from *The Autobiographical Eye*, The Ecco Press, 1992, p. 210. Copyright 1982 by *Antaeus*.

> Goering and Hitler displayed an almost maudlin concern for the welfare of animals; Stalin's favorite work of art was a celluloid musical about Old Vienna, called *The Great Waltz*. And it is not only dictators who divide their thoughts and feelings into unconnected, logic-tight compartments; the whole world lives in a state of chronic and almost systematic inconsistency. Every society is a case of multiple personality and modulates, without a qualm, without even being aware of what it is up to, from Jekyll to Hyde, from the scientist to the magician, from the hardheaded man of affairs to the village idiot.
>
> Aldous Huxley, "Madness, Badness, Sadness," from *Collected Essays*, Harper & Row, 1958, p. 299.

Perhaps the first thing one notices about these examples is that in just three sentences each writer communicates a remarkable amount of information. The second thing one notices is that they do it in different ways. Nancy Mairs uses a popular method for opening a paragraph: a short sentence followed by an even shorter sentence, then a long inclusive sentence that contains much detail and fills in the spaces. We learn a good deal from the writer's daughter's taste in music. The Doors were popular in the early 1970s, so

Abby in 1990 is on a nostalgia trip. (Later in the paragraph Nancy Mairs makes that observation.) The second sentence establishes that the album is not one of the writer's own, original oldies. It's new. And the third sentences clarifies the point, telling us that Abby bought it with her own earnings and that she heard the album, or many of the pieces on it, when she was an infant. The third sentence gives us so much information that by the time we are finished reading it, we know a great deal about Abby, her father, and her mother, who is writing the story. The third sentence works in part because of the balance of its segments, all introduced with "-ing" words: "cutting her teeth and tottering from couch to coffee table to chair and riding on her father's shoulders." The word choices are not exotic, and Mairs includes a certain amount of precision in naming concrete objects in the house and locating the family in the Boston area. The precision—we know the album, who owns it, when she originally heard it, and much more—helps make these three sentences work for us. Even more important to observe is that there is nothing especially magical about this writing. Virtually any writer could use the same method and produce a similar piece of prose.

James Tate is well known as a poet. Whereas Nancy Mairs wants you to understand what she says and how she feels, Tate is intent on expressing his own sense of things in an effort to understand himself. Clarity is not necessarily his uppermost thought. Thus, his sentences are uniformly long: fifty-two, forty-seven, and nineteen words respectively. (Mairs's third sentence is sixty-eight words long but it is balanced by the first two exceptionally brief sentences.) Fifty or sixty words is unusually long for a sentence in modern English. However, when we encounter such sentences we know the writer expects to communicate with a well-read and thoughtful audience. That seems to be the case with Tate. His first sentence describes a hypothetical father who seems confused and possibly even lost—which explains Tate's position in life as a person who does not know his father. For all Tate knows, his father could be in Africa, Europe, South America, or the United States. Each could know the other only from old photographs. Yet, Tate somehow hopes that there is a mystical connection between father and son that would identify them to each other should they somehow meet.

Tate's first sentence begins by saying he always expected to meet his father on the street. Where? Downtown. Where has his father been? Could be any continent. Where would he meet him? At 10th and Magee. Each segment of this and the following sentences is brief, but all are coherent and clear. Coherence, or connectivity, makes all the difference in intelligibility in these long, thoughtful sentences. What they ultimately reveal is the fantasy of a small boy who longs to know his father. As the essay continues, we learn that Tate's father was a bomber pilot shot down in action, but never accounted for. Thus, anything was possible in a child's imagination.

Aldous Huxley's concern for ideas presses him toward long, carefully balanced sentences. He does not use Mairs's technique of contrasting very short with very long sentences, nor do his sentences show quite as much variety as those of James Tate. The three sentences have an intelligible progression, moving from specific people, "Goering and Hitler," through the more generalized "dictators," all the way to "Every society."

Huxley's skill in these sentences is extraordinary. We can all learn something from studying his writing, for example, this progression from the specific to the general, a progression that could just as easily be reversed from the general to the specific. In the third sentence Huxley uses the parallel structure of three phrases:

1. from Jekyll to Hyde
2. from the scientist to the magician
3. from the hardheaded man of affairs to the village idiot

Each of these is grammatically the same (a phrase with nouns, but no verbs) and logically the same in that each phrase proposes opposites that are in many ways linked. Parallelism does not need imaginative genius. Parallelism needs only attention to structural details.

Sentence Rhythms

Rhythm is subtle, whether in music or writing. The qualities of rhythm that we can profitably discuss in relation to sentences are two: emphasis and pacing. Emphasis is achieved by placing words in such a way as to receive an accent in normal speech. This may involve the use of rhyme, alliteration (the repetition of letters at the beginning, middle, or end of words), or repetition of words or word endings. Pacing is achieved by punctuation or its absence, or by balancing short and long words with one another.

The extraordinary thing about rhythmic sentences is that they seem as if they were destined to be expressed as they are. For example, the first sentence of "The Gettysburg Address" seems inevitable. The emphases are here marked with accents:

> Fóur scóre and sevén yeárs agó our fáthers bróught fórth on thís cóntinent, a néw natión,
> concéived in Líberty, and dédicáted to the própositíon that áll mén are creáted équal.

The rhyming of "four" and "score" intensifies the emphasis on those words, as does the alliteration of the "f" sound in "Four," "fathers," and "forth." A more subtle alliteration of the "n" sound in "seven," "on," "continent," and especially "new nation," "proposition" and "men" gives even more emphasis to those words. The pacing of the first thirteen words is swift, with no interruption until the commas that force us to slow down for "a new nation, conceived in Liberty."

Lincoln breaks a number of writing rules here. For one thing, this sentence is the entire first paragraph of the address. For another thing, the commas he uses are not really justified by grammatical needs. They serve only to pace the sentence. Go back over it and read it with attention to the balance of longer words, such as "proposition" (which implies his argument is open to examination), and shorter words, such as "men." Then go on to read the next sentences in the "Gettysburg Address." What such a reading reveals is that Lincoln was very careful to adjust his emphases and pacing. He uses the techniques mentioned above in the most famous moments of the "Address": "The world will little note, nor long remember what we say here, but it can never forget what they did here" and "that government of the people, by the people, and for the people, shall not perish from the earth." Compare the "Address" with the rhythms in Lincoln's letter to John Johnston. Lincoln chose consciously the rhythms of his prose.

Of course, we expect careful rhythmic effects from famous

speeches. Indeed, if we do not get them we often tune out. Leaders are sometimes felt to be charismatic on the basis of their delivery of what begins as written prose. John F. Kennedy's famous line, "Ask not what your country can do for you, ask what you can do for your country," is a memorable example that adds the use of careful repetition to achieve emphasis. This particular technique is called chiasmus: the first part of the sentence follows "country" with "you," while the second part reverses the order, following "you" with "country." Frequently, leaders who have a difficult time hearing and producing rhythmic emphasis and dramatic pacing in their speeches are thought to be dull and uninteresting.

Aldous Huxley did not intend the paragraph used as an example as a speech, but he nonetheless took great pains to intensify the rhythms of his prose. Consider just the last sentences:

> Every society is a case of multiple personality and modulates, without a qualm, without even being aware of what it is up to, from Jekyll to Hyde, from the scientist to the magician, from the hardheaded man of affairs to the village idiot.

You may place accents where you feel they would normally fall and you will find that they come on important parts of important words. Huxley uses alliteration in the "m" of "multiple," "modulates," and "qualm." He uses repetition in the two "without" phrases and three "from" phrases. Finally, he uses balance by opposing terms: "Jekyll and Hyde," "scientist" and "magician," and "hardheaded man of affairs" and "the village idiot." The effect is quite different from Lincoln's, but then so is the way Huxley uses the basic techniques.

You may perform a similar analysis on any example of prose in this book. You will see that writers achieve a wide variety of effects by using the same basic techniques. The rhythm and pacing of their sentences is rarely accidental. Usually, writers aim to produce strong rhythmic effects. Most of us can do the same, but the first step is to understand the techniques that impart emphasis and movement to a sentence. Their application may be done at any stage of the process. The early drafts of the "Gettysburg Address" show that Lincoln's best rhythmic prose came in the first draft. Frank Lentricchia, in the headnote to this chapter, comments on "the shaping of rhythms as I go, myself the rhythm," but other writers defer the polishing of their rhythmic effects until early stages of revision.

Paragraph Choices

Paragraphs offer more opportunities for stylistic differentiation, although most of us regard style as being more observable in the sentence and most obvious in word choice. However, the paragraph is as distinctive an ingredient of style in writing as any other observable element.

There are no set rules for paragraphing—at least none is observable if you judge by what writers are doing in the popular press. Some rules can be helpful, however.

RULES THAT SOMETIMES WORK FOR PARAGRAPHS:

1. Paragraphs should have a minimum number of sentences, usually three.
2. Paragraphs must have a topic sentence.
3. Paragraphs develop only one idea or topic.
4. Long paragraphs should be avoided.

As an advanced writer, you know that rules are made to be broken. But that is not to say that these rules are useless. Sometimes it is good to avoid a one-sentence paragraph—it can sound too brisk and implies a lack of penetration and analysis. Sometimes, or perhaps most of the time, it is good to have a topic sentence. But the awful fact is that when you look closely at a professional writer's work, you will see that the topic sentence is often missing. In that case, we sometimes say it is implied, and perhaps that is true. But whether we want to call it implied or not, it is obvious that good writers can get along without topic sentences much of the time. Likewise, it is not a bad idea to develop only one idea in a paragraph, but frankly, the chance of developing several ideas often arises and sometimes doing so even characterizes the writing of professionals. Finally, many good writers—Aldous Huxley is one—luxuriate in long paragraphs that virtually take on the character of a small adventure in prose. If you have a good reason for writing long paragraphs, by all means do so.

The problem with rules in writing—apart from the fact that good writers break them consistently—is that they are set up ahead of time and do not account for the purposes we as writers discover in the act of writing. They are arbitrary and ignore our needs. We do not know in advance what we will want to do in a given piece of writing, nor do we know what opportunities good luck will make available for us as we write.

Three Writers: Three Opening Paragraphs

Instead of rules, let us look at experience and see what we can learn. The following examples, all by important modern writers, are very different in style. All are the opening paragraphs of a longer piece of writing.

> The last time I spoke to Nabeel was over a year ago. He was in Baghdad. I was in New York. It wasn't easy getting through. The directory listed a code for Baghdad, but after days of trying, all I'd got was a recorded message telling me that the number I'd dialed didn't exist.
>
> In the end I had to book a call with the operator. She took a while, but eventually there was a voice at the other end, speaking in the blunt, rounded Arabic of Iraq: "Yes? Who is it?"
>
> Nabeel's family had told me that he was working as an assistant in a photographer's shop. The owner was an Iraqi and Nabeel had been working for him since 1986, when he left his village in Egypt and went to Iraq. There was a telephone in the shop and the owner was relatively kind, a relatively kind Iraqi, and he allowed Nabeel to receive calls.
>
> Amitav Ghosh, "An Egyptian in Baghdad," *Granta*, vol. 34, Autumn 1990, p. 174.

The first thing to notice about this example is that the three paragraphs form one unit of thought. If Ghosh had been writing in 1894, this would have been one paragraph. If you were to look for a topic sentence in any of the paragraphs, you would have some difficulty, although it is not difficult to know what the general subject of all three paragraphs is: locating Nabeel and getting his telephone number. The paragraphs are also somewhat disjointed, stopping and starting. In that sense, they reflect Ghosh's difficulties in locating his friend. In reading the paragraphs you experience some of his problems.

You might ask yourself what is gained by having each of these paragraphs in the form Ghosh chose. First, it is easy to follow his thoughts, and second, the passage is inviting. The reader is interested in continuing, finding out whether the author really talked with Nabeel, and what they said to each other. The detail about Nabeel and his whereabouts is designed to pique the reader's interest.

The style of the individual sentences is essentially casual and informal, and the style at the level of word choice is also very informal, especially marked by the use of contractions, such as "wasn't." The same is true of the group of paragraphs: the method of development is limited to heaping up a pile of details. Later, we hope, these details will become relevant and meaningful, although even at this early stage, they help us understand where Nabeel is and perhaps give us a clue as to what kind of person he is. The details could be given to us in almost any order—there is nothing special about the order Ghosh chooses. Although the order of events is easy to follow, because it focuses on reaching Nabeel, it skips from a look backward in paragraph one to a look to the end of the efforts to reach Nabeel in paragraph two, and then to a digression with background on Nabeel's whereabouts in paragraph three.

One of the most important aims of a writer, especially in the beginning of a piece, is to stimulate the reader to continue reading. Here the way the paragraphs break the information seems designed to keep the reader's interest level high.

The next example takes a slightly different approach.

> Moths that fly by day are not properly to be called moths; they do not excite that pleasant sense of dark autumn nights and ivy-blossom which the commonest yellow-underwing asleep in the shadow of the curtain never fails to rouse in us. They are hybrid creatures, neither gay like butterflies nor somber like their own species. Nevertheless the present specimen, with his narrow hay-colored wings, fringed with a tassel of the same color, seemed to be content with life. It was a pleasant morning, mid-September, mild, benignant, yet with a keener breath than that of the summer months. The plough was already scoring the field opposite the window, and where the share had been, the earth was pressed flat and gleamed with moisture. Such vigor came rolling in from the fields and the down beyond that it was difficult to keep the eyes strictly turned upon the book. The rooks too were keeping one of their annual festivities; soaring round the tree tops until it looked as if a vast net with thousands of black knots in it had been cast up into the air; which, after a few moments, sank slowly down upon the trees until every twig seemed to have a knot at the end of it. Then, suddenly, the net would be thrown into the air again in a wider circle this time, with the utmost clamor and vociferation, as though to be thrown into the air and settle slowly down upon the tree tops were a tremendously exciting experience.
>
> Virginia Woolf, "The Death of the Moth," from *The Death of the Moth and Other Essays* by Virginia Woolf. Copyright © 1942 by Harcourt Brace Publishers.

The effect of this paragraph is radically different from that of Ghosh's example. Woolf begins by talking about moths and butterflies and ends by talking about rooks—crows—who seem to be flying and gathering on tree branches with extraordinary activity. Where is the topic sentence that binds these flying creatures together? Woolf seems unaware that such a sentence would do her much good in this paragraph. Her style is sometimes described as loose or open, which implies not that it is unstructured, but that it is capacious and can accept a great many untethered details. Certainly, this example contains many details and observations.

Woolf begins by letting us think she is trying to establish whether day-flying moths are really moths. She compares them with butterflies to begin to settle the question. In the process she examines a specific moth with "narrow-hay-colored wings" and observes that, whatever she calls it, it is "content with life." When she tells us "It was a pleasant morning, mid-September," we realize she is reminiscing about a specific moment when she held a moth and was reading a book. She then describes the season, the plow (note she uses the English spelling, "plough") in the field, and the raucous activity of the crows. First they all fly wildly, then they settle on the ends of tree limbs, then they suddenly take off again.

The style of the paragraph differs from that of Ghosh in that it is not broken into several parts—although it could be broken in almost the same manner as Ghosh's. Woolf's individual word choices seem more formal, with words such as "benignant," and "vociferation." The length of the paragraph also implies that Woolf is not fearful that her opening will be too bulky to encourage readers to keep reading.

One hallmark of Woolf's style is elevated sensuousness. She describes the moth and butterflies in such a way as to stimulate our visual senses. She describes color and shape with some care. She describes the earth so that we might imagine touching it. The trees are alive with the rooks, and we can imagine them in motion, then at rest, then in motion. Woolf's paragraph helps establish the principle of development of the paragraph. Woolf is not defining anything, not following a logical progression of actions from a cause to an effect, nor is she telling us a story that begins somewhere and then moves on in a time sequence, as does Ghosh. Instead, she helps us live through a moment she experienced one September morning.

Is the style formal? Is the paragraph difficult to read? Do you wish to continue reading to the end of the essay? Your answers to these questions depend on your own style of reading and your personal preferences. Woolf's essay was written in the late 1930s and it was popular in its time. It is an example of money-making prose: Woolf was a writer of essays for which she was paid enough to live on. But her style is different from that of writers who currently publish in major magazines and newspapers. Most of them would choose much shorter paragraphs. They would break this paragraph down into several smaller ones, although they might make very few changes beyond that.

This third example is somewhat different from the two preceding examples.

> In my Depression childhood, whenever I had a new dress, my cousin Sarah would get suspicious. The nicer the dress was, and especially the more expensive it looked, the more suspicious she would get. Finally she would lift the hem and check the seams. This was to see if the dress had been bought or if my mother had sewed it. Sarah could always tell. My mother's sewing had elegant outsides, but there was something catch-as-catch-can about the insides. Sarah's sewing, by contrast, was as impeccably finished inside as out; not one stray thread dangled.
>
> Cynthia Ozick, "The Seam of the Snail," from *Metaphor and Memory*. Copyright © 1989, Alfred Knopf.

Cynthia Ozick differs from both Ghosh and Woolf by beginning with a very clear topic sentence: "In my Depression childhood, whenever I had a new dress, my cousin Sarah would get suspicious." Unlike the other examples, this paragraph could not easily be broken into shorter paragraphs. If it were, the reader would know almost immediately that the breaks were artificial and ultimately unsatisfactory. The focus of the paragraph is on Sarah's suspicions, and every sentence relates somehow to the opening statement. When a paragraph is structured in this fashion, it is the opposite of loose: its elements are tightly fitted and everything seems essential.

Many writers aspire to this kind of style, and it certainly has its rewards. Ozick's writing seems finished, clear, focused. Its economy is remarkable and admirable. But it should be obvious that while Virginia Woolf might have admired it, she would not have emulated it. You may disagree depending on your reactions to Woolf's and

Ozick's passages. Both have great strengths and both are strong examples of good style.

Your judgment regarding these examples depends on your own approach to writing and thinking. Each example represents a different way of thinking, just as the choices you make when you write reflect your own ways of thinking. But you can learn a great deal about what choices are available when you examine other writers' paragraphs.

It is said that writing can be learned, but not taught. That is a mild paradox, but it is generally accepted. However, it conceals some of the truth. While it is true that no one can instruct you precisely in how to write, any good teacher can instruct you to recognize principles of good writing and help you learn from them. This process begins with examining writing that you and others admire. Before there were schools that taught writing and composition, there were writers who studied the best writing they knew and tried to learn the skill of writing by imitation and emulation. A variant of that method involves some of the approaches used in this book: the examination of a variety of writing with an eye to analyzing the techniques used in order to acquire more options in writing. Writing is an art, and the path of learning most arts is by observing masters and following some basic instructions. Writing is learned by example and by doing. When you understand the example, and realize that most writers' performance is well within your grasp, you can start to learn what you need to know.

The analyses that appear throughout this book clarify what has been done in the samples of writing and help you decide whether you want to use some of those techniques. For example, you may find that the three paragraphs just discussed are not equally effective. Given the way most of us have been taught to write, the last of the paragraphs may seem to you the most interesting from the standpoint of technique. It has a single subject matter, a clear opening statement that focuses attention, and a clear range of statement and conclusion regarding Sarah's attitude toward how to make and evaluate clothes. You may find yourself especially comfortable using that structure for some of your paragraphs.

But you should also note that the other paragraphs have a relaxed and persuasive charm. They, too, have clear subjects, although they are not as sharply focused. Ghosh and Woolf can write without worrying about strict topic sentences and strict limits to paragraph development. As an advanced writer, you may also find it unnecessary to have topic sentences and narrowly structured paragraphs. Fine. You have Ghosh and Woolf as models. However, you might observe that instead of a topic sentence, they provide detail, sensory experience, a fullness of description, and specific information. Some people will say the topic sentence is implied in these paragraphs. After all, we have no trouble following what either writer has to say and we do not feel that the writers wander off or that they have no sense of focus.

We will have considerable opportunity to examine other paragraphs as we discuss individual writers and their work. Good writers will take many different approaches to structuring their paragraphs, and every decision about structure represents a stylistic choice. Some may be made unconsciously, especially in the first draft, but as a writer revises and redrafts a piece, decisions about style become more and more conscious.

Linking Paragraphs Together

Looking at a few paragraphs at a time helps us understand certain stylistic choices, but it is very important to look at an entire piece in order to grasp some of the most important qualities of style. One of the rules you may have heard frequently about linking paragraphs together is to use transition phrases. Well, sometimes such phrases work very well, but they are not the first choice of most current writers. Some typical transitional expressions recommended in grammar handbooks are: "suddenly," "later," "afterward," "but," "and," "however," "nonetheless," "on the other hand," and other expressive variants of time, place, and sequence. Unfortunately, these can be overused, and you may already have noticed that you have a penchant for overusing certain of them.

Watch for the ways in which good writers link their paragraphs. Sometimes they will use transition expressions. Naturally, such expressions can add some grace to a paragraph, but they must be used sparingly. Instead of worrying over the special function of expressions to produce transitions, you might study the way a writer such as Amitav Ghosh moves from paragraph to paragraph. He begins with a statement of time, "The last time I spoke to Nabeel. . . ," almost as if he were making a transition from another piece of writing. The second paragraph begins with "In the end," also a connector referring to time, so a clear transition is made from one paragraph to the next. However, there is no transition between the second and third paragraph, which begins: "Nabeel's family had told me . . . ." Ghosh did not feel the third paragraph needed a transition because his strategy was basically that of an interruption. He wanted to tell us something about Nabeel and his family, and he was able to do so with the full understanding that we could follow his progress from paragraph to paragraph. After all, he continued to talk about Nabeel and continued to work out his thoughts in a natural (if not expressly logical) way. Ghosh creates the effect of a person speaking, with ideas moving in something of the way they often do in conversation.

Developing Your Own Sense of Style

Your analysis of the style of the writings in this book can help you craft your own personal style. Writers study each other looking for new tricks partly because an apprenticeship in writing involves a great deal of reading. As you read, you will have your own distinctive impressions of how sentences affect you. Your personal feelings signal your individuality. When you want your writing to produce a specific impression, your decisions about word choice, sentence length, parallelism, balance, rhythm, and other stylistic issues will eventually help produce your own individual style.

A great many issues come up when we speak about the style of sentences, even when we want to focus primarily on sentence length. In the examples given, we began talking about the use of variety in the length and complexity of sentences, which in turn translates roughly into complexity of thought. We later turned to the subtleties of rhythm and pacing. The sentences also reveal interesting approaches to the use of description, the differences between concrete examples and abstract statements, the choice of sentence rhythms, and decisions about balance and parallelism. All these details help us distinguish style. Happily, there are no rules for making specific choices. As we discuss and analyze the work of good writers, you will begin to judge the kinds of opportunities that are always available to you. Writing is a process, and learning to write well is a process, too. It begins in general observation, proceeds to exceptionally close observation, and ends in awareness. The awareness consists first of recognizing what a good writer is doing, then of realizing that you can make use of most of the same techniques, employing them as you will, when you will, to what ends you will. No two people will ever observe a writer's work in the same way, nor make the same realizations about style or process. Consequently, the process of observing, analyzing, and realizing produces wonderfully different responses in different people. In other words, it produces an individual approach to style.

How Writers Work

The blank page affects all writers in more or less the same way: it is intimidating. Some writers actually begin their day's work by writing a line of nonsense syllables across the top of the first page. Others write a formulaic phrase, such as "Once upon a time . . . ." Almost anything will do to get started, since you know that whatever you are writing at first will be revised later. Just getting going is the important thing. Once you've gotten under way, however, some "tricks of the trade" can come in handy. One is to jot some notes at the bottom of the last page of a session, or on the next "blank" page to come. Such notes give direction for the next session's work. Most advanced writers need only a few words of direction to get up and going. Another trick, one that Ernest Hemingway used and which will work for any writer, is to end a day's work in the middle of a sentence. For example, make the last thing you write go something like this: "The problem of homelessness among children in Brazil is so severe that some authorities form killing squads and actually go out and. . . ." When you come to that sentence the next day, its conclusion will be obvious to you and you will immediately be under way in the day's session.

The Course in Advanced Writing

All writers, advanced or beginners, use most of the same methods. Advanced writers, for the purpose of this book, are those who have had both some experience in writing and writing instruction and some present need to write, whether for school, business, or personal satisfaction. I sometimes tell my students in Advanced Writing that one reason they elected the course is that if they are lucky they may someday be asked to write reports, descriptions, proposals, journals, observations, contracts, or letters essential to their work. Such a request will place them in a position of independence, which tells them that their ideas and thoughts are valuable to others. Consequently the course in Advanced Writing will make them ready to accept the opportunity when it comes their way. If they perform well and impress the people who read their work, then they will have new opportunities and assume a role of importance appropriate to their sense of themselves.

Advanced writers, like beginning writers, often puzzle over details of correctness, such as knowing when to use an apostrophe ("its" when you mean "its own name," but "it's" when you mean "it's not enough to live on") and keeping subjects and verbs in agreement ("The recent criteria [plural noun] satisfy the requirements for success in this work"). In the eyes of many writing instructors and language theorists, such details are trivial. However, in the world at large they can take on considerable importance. One advertisement for a job in publishing in Boston attracted almost 250 letters of application. More than 150 were completely disregarded because of otherwise trivial errors in accuracy. This may be extreme, but the message is clear: correctness is desirable even if it is not the most important aspect of good writing.

This book is essentially practical in its advice. Its assumptions are based on the facts that the writing process involves a wide range of skills and that the ultimate product of your writing can be shaped according to well understood techniques. This book will give you extensive opportunities to develop a range of useful styles that will both reflect your personal sensibilities and permit clear and effective expression of thought.

2

Writing the Personal Essay

The personal essay represents one of the most important kinds of writing in the life of any writer. Partly because most people like to talk about themselves, and partly because people write best about what they know best, autobiography is among the most common forms of writing. If you consider that psychological therapy consists almost entirely of talking about oneself, it should become clear why autobiography is so important. Study and reflection on oneself lead to self-knowledge, and self-knowledge is the reward of the most serious philosophies we know. Socrates said, "Know thyself," and theologians in the late modern period insist that self-knowledge can lead us to a knowledge of God.

The personal essay may not represent such grand goals for all of us. But even more modest goals should help you develop a better understanding of how you have become the person you are. Even if that purpose is not fully achieved, one of the gifts of personal writing is letting friends know more about you. Basic human curiosity leads us to inquire about our friends and to let them know about ourselves.

Maintaining a Journal or Diary

Journal keeping, or writing in one's diary, has become a hallmark of many writers. Writers often identify themselves as "inveterate journal keepers," meaning that they jot down ideas, events, names, things to remember, descriptions of things that have happened to them and others, responses to moments in a day, even recollections of past events, in order to have something to write about. Journals and diaries are raw material like ore. What they contain may be reworked, transformed, and molded to fit new situations.

Diaries and journals come in all forms. Some people keep an appointment book with only a few lines for each day. They fill in the details for the day with short comments on what they did or what they wished to do. Other people write an extensive commentary, sometimes at the end of the day, describing events, reflecting on what they did, and analyzing their experience. One approach is to keep theater stubs and programs, movie tickets, receipts from restaurants, photographs, postcards either from places you visit or from friends who remember you—anything that is associated with the period in question. Many people keep a daily journal in notebooks that they date and keep together, writing about many different subjects, copying in important quotations or passages from favorite authors. In the seventeenth century, writers often kept "commonplace books" filled with quotations, poems, short observations, and plans for longer pieces of writing. Journals come in many forms. If you decide to follow the pattern of many writers and keep a journal, you may find the following tips helpful.

TIPS FOR KEEPING A JOURNAL

1. Set up a regular time each day for writing in your journal. If you miss a day do your best to recapture some details from the missing period of time.
2. Date each entry in your journal. Mention the weather and be sure to write down where you are during the day.
3. Keep track of the highlights of the day, but be sure to write about the ordinary events in your life. The ordinary events are really of immense importance to everyone, and unfortunately most of us take them for granted even when keeping a journal.
4. If possible, use photographs or other visuals to jog your memory at a later date. Drawings are also very useful in a journal.
5. Creative writing, such as poetry or fiction, is also appropriate in a journal, especially if it is related to the events of the day.
6. Don't be afraid to write fragments. It is not important to produce finished writing in a journal.
7. Decide right away if you expect anyone else to read your journal—then write accordingly. Either you are the sole audience of your journal, or else you and a range of people will be its readers.
8. Plan to keep your journal throughout your life. And for that reason be sure to clarify details that might become obscure in later

life. Be sure to name names and identify the people who figure in your daily life.

9. When possible write down the things people say. Try to be as accurate as possible, but do not worry about being perfect.
10. Try to capture your own opinions and feeling states as much as possible.

Sample Journal Entries

Edward Weston

The following excerpt is from a journal maintained by Edward Weston, one of the great modern photographers. He kept his daybooks, as he called them, for more than fifteen years beginning in 1920, when he was in Mexico. He did not intend to publish it, although he eventually took a few segments out for publication in journals and went back late in life and edited portions, aware that he was well known. The daybooks were published in full three years after his death.

January 26 [1924]. After four cloudy days, gentle rain is falling, much like a January day in California. A sitting was postponed because the young lady could not wash her hair. I wore a smiling mask and changed the date; a cloudy day and a pretty girl's unwashed hair might change another's life,—tomorrow's tortillas depended on that sitting.

The gods always save me at some crucial moment, this time through Flora, who wired me $200. I hope she sold no land at a loss.

Strange not to hear from Ramiel—over a month since he wrote me of his accident, and six weeks since Margarethe wrote "God help me to write you tonight." From both I should have heard, and for not merely sentimental reasons. May's appendix in the slop pail! Dearest sis, when shall I see you again! Johan may be alive or dead, for aught I know; not a line since I have been in Mexico.

Senator Galván in last night to say hasta luego—see you soon. He leaves for the front this morning. His talk of the Indians was refreshing, especially after the depressing opinions from other Mexicans related the last few days,—one felt not only hope, but desire to help. For today, at least, I am a "Callista."

We sat in Monotes talking. "We are going to make Diego Rivera a deputy," said Galván (deputy is similar to congressman in the U.S.). "But you will spoil a great artist," said Tina. "No, he can still go on painting," replied Galván. "Anyhow, Diego is even greater as a statesman."

Interesting faces at Monotes, the derelicts, the dreamers, the useless riff-raff of the world, artists, poets, etc. Always good food there, tamales de pollo y atole, tostadas sabrosas.

Then we went to El Teatro Lírico—Lupe Rivas Cacho y Compañía. I had heard much of her and was not disappointed. The last scene was spectacular, backgrounds, costumes entirely made from sarapes, a dazzling prismatic effect. Everything, it seems, is right in the proper place or at the proper time. Before, I had not cared for the crude colors of the *modern* sarape, but here the ensemble was stunning.

Weston was in Mexico at an exciting time, during a revolution. His friend, Diego Rivera, was one of the greatest of modern Mexican painters, but he was also a political man and had taken sides in the current war. He was also married to one of the most important painters of his time, Frieda Kahlo, whom Weston knew. As an American, Weston had stayed clear of politics, but as he says in this entry, for the evening he was able to side with his friends. What Weston has done in this entry is to keep track of the names of his friends, the food that he ate, the subjects of the discussions, and the events of the day, including visiting the theater for an experience that changed his mind about sarapes. Weston did not go on to write autobiography, but if he were to have done so, he would have had a great deal of material here to draw from. He recognizes the emotional mood of the time, the atmosphere, the subjects that concerned people. He writes about people whom we would know only if we read the entire journal, but for him each of these names is like a talisman that brings back specific memories.

Anne Frank

Probably the most celebrated of modern diaries is the diary of Anne Frank, who kept writing in the most hopeless of circumstances. She kept her diary in a first version, then revised it. She also created a version called *Tales from the Secret Annex*, which was the basis of the original publication of *Anne Frank: The Diary of a Young Girl* in 1952. Her life while she kept her diary, in the form of letters to an imaginary Kitty, was constrained because she and her family were in hiding from the Nazis in Amsterdam. They were holed up for roughly two years. The excerpt that follows is from the most current translation of the revised diary.

> Dear Kitty, Sunday 2 Jan 1944.
>
> This morning when I had nothing to do, I turned over some of the pages of my diary and several times I came across letters dealing with the subject "Mummy" in such a hotheaded way that it quite shocked me and I asked myself: "Anne, is it really you who mentioned hate? Oh, Anne, how could you?" I remained sitting with the open page in my hand, and thought about it and how it came about that I should have been so brimful of rage and really so filled with such a thing as hate that I had to confide it all in you. I have been trying to understand the Anne of a year ago and to excuse her, because my conscience isn't clear as long as I leave you with these accusations, without being able to explain, on looking back, how it happened.
>
> I suffer now—and suffered then—from moods which kept my head under water (so to speak that is) and only allowed me to see things subjectively without enabling me to consider quietly the words of the other side, and to answer them as the words of one whom I, with my hotheaded temperament, had offended or made unhappy.
>
> I hid myself within myself, I only considered myself and quietly wrote down all my joys, sorrows and contempt in my diary. This diary is of great value to me, because it has become a book of memoirs in many places, but on a good many pages I could certainly put "past and done with."
>
> Anne Frank, *The Diary of Anne Frank*, The Critical Edition, prepared by the Netherlands State Institute for War Documentation, translated by Arnold J. Pomerans and B. M. Mooyaart-Doubleday. New York: Doubleday, 1989, page 438.

Anne Frank speaks to her diary as if it were an old friend. She records the date, but because she cannot leave her dwelling, she makes no mention of the place. The most concrete references are to herself, her mother, and her diary. She realizes as she writes that her diary is an intimate portrait of her emotional and psychological growth. She had begun her diary in June 1942, before she went into hiding. Even then she reflected on the act of keeping a diary, which she thought odd because: "it seems to me that neither I—nor for that matter anyone else—will be interested in the unbosomings of a thirteen-year-old schoolgirl. Still, what does that matter? I want to write, but more than that, I want to bring out all kinds of things that lie buried deep in my heart." (Saturday, June 20, 1942) [p. 180]. Because she died in the Nazi death camps she has become an especially poignant figure in modern history. But she is typical of many writers. She recognized in herself a desire to use a talent that had already shown itself in her delight in reading Dickens and many contemporary writers.

Harold Nicolson

Harold Nicolson, an aristocratic Englishman who maintained himself in important political circles before World War II, kept an entirely different kind of diary.

> DIARY 14th June, 1939
>
> Dine with Kenneth Clark. The Walter Lippmanns are there: also the Julian Huxleys and Winston Churchill as the guest of honour. Winston is horrified by Lippmann saying that the American Ambassador, Jo Kennedy, had informed him that war was inevitable and that we should be licked. Winston is stirred by this defeatism into a magnificent oration. He sits hunched there, waving his whisky-and-soda to mark his periods, stubbing his cigar with the other hand.
>
> "It may be true, it may well be true," he says, "that this country will at the outset of this coming and to my mind almost inevitable war be exposed to dire peril and fierce ordeals. It may be true that steel and fire will rain down upon us day and night scattering death and destruction far and wide. It may be true that our sea-communications will be imperilled and our food-supplies placed in jeopardy. Yet these trials and disasters, I ask you to believe me, Mr. Lippmann, will but serve to steel the resolution of the British people and to enhance our will for victory. No, the Ambassador should not have spoken so, Mr Lippmann; he should not have said that dreadful word. Yet supposing (as I do not for one moment suppose) that Mr Kennedy were correct in his tragic utterance, then I for one would willingly lay down my life in combat, rather than, in fear of defeat, surrender to the menaces of these most sinister men. It will then be for you, for the Americans, to preserve and to maintain the great heritage of the English-speaking peoples. It will be for you to think imperially, which means to think always of something higher and more vast than one's own national interests. Nor should I die happy in the great struggle which I see before me, were I not convinced that if we in this dear dear island succumb to the ferocity and might of our enemies, over there in your distant and immune continent the torch of liberty will burn untarnished and (I trust and hope) undismayed."
>
> We then change the subject and speak about the Giant Panda.
>
> Harold Nicolson, *Harold Nicolson: Diaries and Letters 1930–1939*, edited by Nigel Nicolson. New York: Atheneum, 1966, page 438.

Harold Nicolson was a prodigious writer with at least twenty-eight books to his credit. His ability to note such a lengthy quotation from Winston Churchill in his diary was probably not unusual because it was a habit of his to write down people's words. Of course, his own ability as a writer may well have contributed to the phrases attributed to Churchill. But whether his recording of the speech was 100 percent accurate or not is less important than the fact that he made an effort to record it. One obvious use of a diary is to keep track of what people say as well as what we say ourselves. Judging from what we know of Churchill, such a speech would have been quite in order for him, and Nicolson's recollection seems reasonable as well as passionate and convincing.

The Personal Essay

Frederick Douglass

Writing with a journal as a basis for your memories is probably the preferable way of developing the personal essay. However, there are times and situations that make it impossible to keep a diary. Frederick Douglass, during much of the period covered in his remarkable *Life of an American Slave*, was unable to write regularly because it was a crime for slaves to read and write. Consequently, he relied on his memory for details, and his personal writing is certainly more polished and complete than we would find in a journal. Douglass was a gifted speaker and a gifted writer, but in the paragraph that follows he does what most writers of personal narratives do. He recalls a particularly memorable incident and tells us about it. He describes a period during which he was "hired out" and gave thought to escaping to freedom.

> In the early part of the year 1838, I became quite restless. I could see no reason why I should, at the end of each week, pour the reward of my toil into the purse of my master. When I carried to him my weekly wages, he would, after counting the money, look me in the face with a robber-like fierceness, and ask, "Is this all?" He was satisfied with nothing less than the last cent. He would, however, when I made him six dollars, sometimes give me six cents, to encourage me. It had the opposite effect. I regarded it as a sort of admission of my right to the whole. The fact that he gave me any part of my wages was proof, to my mind, that he believed me entitled to the whole of them. I always felt worse for having received anything; for I feared that the giving me a few cents would ease his conscience, and make him feel himself to be a pretty honorable sort of robber. My discontent grew upon me. I was ever on the look-out for means of escape; and, finding no direct means, I determined to try to hire my time, with a view of getting money with which to make my escape. In the spring of 1838, when Master Thomas came to Bal-

> timore to purchase his spring goods, I got an opportunity, and applied to him to allow me to hire my time. He unhesitatingly refused my request, and told me this was another stratagem by which to escape. He told me I could go nowhere but that he could get me; and that, in the event of my running away, he should spare no pains in his efforts to catch me. He exhorted me to content myself, and be obedient. He told me, if I would be happy, I must lay out no plans for the future. He said, if I behaved myself properly, he would take care of me. Indeed, he advised me to complete thoughtlessness of the future, and taught me to depend solely upon him for happiness. He seemed to see fully the pressing necessity of setting aside my intellectual nature, in order to contentment in slavery. But in spite of him, and even in spite of myself, I continued to think, and to think about the injustice of my enslavement, and the means of escape.

Ultimately, Douglass managed to hire himself out and eventually to secure his freedom by taking the place of a seaman and sailing north. This example from his personal narrative is notable for its emphasis on Douglass's thoughts and motivations. He examines his own feelings and his own reactions to circumstances that were horrifying. He does not quote his master directly except for one three-word sentence. Yet, he tells us what his master said to him by quoting him indirectly, thus relieving himself of the responsibility of being absolutely accurate, as we would expect if the speech were in quotation marks. This passage is also remarkable for containing no description. Douglass concentrates so much on his responses and his plans and feelings that he does not point to the physical world in which he lives. His is a mental world filled with pain and discontent. His purposes are to find relief and to live free.

The simplicity of Douglass's style helps convince us of the honesty of his feelings and his report of his experience. His word choices veer toward the plain and simple, with very few unusual words or phrases such as "with robber-like fierceness"; "stratagem"; "He exhorted me." However, Douglass uses the verb "to be" sparingly, preferring simple action verbs such as "*pour* the reward"; "My discontent *grew*"; "he *should spare* no pains"; "he *advised* me." Even the sentence structure is plain and simple, with a great many sentences beginning with "He." In the manner of the age, the sentences are long, but they are not complicated or sinuous. Instead, they are clear and direct. Douglass wanted his audience to understand him completely and to think about his experience rather than admire his style.

Virginia Woolf

Virginia Woolf, in "A Sketch of the Past," writes about a time before she could have thought to keep a journal. Consequently, she concentrates entirely on memory.

—I begin: the first memory.

This was of red and purple flowers on a black ground—my mother's dress; and she was sitting either in a train or in an omnibus, and I was on her lap. I therefore saw the flowers she was wearing very close; and can still see purple and red and blue, I think, against the black; they must have been anemones, I suppose. Perhaps we were going to St Ives; more probably, for from the light it must have been evening, we were coming back to London. But it is more convenient artistically to suppose that we were going to St Ives, for that will lead to my other memory, which also seems to be my first memory, and in fact it is the most important of all my memories. If life has a base that it stands upon, if it is a bowl that one fills and fills and fills—then my bowl without a doubt stands upon this memory. It is of lying half asleep, half awake, in bed in the nursery at St Ives. It is of hearing the waves breaking, one, two, one, two, and sending a splash of water over the beach; and then breaking, one, two, one, two behind a yellow blind. It is of hearing the blind draw its little acorn across the floor as the wind blew the blind out. It is of lying and hearing this splash and seeing this light, and feeling, it is almost impossible that I should be here; of feeling the purest ecstasy I can conceive.

I could spend hours trying to write that as it should be written, in order to give the feeling which is even at this moment very strong in me. But I should fail (unless I had some wonderful luck); I dare say I should only succeed in having the luck if I had begun by describing Virginia herself.

Here I come to one of the memoir writer's difficulties—one of the reasons why, though I read so many, so many are failures. They leave out the person to whom things happened. The reason is that it is so difficult to describe any human being. So they say: "This is what happened"; but they do not say what the person was like to whom it happened. And the events mean very little unless we know first to whom they happened. Who was I then? Adeline Virginia Stephen, the second daughter of Leslie and Julia Prinsep Stephen, born on 25th January 1882, descended from a great many people, some famous, others obscure; born into a large connection, born not of rich parents, but of well-to-do parents, born into a very communicative, literate, letter writing, visiting, articulate, late nineteenth century world; so that I could if I liked to take the trouble, write a great deal here not only about my mother and father but about uncles and aunts, cousins and friends. But I do not know how much of this, or what part of this, made me feel what I felt in the nursery at St Ives. I do not know how far I differ from other people. That is another memoir writer's difficulty. Yet to describe oneself truly one must have some standard of comparison; was I clever, stupid, good looking, ugly, passionate, cold—? Owing partly to the fact that I was never at school, never

> competed in any way with children of my own age, I have never been able to compare my gifts and defects with other people's. But of course there was one external reason for the intensity of this first impression: the impression of the waves and the acorn on the blind; the feeling, as I describe it sometimes to myself, of lying in a grape and seeing through a film of semi-transparent yellow—it was due partly to the many months we spent in London. The change of nursery was a great change. And there was the long train journey; and the excitement. I remember the dark; the light; the stir of going up to bed.
>
> Virginia Woolf, "A Sketch Pad," from *Moments of Being*. Reprinted by permission of the Executors of the Virginia Woolf Estate and The Hogarth Press.

Unlike Frederick Douglass, Virginia Woolf (maiden name Virginia Stephen) was a professional writer concerned with style and the affect of her prose. She reveals that to us when she reflects on the act of writing, explaining what she likes and dislikes in other people's memoirs. Her most important insight, at least for the majority of other writers, is the fact that many memoirists tell us all about what happened, but almost nothing about the person to whom it happened. Therefore, she begins appropriately with her first memory, then goes on to tell us some important details about herself. She reflects on the fact that she was educated at home—as she says elsewhere, in her father's library—and therefore did not experience the competitive pressures that are present in all schools. She did not compete for attention, grades, or athletic prizes. That detail alone tells us a great deal about young Virginia Stephen. For one thing it implies that the act of writing this narrative is designed to help her see herself better, to act, in other words, as a mirror in which to observe herself in comparison with other memorists.

Another informative detail surfaces in the structure and character of her memory. She connects herself to her mother, especially the dress she wears; she then connects herself to her nursery and the yellow blinds that rustle in the wind. Unlike Douglass, Woolf is connected profoundly to the physical world and observes it in terms of colors, sounds, and sensory experiences. Like Douglass, she internalizes experience, but her concentration is on dredging up memories which will give a clue as to what kind of child she was and those memories exist in terms of physical experience.

In asking the question "Who was I then?" Woolf offers all of us a guide to writing the personal narrative. One job that any writer of a memoir has is discovering the self, trying to find out what we were like "then." We discover something about Virginia Woolf in this passage not in terms of things she did or adventures she had. Rather, we learn in terms of things she tells us about herself and in terms of the nature of her observation of the world around her.

Personal essays come in all forms, naturally, but they usually depend on careful recollection and the management of details that, at the time they occurred, may not have seemed as important as they turned out to be. As you can see, not all writers refer to diaries or journals, although a great many do. Those who do not have prodigious memories or else go back and recapture details from other people's memories or from documents such as newspaper clippings, letters, even bills and various task lists. The following complete essay is important for its ability to capture the past and the feelings of those who lived through its events.

Richard Ford

"Accommodations," published in *Banana Republic Trips*, is very personal, a memoir of childhood experiences and people Richard Ford knew as a child. If Ford did not consult a diary or journal, the details of this piece must have lived in his memory for years. Ford brings back the character and feel of the 1950s in middle America. He mentions places, names of people popular in another day, important details about how people made their living, and details about the way he and his family got by.

RICHARD FORD

Accommodations

And what was it like to live there? From my childhood, this memory: I am in bed. It is one o'clock in the morning. I am eleven years old, and in a room inside my grandfather's hotel—the room connecting to his. I am

*Richard Ford, "Accommodations," from *Banana Republic Trips* by Richard Ford. Copyright

awake, listening. This is what I hear. Someplace, through walls, an argument is going on. A man and a woman are arguing. I hear some dishes rattle and then break. The words "You don't care. No, you don't" spoken by a woman. How far away this goes on I can't tell. Rooms away is all. I heard a door open into the hall, and a voice that's louder—the man's—say, "Better you than me in this is what I know. You bet." I hear keys jingling, a door close softly, then footsteps over the carpeted hallway. And then a smell of sweet perfume in my room, an orchid smell, all around me where I'm alone and in the dark, lying still. I hear an elevator grate drawn back. A second woman's foice farther away, talking softly, then the door closes, and it's quiet again inside. I hear a bus hiss at the station across the city street. A car horn blows. Somewhere outside someone begins to laugh, the laughter coming up off the empty pavement and into the night. Then no more noises. The perfume drifts through my room, stays in the air. I hear my grandfather turn in his sleep and sigh. Then sleep comes back.

This was the fifties, and my grandfather ran the hotel where we lived—in Little Rock, a town neither exactly south nor exactly west, just as it still is. To live in a hotel promotes a cool two-mindedness: one is both steady and in a sea that passes with tides. Accommodation is what's wanted, a replenished idea of permanence and transience; familiarity overcoming the continual irregularity in things.

The hotel was named the Marion, and it was not a small place. Little Rock was a mealy, low-rise town on a slow river, and the hotel was the toniest, plushest place in it. And still it was blowsy, a hotel for conventioneers and pols, salesmen and late-night party givers. There was a curving marble fish pond in the lobby; a tranquil, banistered mezzanine with escritoires and soft lights; a jet marble front desk; long, green leather couches, green carpets, bellboys with green twill uniforms and short memories. It was a columned brownstone with a porte-cochère, built in the twenties, with seven stories, three hundred rooms. Ladies from the Delta stayed in on shopping trips. The Optimists and the Rotarians met. Assignations between state officials went on upstairs. Senator McClellan kept a room. Visiting famous people stayed, and my grandfather kept their pictures on his office wall—Rex Allen the cowboy, Jack Dempsey the boxing champion, June Allyson and Dick Powell, Harry Truman (whose photograph I have, still), Ricky Nelson, Chill Wills. Salesmen rented sample rooms, suicides took singles. There were hospitality suites, honeymoon suites, a Presidential, a Miss America, Murphy beds, silver service, Irish napkins. There was a bakery, a print shop, an upholsterer, ten rooms (the Rendezvous, the Continental) for intimate parties, six more for large, and a ballroom with a Hammond organ for banquets. There was a beer bar in the lower lobby, a two-chair barbershop, a cigar stand, a florist, a travel agent, a news agent, a garage where you parked for nothing while you stayed. There was a drummer's rate, a serviceman's rate, a monthly rate, a day rate, even an hourly rate if you knew my grandfather. Everything happened there, at all hours. Privacy had a high value. To live in a hotel as a boy knowing nothing was to see what adults did to each other and themselves when only adults were present.

My grandfather, Ben Shelley, was a man of strong appetites—food, but other things, too. The usual things. He was a fatty who played winter golf in pleated gabardines, shot pool and quail. He qualified as a sport, a Shriner, a wide, public man, a toddling character in a blue suit with change in his pockets and a money clip. To me, he was the exotic brought to common earth, and I loved him. "The latchstring is always on the outside" was his motto, and he winked at you when he said that, smiled between his thick amorous lips, as though his words meant something else, which they may have. I could think different of him now, see him through new eyes, revise history, take a narrower, latter-day view. But why?

He had been a boxer—a featherweight, a club fighter; worked dining cars on the Rock Island as far as Tucumcari, waited tables in El Reno, been a caterer's assistant at the famous Muehlebach in Kansas City. That was the way up in the hotel business, and such work was his by nature. Service. That word meant something it doesn't mean now.

What his skills were, his acumen, his genius that got him down to Little Rock and into a good job in 1947, I don't know. Loyalty and firmness, I imagine. Discretion, certainly. A lack of frankness. Gratitude. Still good qualities. People liked him, liked staying there—which were similar experiences. Everyone approached him smiling, as if he knew something private about them, which he undoubtedly did. They were in his house when they were in his hotel, and he spoke to them at close range, in cagey whispers, his big stomach touching them. He held their arm, cradled their elbow, spoke while he seemed to look away, smiling. He knew the joke, that was his business, exactly. Nothing in the private sector deserves privacy but sex. And that was in the air about him and the whole place. A hotel is for that as much as —maybe more than—anything. And he knew it mattered less what you did than whether someone knew about it.

Normal life, I know now, is life that can be explained in one sentence. No questions needed. And that, I lacked. "You live right here in the hotel?" is what I heard. Afterwards, a smile. These were Southerners, guests I met briefly. They wanted their own straight line on the eccentric, which is what I was to them; wanted as always to compare and contrast lives to their own. It is the Southerner's favorite habit. My story, though, took too long to get into, and I wouldn't: my father was sick; he traveled for a living; my mother drove him; I was from another city, not here; these were my grandparents; I liked it here. It was only that complicated, but I left it alone. Accommodating your own small eccentricity to yourself is enough. And even that moves you toward remoteness, toward affection for half-truths, makes you conspiratorial, a secret-keeper.

Certain things *were* acknowledged lacking. Neighbors. There were none of those. Only employees, guests, "the Permanents" (old bachelors, old shopkeepers, old married couples in cheap rooms with no better homes to hold on to), lobby lizards—older men with baffling nicknames like Spider, Goldie, Ish—men who lived out in town but showed up each day. These were all. No one was my age ever. There was no neighborhood of other houses, no normal views out windows, no normal quiets or light. We were downtown, detached from normal residential lives. Town—the real city, the coarse town mix—started just outside the lobby door: a liquor store, two cheap movies, a pool room, a less-good hotel with whores, the bus depot. Everything was immediate. No delays. At night, out my window from floor six, I could see the town signs with black sky behind, a green beacon farther off, could hear the Trailways heave in and out. I saw sailors, single women, older black couples standing down on the pavement stretching, taking their look around at a strange city, using the phone on the wall, the bathroom, staring across Markham Street at the hotel where they weren't staying the night. Then getting on the bus again for St. Louis or Texas or Memphis. Then gone. Was it lonely for me? No. Never. It is not bad or lonely to see that life goes on at all times, with you or without you. Home is finally a variable concept.

Travelers—our guests—were people I did not know. They appeared with bags, wives, and kids—their cars outside. They looked around the lobby, glanced into the fish pond, sniffed the air, checked in, *became* guests, walked toward the elevators and disappeared. I almost never noticed them again, did not even imagine them—their days, their houses in other states, their fatigues, where they'd already been that day, where they lunched, whether they'd argued or why, where they might go next. I resisted them. It might have seemed a conversation would take too long, go nowhere. I did not really like traveling, I think now. Traveling and hotels reflected things different at heart.

And, of course, we lived *in*, in an apartment with four rooms where we did not own the furniture but where we liked it—room and board the highly valued parts of our deal. We ate where we pleased—in the big kitchen downstairs or in the dining room—The Green Room—in our apartment. We ordered room service. Laundry was free. A lot was free. My grandfather kept bird dogs in the basement. We had TV early, our car had a good spot in the garage and got washed every day. The sheets were always clean. We saw few visitors. Complete freedom within limits. But if my grandfather lost his job—always the backstage scare story—we lost it all. How fast we could be "put on the street" for some vague infraction observed by the captious owner was a topic much reviewed by my grandmother, who had been poor, though not by my grandfather, who had been poor, too, but couldn't imagine it anymore, and who too much loved his work. Employment was undemocratic then. It lacked the redress we take for granted now—the doctrine of fairness. Hotels were thought to run best as sufferance, with things in limbo. And every morning in the dark before work, my grandfather would sit in a chair in his underwear, just before lacing his shoes, and pray out loud for his job, thank God for loyal employees, for his good boss, and for the trust he felt he had, pray for the future. I could hear this from my bed in the next room. It seemed prudent to me, as it still does.

Whatever his duties—and they were not so clear-cut to me—he was up at six to do them, gone down the elevator in his loose blue suit to "put in an appearance." Mostly his job was simply that. Being there and only there. A presence and conserver to his employees, a welcoming man to guests. He "toured the house," saw that operations were operating. That is how a hotel was run. He signed checks. He hired people, fired them. He ate *in* to prove his food was good, lived in for the same reason. His prosperity (in conspicuous evidence, always) promised others the same. In this he was not an *hôtelier*, not an inn-keeper, he was a hotelman. He would not have been happy to manage something else—a store or a row of trailers. He did not look forward to advancement, only to more of the same. Time has gone when men inhabited their jobs in that way, when occupation signaled that.

And what did I do. Little. I was there, too. I lived *inside* and did not think of outside. I took few duties. I stood, I watched things pass by me. I rode the elevators, I chatted up bellboys and waiters and room clerks. I slouched around, watched lights light up on the PBX, saw operations operating over and over. I fed the fish. I was prized for my manners, for my height, for the fact that my father was sick and I was here—bravely and indefinitely. I was thought to be interested in hotel work and said that I was. I was curious, unperplexed, un-self-centered, as useless as any boy who sees the surface of life close and reclose over facts that are often not easily simplifiable. We can become familiar with a great many things.

To make regular life seem regular need not always be to bleach the strong colors out. But just for a time it can help. When you look for what's unique and also true of life, you're lucky to find less than you imagined.

How permanent is real life? That's the question, isn't it? The one we both want and don't quite want to hear told. Queasy, melancholic, obvious answers are there. In the hotel there was no center to things, nor was I one. It was the floating life, days erasing other days almost completely, as should be. The place was a hollow place, like any home, in which things went on, a setting where situations developed and ended. And I simply stood alongside that for a while in my young life—neither behind the scenes nor in front. What I saw then—and I saw more than I can say, more than I remember—matters less than what I thought about it. And what I thought about it was this: this is the actual life now, not a stopover, a diversion, or an oddment in time, but the permanent life, the one that will provide history, memory, the one I'll be responsible for in the long run. Everything counts, after all. What else do you need to know?

STYLE IN "ACCOMMODATIONS"

If we look first at words, then sentences, then paragraphs, we can begin to detail some of the characteristics of Ford's style, although we will also have to be prepared to admit that his style transcends all such efforts at breaking his essay down into simple elements. He is too careful, too subtle, and too successful a writer to permit us to nail him down the way some people would nail a bat to a barndoor. Our purposes are not to do a post-mortem on this essay—because it lives and breathes—but to simply point out some of its achievements so we can learn something about how to write personal essays of our own.

Word choices

Ford's word choices are as middle American as his locale. He avoids fancy expressions, technical chatter, jargon, or cliché. He is direct and expressive, colloquial without being crude, immediate without being too familiar. He imagines an interested audience of readers who are much like him, people with a memorable past, people who know what a car is, who have heard keys jingling, who have smelled perfume, and who understand the ambience of small towns and their hotels. He throws in a great many details that are meaningful to him, and which will be unknown to most of his younger readers. But we do not need to know each and every reference he makes in order to make good sense of what he says.

Ford moves from the extremely chummy opening description

of Little Rock to the more amused and amusing description of the interior of the hotel in the third paragraph:

> Little Rock was a mealy, low-rise town on a slow river, and the hotel was the toniest, plushest place in it. And still it was blowsy, a hotel for conventioneers and pols, salesmen and late-night party givers. There was a curving marble fish pond in the lobby; a tranquil, banistered mezzanine with escritoires and soft lights; a jet marble front desk; long, green leather couches, green carpets, bellboys with green twill uniforms and short memories.

The word choices in this passage are extremely careful, just as they are revealing and effective. Calling a town "mealy" and "low-rise" imparts an emotional quality. Contrasting the town with the plushness of the hotel, with the overdone qualities of marble, banisters, leather couches—all color coordinated in green—is complemented marvelously with the use of the formal "escritoires," for little writing tables. The use of French here is pretentious, to match the pretentiousness of the hotel lobby. The description imparts a powerful visual image because Ford has appealed directly to our visual sense. However, at the same time he has included sounds and smells so that we are sensually engaged at an intense level throughout the beginning of the essay.

The word choices may look simple because most of the words are simple, but the simplicity masks the power of the sensory appeal the words make. As you review the first two pages of the essay, notice how many words invoke images of sounds, sights, and smells. Busses hiss, car horns sound, women's voices are audible, laughter mixes with perfume. A multitude of the words are names of things you could see and touch if you were there: dishes, keys, leather, photographs, silver, napkins, barber chairs, and people—people with names, like Senator McClellan, as well as anonymous bellhops and salesmen. All of this named detail implies a vibrancy of life and a vitality that the writing sustains. It is not easy to write like this. But it is utterly impossible to write with such vitality unless you do as Ford does: appeal with your choice of words to the sensory imagination of the reader.

Sentence choices

Ford's sentences are usually short, sometimes unorthodox. He begins the essay with a rhetorical question, then proceeds to answer it. Essentially, the essay is an effort to let us know and feel what it was like to live in his grandfather's hotel. Some sentences are brief and almost in the language of the imagined eleven-year-old boy: "I am awake, listening. This is what I hear." The first paragraph has a number of such sentences as a way of reinforcing the intense memories of a young boy. The first sentence of the second paragraph opens up a bit, leaves the young boy behind and reveals the present Richard Ford, a man who can think in longer, more subtle structures: "This was the fifties, and my grandfather ran the hotel where we lived—in Little Rock, a town neither exactly south nor exactly west, just as it still is."

Ford uses considerable variety in his sentence structures. Some sentences are questions, like the first, and most are simple declarative statements, such as: "There was a drummer's rate, a serviceman's rate, a monthly rate, a day rate, even an hourly rate if you knew my grandfather." But every sentence is carefully chosen to balance the sentence that preceded and the sentence that comes after. It might be possible for an editor to join some of his shorter sentences together into longer ones, but that is not how Ford would want it. Instead, he prefers:

> "Normal life, I know now, is life that can be explained in one sentence. No questions needed. And that, I lacked. 'You live right here in the hotel?' is what I heard. Afterwards, a smile. These were Southerners, guests I met briefly."

Ford is not afraid to use sentence fragments when he needs to, as in "Afterwards, a smile," or in the later one-word sentence, "Service," which follows in the example below.

Paragraph choices

Like Ghosh and Woolf, Ford avoids rigidly structured paragraphs. He does not necessarily rely on topic sentences, and sometimes his paragraph breaks are relatively arbitrary. The paragraphs are rather long. Paragraph one is approximately 235 words long; paragraph two is about 70 words; paragraph three is 335 words; paragraph four is 125 words; and paragraph five is 60 words long. The average length of paragraphs is about 200 words throughout. But let us look at paragraphs four and five, which appear to be arbitrarily broken:

> My grandfather, Ben Shelley, was a man of strong appetites—food, but other things, too. The usual things. He was a fatty who played winter golf in pleated gabardines, shot pool and quail. He qualified as a sport, a Shriner, a wide, public man, a toddling character in a blue suit with change in his pockets and a money clip. To me, he was the exotic brought to common earth, and I loved him. ' The latchstring is always on the outside' was his motto, and he winked at you when he said that, smiled between his thick amorous lips, as though his words meant something else, which they may have. I could think different of him now, see him through new eyes, revise history, take a narrower, latter-day view. But why?
>
> He had been a boxer—a featherweight, a club fighter; worked dining cars on the Rock Island as far as Tucumcari, waited tables in El Reno, been a caterer's assistant at the famous Muehlebach in Kansas City. That was the way up in the hotel business, and such work was his by nature. Service. That word meant something it doesn't mean now.

These paragraphs have his grandfather as their topic; their purpose is to give us an impression of the man and tell us about his character and career. It would be reasonable to see the first sentence of paragraph four as the topic sentence in that it introduces the topic and identifies him. But what is the topic sentence of the fifth paragraph? That paragraph is a list of jobs his grandfather held, with a final comment on service. What is the topic sentence?

One of the best ways of regarding these paragraphs is to see them as both controlled—loosely—by the first topic sentence. They are broken in two to make the paragraphs more inviting to read. Also, paragraph two is logically distinct because it treats the subtopic of the jobs Ford's grandfather held.

The paragraphs are developed first through description (also the main principle of paragraph three) with examples and questions. Then, paragraph two offers a series of occupations with a brief comment. The principle in both cases is accretion of detail. Since every detail relates explicitly to the grandfather, and since there are no digressions, interruptions, or discussions of subtopics, the paragraphs possess a unity and wholeness. They are also relaxed, conversational, natural, and soothing.

Paragraph links

The structure of this essay can be seen clearly by following the opening sentences of each of the paragraphs. That is not to say that the opening sentences are topic sentences—as may sometimes be recommended. Instead, they tend to point to the direction of the next or additional point that is to be made. The boxed material is a simple listing of each opening sentence of each paragraph. You can see how their subject links them from one paragraph to the next, with very few ordinary transitional statements ("And, of course" may be the only candidate).

FORD'S OPENING SENTENCES

And what was it like to live there?

This was the fifties, and my grandfather ran the hotel where we lived—in Little rock, a town neither exactly south nor exactly west, just as it still is.

The hotel was named the Marion, and it was not a small place.

My grandfather, Ben Shelley, was a man of strong appetites—food, but other things, too.

He had been a boxer—a featherweight, a club fighter; worked dining cars on the Rock Island as far as Tucumcari, waited tables in El Reno, been a caterer's assistant at the famous Muehlbach in Kansas City.

Normal life, I know now, is life that can be explained in one sentence.

Certain things *were* acknowledged lacking.

Travelers—our guests—were people I did not know.

And, of course, we lived *in,* in an apartment with four rooms where we did not own the furniture but where we liked it—room and board the highly valued parts of our deal.

Whatever his duties—and they were not so clear-cut to me—he was up at six to do them, gone down the elevator in his loose blue suit 'to put in an appearance.'"

And what did I do?

To make regular life seem regular need not always be to bleach the strong colors out.

How permanent is real life?

These sentences represent the engine that moves this short essay. They vary in structure, length, detail, and tone. When you read them in this fashion, one after another, they imply much that the essay develops. They are not, however, the essay in miniature. They reveal Ford's combination of close observation of his childhood memories with the mature reflection that comes with age and experience. In other words, as implied in his last sentence above, reflecting on this experience has made him philosophical and has awakened in him an inquiring spirit. When you read the entire essay in light of observing these controlling sentences, you realize that Ford has spent a great deal of time describing a place—the Marion—and a person—his grandfather—but he has also revealed quite a bit about the boy that he was and the man he has become.

One of the purposes of writing personal recollections or autobiography is to learn about the person you have become. Just as Freudian psychiatry emphasizes the childhood of the patient as a key or clue to the emotional well-being of the adult, autobiography offers the opportunity to examine the past in an effort to comprehend the present. It may even help shed light on the direction of the future.

Reflections on Richard Ford's Style

Much of the analysis of Ford's style concerns essentially mechanical issues: the types of words, the length and kinds of sentences, the length of paragraphs, the question of topic sentences, methods of development. True, all these are important. But such considerations are something like dissections of cadavers. They describe the thing, but do not give insight into what makes it live.

However, for the purpose of advanced writers, these mechanical concerns are very important. For one thing, they help us observe certain details regarding the way in which Ford writes. And, perhaps most important, they point us to things that we ourselves can benefit from. For example, we can learn from looking at Ford's choices of words. Consider the words in paragraphs three and four. Here are the proper names, some unusual nouns, strong verbs, and interesting modifiers:

Proper names: Ben Shelley; Shriner; Rock Island; Tucumcari; El Reno; Muehlebach; Kansas city

Nouns: appetites; fatty; gabardines; money clip; the exotic; latchstring; history; boxer; featherweight; fighter; Service

Strong verbs: shot; qualified; brought; loved; winked; revise

Modifiers: strong; pleated; wide, public; toddling; thick; amorous; narrower; latter-day

When you go back to reread those paragraphs you will realize how much subtle mileage Ford gets from these careful word choices. He depends on proper names for much of his effect—examine your own writing to see how you do on that score. His nouns are by no means weird or exotic, but they are careful. For example, instead of saying his grandfather was fat, Ford calls him a fatty; instead of saying he played golf in dress trousers, he says gabardines. Every noun gives us concrete information that helps build the portrait of this interesting person. The verbs are cautiously chosen. Weak verbs would include the verb "to be" and its variants, some of which he uses: was (six times); is (once); been (twice). Some advanced writers might avoid using the verb "to be" entirely, while beginning writers seem to depend on it entirely. Ford's use of the verb "to be" is essentially colloquial. It relaxes the reader, but because of its moderate use, it does not throw the reader into a torpor.

Ford's modifiers, essentially adjectives, are not unusual, but they are always timely. Some, like "toddling," are surprising and amusing. We can learn from his practice by noticing that he does not overdo modifiers. One problem characteristic of less experienced writers is that they often use more modifiers than strong nouns or verbs. Ford chooses a limited number of modifiers in relation to nouns and verbs. The result is a powerful style.

Beyond the mechanical issues, Ford's style depends on a point of view, an attitude toward his subject matter and toward his audience. His approach to the audience is to assume people are much like him, that they are curious, and that they will share some of his feelings of nostalgia, and perhaps share a moment of recognition from their own childhood memories. Ford's attitude toward his material is positive, filled with something of a sense of wonder. It is not cynical, cocky, or challenging. All of that comes through in the style because in order to be cynical, he would have to make other word choices and describe his grandfather, the hotel, and his childhood experiences much differently. The child he was is open to experience, filled with the excitement and curiosity of youth. All that is implied in the manner in which he addresses his subject and his audience.

His deep subject, apart from the detailed description and discussion of his grandfather and his hotel, is "normal life." What is normal? For most of us, growing up in a hotel is far from normal, which is one reason we read this and find it interesting. But Ford explains that he was never lonely, never thought things were odd or strange. Certainly, some things were different. There were few neighbors as such, and no other children his age to spend time with. And what did he do all the while he was in the hotel? As he says, he "saw operations over and over." He "was prized for my manners, for my height, for the fact that my father was sick and I was here—bravely and indefinitely."

The Search for Significance

One goal of autobiographical writing is discovering meaning in personal experience, the significance of the personal narrative. For example, it is possible to write about everyday personal issues, but shaping the narrative will give some point to your story. The significance of Ford's essay lies in his deepened awareness of himself in relation to relatives who really mattered to him. He tells us about them in such a way as to make us feel their importance as well. Good personal essays will usually try to do the same.

The one thing you do not want people to say about your autobiographical piece is: "So what?" Ford wants you to understand that he is no longer the boy he once was, and that the early experiences he had went into making him the observant person he is today. We are shaped by past experiences, but how? Which experiences seem to get which results? We are always interested in the answer to such questions. Part of the pleasure of writing an autobiographical piece lies in the possibility that you will see the significance of a series of events and come to a better understanding of yourself.

Let Your Story Unfold

Some writers assume the significance of a personal essay can reside in a motto, such as "Do unto others as you would have them do unto you." But in practice such a device is unnecessary. Personal stories accrue their own meaning. Life is too complicated for most of us. Instead, you need to be willing to let your story unfold as it must and as you write or rewrite, move it toward revealing its own meaning both to writer and reader. That is difficult advice, but it is meant in the spirit of avoiding work that is likely to reduce rather than elevate the understanding of complex moments of life. There is no way to boil Ford's piece down into a simple statement that has any of the significance of the entire essay. If anything, the significance of the piece is never entirely clear until we, as the readers, reflect upon it. Yet, it is significant because it reveals the nature of the writer and the person the writer was at the time Ford wrote about him. That is largely a result of Ford's honest portrayal and his capacity to provide enough details for us to relive the experience with him.

The box material sums up the discussion about writing the personal essay covered in this chapter.

TIPS FOR WRITING A PERSONAL ESSAY

1. Choose a limited moment of experience or a limited period of time and decide how to tell your story. Focus your attention so as to focus your reader's attention.
2. Your essay need not center on exceptional experiences, such as triumphs or catastrophes. Instead, the ordinary events of growing up, making friends, learning new things, cooking meals, anticipation of people's behavior, and the development of understanding between you and family members make wonderful subjects for a personal essay.
3. Use conventional narrative techniques where they seem appropriate, for example beginning in the middle of the action, then pausing to bring the reader up to date. Use flashbacks where necessary. It is also appropriate to start at the beginning and go to the end, telling the story in chronological order.
4. Emphasize details such as the names of places, the names and description of people.
5. Use sensory details as appropriate. Keep a checklist of the five senses and see that you include the most important.
6. Use direct and indirect quotation. Be as accurate as possible.
7. Include personal reflections on your experience and aim for honesty in portraying yourself and others. Use your own voice.
8. If you have maintained a journal or diary, make use of it by reviewing entries before and after the events you include in your essay.
9. Write your first draft quickly and get your ideas out on paper.
10. When you revise, examine your style on the levels of word choice, sentences, and paragraphs. Revise for a simple, direct, and efficient style.

3

Writing the Biographical Essay

Another Person's Life

The section in libraries labeled "Biography" holds multivolume books that cover the lives of famous people from their birth to their death. Some people written about in those books seem to have helped change the world. Others appeared ordinary enough while they lived, but on close examination reveal a complex and rich quality that stimulates our attention. The huge biographies are comprehensive. However, shorter biographical essays usually focus on a single quality of a person's life, or on a brief moment in that life. Sometimes it is a moment of crisis and great decision making, and sometimes it is a moment that reveals a surprising, and perhaps tender, quality that the world may not have appreciated. The brief biographical essay succeeds because of its focus and its detail. But it also succeeds generally because most of us are interested in knowing how other people live.

Often we want to know more about admirable people, such as sports stars Jackie Robinson, Michael Jordan, "Babe" Didrickson, "Tiger" Woods, Jennifer Capriati, or Michelle Kwan. Sometimes we simply wish to pay homage by learning about a person's life, as in the case of Jacqueline Kennedy Onassis. Then there are people who fascinate us because of their horrible deeds. The many biographies of Bonny and Clyde, John Dillinger, the Boston Strangler, and other serial killers, such as John Wayne Gayce, hardly begin to satisfy the public's morbid curiosity. People who prey on their fellow humans are not the norm, and many of us try to understand the norms of human behavior by reading about the abnormal. Or at least, we need reassurance that such frightening criminals are different from us.

What We Learn from Writing About People

It may be a cliché, but we always learn something about ourselves from reading biography. The reason is simple: in biography we have a point of comparison. When we read Paul Theroux talking about his fellow travel writer Bruce Chatwin, in the essay that appears later in the chapter, we know that Chatwin set some kind of benchmark for nonstop talking and subtle self-promotion. Theroux's value judgment regarding such behavior gives us a measure of what other people can tolerate in big talkers. Reading about Chatwin we ask ourselves, "Am I like that?"

Writing about other people helps us express generosity, clarify our own values, and study behavior more objectively than when we examine ourselves. It also gives us a chance to reflect on the meaning of a life or the effect that individuals can have on others and on history itself. The study of the human spirit is one of the most compelling studies that we conduct. It is sometimes inspiring, sometimes appalling, but always interesting.

Catherine S. Manegold's very brief biographical essay "Kara S. Hultgreen: The Short Flight of a Fighter Pilot," is a homage of appreciation, but it is tinged with sadness and with a sense of loss.

CATHERINE S. MANEGOLD

Kara S. Hultgreen
THE SHORT FLIGHT OF A FIGHTER PILOT

Hers was a dream denied, then deferred and finally granted, to fly with the elite in a fighter jet so fast, so complex and so advanced that its wings heave back and forth along its glinting body, shifting angles for attack, landing, takeoff and approach, a machine hurtling 35 tons of metal, raw speed and unspent ammunition toward a combat target or a floating landing field called home.

To fly an F-14 has always been for the few. Kara Spears Hultgreen fought for the privilege. Again and again, the system closed its doors, but systems change. When the ban on women in combat was finally lifted, Hultgreen was prepared. She had a Navy post, about 1,000 hours of flight experience and a reputation as a pilot unfazed by the rigors of life along the thin blue line of the earth's atmosphere.

When she was a college senior, her mother, Sally Spears, thought she would make a stunning debutante. Instead, she joined the Navy and became a stunning fighter pilot—5 foot 10, lean, with silk brown hair, vivacious, with a ready smile. She also had an edge when edge was needed and a sky-time nickname, Fang.

Once, after landing on an aircraft carrier off Key West, she was striding down the deck when the flight bosses noticed her hair tumbling below her helmet. They said it was a safety hazard and she was told to cut it short. She balked: "You don't want to keep me from exploring my feminine side, do you?" The Pentagon spent hundreds of thousands of dollars studying the problem. But Hultgreen did not wait for the result. Instead, she bought a race-car helmet, which solved the problem. And that ended that.

"Yes, it's a macho job in a number of ways," the 29-year-old flyer told Scott Watkins, a senior editor at Woman Pilot magazine, several weeks before she died. "But that's not why I wanted to do it. I did this to become a fighter pilot. It makes me feel no less feminine and it should not make men feel less masculine. The F-14 is a humbling jet and I've been humbled."

From the start, she had wanted to fly the fastest, damnedest jets in the force, hoping, one day, to become an astronaut. She had hoped for an F-18, the sharpest of the lot, but the Navy assigned her to the less glamorous EA-6A, an electronic warfare plane used to simulate enemy aircraft. She excelled. In 1992, while ending a routine flight in the blue skies over the Florida Keys, Lieutenant Hultgreen came in with crippled landing gear. A man on the ground taped the smooth landing. It was, says Comdr. Stephen Pietropaoli, a Navy spokesman who watched that feat on tape, "a neat piece of flying."

Eighteen months later, as Navy regulations eased, Hultgreen was on her way to California to sit at the controls of her first F-14. For all its speed and fury, she would say, the jet was heavy and intractable. She compared it to an elephant. "You can ease it over to the right and sort of nudge it over to the left," she said. "But when it decides it's going to sit down, there's nothing you can do about it."

At the San Diego base, Hultgreen earned her F-14 carrier qualification after a narrow failure on her first attempt. An exhausting round of exercises at a naval war-combat school in Nevada in early October was followed by a stint with an aircraft carrier, the Abraham Lincoln. Then, on Oct. 25, as Hultgreen came in for a landing, the left engine sputtered and seemed to fail. The jet rolled. The radar-intercept officer ejected. Less than a half-second later, the pilot's seat was automatically expelled. The F-14 was only about 150 feet above the water then and Hultgreen slammed into the sea at three times highway speeds. She died on impact and the jet sank, wasting, in a fraction of a second, one extraordinary pilot's life.

This essay portrays an unnecessary death that seems, in light of the struggles of Kara Hultgreen, tragic. But the essay is also about overcoming obstacles. The opening line: "Hers was a dream denied, then deferred and finally granted," alludes to Langston Hughes' poem that talks about the struggle of African-Americans, what he called "A dream deferred." The allusion reminds the reader that prejudice comes in many forms, and one of them is the male macho prejudice against women fighter pilots.

Once having read the essay, what do we know about Kara Hultgreen? Some of the most important details are:

- She was 29, a pilot with more than 1,000 hours experience.
- She was a beautiful woman from a privileged background.
- She was a problem-solver who valued her feminine side.
- She was a skilled pilot, as witnessed by her landing a crippled plane in brilliant fashion.
- She had problems with her challenging F-14 plane and was killed in her approach to an aircraft carrier.

What we do not know much about are her feelings, her inner concerns. This brief essay gives us the details of the events, but no details of her motivations. Why did she want to fly? And why did she want to be a fighter pilot? We can presume that it was the challenge, the excitement—in fact the very things that might draw anyone into wanting to become a fighter pilot. Manegold uses the example of Kara Hultgreen as an argument for treating men and women in the air force equally.

Hultgreen's job, until recently, had been reserved for men. The very fact that we do not normally expect women to be flying high-powered jets in combat makes this brief life interesting. That she died doing what she enjoyed most is terrible, but we admire what she accomplished. What Manegold may not have known is that between 1992 and the end of 1994 ten F-14 aviators died in accidents. Kara Hultgreen is only one of them. Also, the Navy blamed her for the crash until an investigation, completed in February 1995, exonerated her when it was discovered that her engine had failed.

Following Personal Interests

As a writer of biography you have a wide range of choices for a subject. We can tell that Catherine Manegold wrote about Kara Hultgreen because Hultgreen was a high achiever in a "man's world." You may have some special interests that would lead you in a similar direction. You also may have some special resources that other writers would not have, such as letters or notebooks of someone whom you feel you would like to know. Often, families have caches of material that belonged to ancestors who are now only shadowy figures. Writing about them and using their own words as resource material can make a biographical essay fascinating. Photographs enrich biographies and contain visual information not present in letters and memoirs. Ours is a highly visual age, and since the photograph has been with us for more than 150 years, you may have access to some rich material in your own family household.

You may also be involved in an activity that has produced some interesting people. For example, if you are a chess player, you will run across names such as Paul Morphy, the first American world champion. You will probably be familiar with the name Bobby Fischer, the most recent American world champion. Both of these men are fascinating for their unorthodox lifestyles. If you play tennis you may be curious about Andre Agassi or Martina Navritilova, both media stars as well as champions. If you are interested in basketball, you may want to write about Magic Johnson, Shaquille O'Neill, Larry Bird, or Michael Jordan. You may also know of women basketball stars such as Rebecca Lobo in a new professional league. In medicine, you may want to know more about Jonas Salk, who found the cure for polio. There are many famous medical people, both past and present. If you are interested in researching famous contemporary women writers, you might choose from Alice Walker, Toni Morrison, Gwendolyn Brooks, bell hooks, Gloria Steinem, Margaret Atwood, or Doris Lessing.

In certain arenas, such as entertainment, people achieve fame through the power of personal charisma. Marilyn Monroe, Elvis Presley, and James Dean fascinated an entire era in America. They all now appear on U.S. postage stamps. You may find yourself curious about how they lived, what they thought, what made them interesting. Politicians, such as Franklin D. Roosevelt, Winston Churchill, and John F. Kennedy, interest us for the way they affected our own history. In writing a biographical essay, think through aspects of your own life and the people who have had an influence in areas that concern you.

What Makes Someone Interesting?

Achievement makes a public figure interesting. What a great politician achieves will have an influence on the lives of many people, and we always want to know what kind of person makes earth-shaking decisions. Is the person totally in control of things, or is it a case of the person moving with the right flow at the right time? What kind of principles does a politician hold to? How were they formed? What is the measure of courage for someone who makes unpopular political decisions? In the case of politics, power is the ultimate issue, and we want to know how our politicians handle power, how they value it, and whether they respect it enough to use it sparingly.

Difference is another source of interest in people. If you had a chance to spend some time gathering information about a group of Bornean head-hunters (and you knew you'd come out of it alive), you would probably go. Just the chance to see how people totally different from you behave on a daily basis and how they react to your habits would appeal to many people. Some of us do not have enough curiosity about people to go off and live with them. But *The National Geographic* has been a successful publication for more than a century because of our general curiosity in how other people live. When we consider the lives of Native Americans, such as the Apache, the Sioux, the Chippewa, the Pueblo, the Zuñi, and many other smaller tribes, we realize that there are alternatives to the way we live today. Writing about an individual member of one of those tribes would give us insight into some of those alternatives, and thus broaden choices in our own lives.

A third source of interest is a quality or qualities we want to emulate. We have all seen monkeys imitating people or other monkeys. Seagulls learn from other seagulls how to snatch up clams from the edge of the sea and drop them on something hard from a great height. That is not an instinct: it is learned behavior. We learn from our parents, friends, teachers, and relatives, and sometimes from total strangers. When we learn to play baseball, tennis, golf, hockey, or any other sport, we usually pick up a good many tips from people already good at it. When we read biography, we are also capable of learning how to react to certain difficult or crucial situations that might show up in our own life. It could help many of us to know how President Roosevelt dealt with crippling polio while running for president. He tried to convince the country during the Depression that it could stand on its own legs at a time when he could not stand on his.

Scandal is another source of interest in public figures. We are almost always drawn to want to know more about people whose lives are marked by "having been caught" in some form of unsanctioned behavior. When word leaked out that John F. Kennedy was having affairs with a variety of women while he was in the White House, the public took notice. Scandal is interesting when it touches people we think ought to be positive role models. Some public figures, such as Madonna or Johnny Rotten, might be helped by a touch of scandal, since we do not expect them to live exemplary lives. The mixed reactions to Michael Jackson's legal problems in his relations with children, on the other hand, had a negative effect on his career. Our interest in scandal comes under the heading of morbid curiosity. We may feel a bit ashamed of ourselves for paying attention to charges and innuendoes against famous people, but we are fascinated by questionable behavior.

Gathering Sources for a Biography

Obviously, the better the sources, the better your biography is likely to be. To begin with, there are two possibilities: (1) If you know the subject of your essay and can gather materials directly from him or her, then your sources will be local and varied. (2) If you do not know your subject, you may have to rely entirely on printed material such as books and articles. In the first instance, you rely on primary sources. In the second instance, you rely on secondary sources.

The Personal Interview

If we assume that you have chosen a person as your subject with whom you can meet and talk, you have a number of possibilities for the sources you can use. Your own personal experiences with your subject are of first importance. If, for example, you decide to write about a parent or a grandparent, you can draw from memories, as did Richard Ford in "Accommodations." You may also want to gather materials from personal albums, letters, and conversations with your subject. All first-hand information is of value to the biographer, since that material will be reliable and not widely know. If you choose to write about a family member, you may also rely on the recollections of others in the family. In many cases you may have correspondence, diaries, daybooks, checks and checkbooks, and photographs to help make your biography more detailed and authoritative.

To your personal experience, you may add material from an interview or interviews. The personal interview should follow your examination of any written information or photographs that might help your biography. If you can draw on personal experiences, you might make a list of the most memorable so that during the interview you can mention them to see if your memories coincide with those of your subject. Again, it is the principle of being concrete.

One of the most important preparations for an interview is writing down a list of questions that you feel are important and revealing. Pare the list to the most important and have them ready when you talk with your subject. Another important preparation involves finding out what you can about your subject's background so you can demonstrate that you are interested enough to be ready to talk seriously about the things that interest you.

Biographical References

When you wish to write a short biography on someone you do not know, the resources at your disposal are numerous. The place to start is the reference section of your library, where you might be directed to consult some of the sources listed here as box text.

GENERAL BIOGRAPHICAL RESOURCES

Biography Index. This widely available resource provides an index of books about people and articles in journals. It is the first place to look.

Your library's catalog will give you titles of holdings on your subject.

Chamber's Biographical Dictionary (New York: Two Continents, 1974). A good general source for a quick biography of people in many fields.
Contemporary Authors (Detroit: Gale, 1967–). Exists in several editions and is constantly updated. If your subject is an author, this resource may help find key information.
Current Biography (New York: Wilson, 1940–). Monthly issues that contain eighteen or twenty short biographies of people of current interest.
Dictionary of American Biography, 16 vols. (New York: Scribner's, 1927–). Famous dead Americans, updated with supplements.
Who's Who in America, 1899–, biennial (Chicago: Marquis Who's Who). Living Americans. Specialized and regionalized editions.
Dictionary of American Negro Biography (New York: Norton, 1982).
Dictionary of National Biography, 22 vols. (New York: Oxford, 1882–1986). Famous dead British subjects.
Dictionary of Scientific Biography, 8 vols. (New York: Macmillan, 1981).
New Encyclopedia Britannica. 32 vols. (Chicago: Britannica, 1985). Provides biographies, as do specialized encyclopedias.

These resources are meant to serve a general public interested in basic information, primarily the facts surrounding an individual's life. Consequently, they must be regarded as places in which you begin your research. They may provide you with some useful leads, such as giving you titles of books about your subject, commenting on the reliability of information about your subject, and/or providing you with names of people who were close to your subject and who may have included observations useful to you in their own autobiographies or other writings.

Books, Biased and Unbiased: The Case of Sylvia Plath

The most generally useful titles you will find will be book-length studies of your subject. Since biography is one of the most common forms of publication, it comes as no surprise to find that almost everyone of note has inspired one or more biographies. You may assume that everything in a biography is absolutely reliable. However, a given biographer may have an axe to grind by proposing a specific view of a controversial person. Biographies often try to settle the controversies (or start one), and therefore two or more biographies can easily produce distinctly different portraits of the same person.

An interesting case in point is the range of interpretation of the life of the American poet Sylvia Plath (1932–1963), who killed herself in London, despondent over having been left by her husband, Ted Hughes, the British poet. Plath was emotionally unstable as a young woman, and her death raised so many questions about loyalty and talent that she has become an object of fascination for many young writers. Sylvia had two young children but was essentially alone in London, unsure of her future. Some people blame Hughes, but others point to the fact that Plath had attempted suicide earlier and that even with him, she might have done exactly what she did. Moreover, some people assert that Sylvia Plath would not be considered an important poet today except for the fact that she committed suicide so young. In a sense, they say, she martyred herself for art and has therefore become an object of morbid fascination.

Each of the following works on Sylvia Plath takes a specific position in the debate:

Jacqueline Rose, *The Haunting of Sylvia Plath* (Cambridge, Mass.: Harvard University Press, 1991). This book is antagonistic toward views held by Ted Hughes and his sister Olwyn Hughes.

A. Alvarez, "A Poet and Her Myths," *New York Review of Books*, September 28, 1989. Alvarez has generally been pro-Hughes. He knew Sylvia personally.

Olwyn Hughes, "The Plath Myth and the Reviewing of *Bitter Fame*. *Poetry Review*, vol. 80, no. 3 (Autumn 1990). Written by Hughes's sister.

Anne Stevenson, *Bitter Fame: A Life of Sylvia Plath* (Boston: Houghton Mifflin, 1989). Stevenson was given access to family papers by Olwyn Hughes and says she was forced to rewrite her book five times to satisfy Olwyn Hughes, who was still unhappy with the result.

Linda Wagner, *Sylvia Plath: A Biography* (London: Chatto &

Windus, 1988). This book was attacked by Olwyn Hughes as being crudely feminist.

Janet Malcolm, *The Silent Woman: Sylvia Plath and Ted Hughes* (New York: Random House, 1994). Malcolm wrote a book about writing a biography about Plath. In the process, she developed a strong sympathy for Ted Hughes. She also critiques each of the major biographies.

If you were to write a brief biography of Sylvia Plath, you might approach these books as if they were all equal in importance and value. You might not discover they are all part of a complex controversy until rather late in your reading. Such controversies exist for many people who have been subject of biographies, and the only way to make sure that your sources are reliable is to go to the *Book Review Digest* in your library and look up two or three reviews of the books you plan to use. The reviews will give you a sense of the reliability of the books, but they will also point to other titles that will be relevant to your researches. Most people writing a short biography would probably skip that process—but you should not. It is a key to making your biography valuable to you and your readers.

Autobiographies

Many subjects of biographies have prepared their own autobiography. For a biographer, an autobiography offers wonderful opportunities to see how the subject regards experience and what the subject thinks is important about his or her life. But one thing is always clear about autobiography: it presents the best view of the subject—or at least the view that the writer is most interested in having other people see. Consequently, autobiographies need to be read carefully and skeptically. Usually the bare record of events is more or less the same in an autobiography as in a biography, but the interior events—the moral decisions, the motivations, the emotional baggage—all these will be worth close scrutiny in an autobiography.

If you were researching Sylvia Plath, you would find two very interesting sources that approximate autobiography. One is *The Journals of Sylvia Plath* (New York: Random House, 1982). However, when you examine the book you will discover that it was published after Plath's death and that its consulting editor is Ted Hughes. Ted Hughes omitted many passages in the journals, and consequently the book's value may be somewhat limited. The second source is *Letters Home: Correspondence 1950–1963*. These were edited by Aurelia Schober Plath, Sylvia's mother. These letters from Sylvia to her mother were also edited to omit some passages Aurelia Plath did not want read. Both of these sources may be of limited value.

The point of all this is that in the area of biography, deep feelings, personal concerns, even vanity and pride, become a major consideration. All these get factored into every biography, every autobiography, and every observation on a person's life. Ultimately, your own biographical writing will reflect some of these values as filtered through your views and your personal concerns. Even the most careful biographer will find it difficult to interpret a life and remain completely objective. Indeed, it is probably impossible to do so.

The Media Image

Some popular journals such as *People Magazine* and *Us* as well as tabloid newspapers such as *The National Enquirer* thrive on telling us about people in the public eye. Naturally, these publications either puff their subjects to make them sometimes seem superhuman, or they dwell on scandal in hopes of titillating our interest. The popular media aim to stimulate their audience more than to give an objective, detailed portrait of the people they discuss. Consequently, these publications are often accused of distortion and sometimes are sued for libel.

That does not mean we cannot learn from the media. *Rolling Stone*, *Spin*, *Forbes*, *Business Week*, *Time*, *The New Yorker*, *Newsweek*, and other specialized magazines all present portraits of people they feel their readers should know about. The Sunday magazine sections of major newspapers do the same. However, you will note that most of the journalistic biographies look for some kind of "hook," a striking detail to get your attention and keep you reading. The "hook" may be shocking, amusing, or touching—but much of the time it will distort the picture. In the case of Catherine Manegold's essay it is the very fact of a woman flying a fighter plane. In Paul Theroux's essay on Bruce Chatwin, the first paragraph comments on overhearing Chatwin talk about mountain climbing when Theroux knew he "had never been much of a mountaineer." Such details pique our curiosity.

The popular media tell us that it is not enough to sit down and dryly tell the story of your subject, beginning with birth date and following with the key statistical information of schooling, marriage, and profession. One of the best ways to start a biography is by putting your subject into action, showing the reader a key moment in the subject's day, then going back and taking the time to fill in the information that will make your story complete. The popular media can also help us learn that you need an angle—a personal view of what you think is true when you write a biography. Ideally, you will have researched your subject enough so that you will have a strong opinion about his or her life. Your biography should defend that position with a good interpretation of the evidence. Popular biography may be sleazy at times, and it may be sensational at times, but its one lesson is important: it tries not to be dull.

Judging Someone's Life

Biography involves judgments. Most biographers are confronted by evidence and issues that conflict or confound. People live complex lives that do not on the surface always add up to what they seem. Biographers have important choices. They can maintain an objectivity that emphasizes only the known facts, permitting readers to draw their own conclusions. Or, the biographer can present the evidence and material in a way that argues for one or another view of the subject. Biographers of Elvis Presley must cope with the image at the end of his life of a bloated, drug-using Elvis. How can they square that with the almost religious devotion that Elvis inspired in his fans? Simply listing the known facts will not serve the purpose. Interpreting the facts in light of the evidence may be the only choice.

The following essay recalls a friend. Paul Theroux, the author and noted travel writer, has lived in Italy, Malawi, Uganda, and Singapore. His *The Old Patagonian Express* (1979) is well known. Bruce Chatwin is also famous as a travel writer. His *In Patagonia* (1980) mixes history and his personal experiences in Patagonia, the southern part of Argentina. Because the two had Patagonian experiences in common, and because they shared the same professional interests, Theroux and Chatwin were capable of a close friendship. But that does not mean Theroux's memoir is without a judgment regarding his friend. We see Chatwin not as an object of adulation, but as a person whose faults are as interesting as his virtues.

PAUL THEROUX

Chatwin Revisited

When I think of Bruce Chatwin, who was my friend, I am always reminded of a particular night, a dinner at the Royal Geographical Society, hearing him speaking animatedly about various high mountains he had climbed. And that struck me as very odd, because I knew he had never been much of a mountaineer.

I was some way down the table but I heard him clearly. He spoke in his usual way, very rapidly and insistently, stuttering and interrupting and laughing, until he had commanded enough attention to begin speechifying. Being Chatwin, he did not stop at the peaks he scaled. He had plans for further assaults and expeditions—all of them one-man affairs, no oxygen, minimum equipment, rush the summit—and as he appeared to be holding his listeners spellbound (they were murmuring, "Of course" and "Extraordinary" and "Quite right"), I peeked over to see their faces. On Chatwin's right was Chris Bonington, conqueror of Nanga Parbat and numerous other twenty-thousand-footers, and on his left, Lord Hunt, leader of the first successful expedition up Everest.

"Chatter, chatter, chatter, Chatwin," a mutual friend once said to me. He was smiling, but you could tell his head still hurt. Bruce had just been his houseguest for a week. "He simply never stops."

This talking was the most striking thing about him, yet there were so many other aspects of him that made an immediate impression. He was handsome, he had piercing eyes; he was very quick—full of nervous gestures, a rapid walker; he was often surprisingly mocking of the English. Of course, Bruce talks a lot, people said. It's because he's alone so much of the time. It was true that he was intensely solitary—he was given to sudden disappearances, that is, and everyone assumed he was alone. But even so, I believe he talked to himself, probably yakked nonstop, rehearsing his stories and practicing funny accents and mimicry: it is a habit of many writers and travelers. I am sorry I never asked him whether he did this. I am sure he would have let out his screeching laugh and said, "Constantly!"

He was such a darter he seldom stayed still long enough for anyone to sum him up, but when he died many people published their memories of him—and the portraits were so different. It was amazing how many people, old and young, many of them distinguished, a number of them glamorous, gathered to mourn him, in a Greek Orthodox church in London. Salman Rushdie sat in the pew in front of me with his then wife. It was Valentine's Day 1989, the day after the ayatollah condemned Salman to death—I thought it was a hollow condemnation, and I joked about it. Judging from the congregation, Bruce had known everyone in London. But he had flitted from one to another, keeping people separate, making a point of not introducing them to each other, but often dropping their names.

He did not only drop Francis Bacon's name: he went one better and mimicked him—which suggested just how well he knew him. "Oh, dear," he would say, with an epicene hiss, "a million quid for one of my paintings—I'll just spend it on champagne." He could get two or three boasts into a single statement, as in "Werner Herzog and I just hiked two hundred miles in Dahomey," or "David Hockney told me that his favorite painter is Liotard, a seventeenth-century Swiss. He's brilliant. I often go to the Rijksmuseum just to look at his work." (This must have been true, because one day in Amsterdam, Bruce showed me a Liotard painting.)

Postcards are the preferred medium for many boasters, combining vividness, cheapness, and an economy of effort—something like a miniature billboard. Bruce was a great sender of postcards. He sent them to me from France, from China, from Australia, and from the artists' colony Yaddo—*Feverish lesbian sculptors doing vulvaic iconography in plastic.* He encapsulated a theory about an Italian writer in Yunnan. From Australia he wrote, *You must come here. The men are awful, like bits of cardboard, but the women are splendid.* And on another postcard (this one of a bushranger), *Have become interested in an extreme situation—of Spanish monks in an Aboriginal mission and am about to start sketching an outline. Anyway the crisis of the "shall-never-write-another-line" sort is now over.*

In terms of writing, he was in a state of permanent crisis. Perhaps he had started to write too late in his life, perhaps he lacked confidence. A writer talking to another writer about the difficulty of writing is hardly riveting. Bruce was at his least interesting bemoaning his writer's block, and I often felt that he was not really bemoaning it at all, but rather boasting about the subtlety of his special gift, the implication being that it was so finely tuned it occasionally emitted a high-pitched squeal and seemed to go dead; but no, it was still pulsing like a laser—it had simply drifted an instant from his sights. I had no such story to tell—I was producing a book a year, turning the big wooden crank on my chomping meatgrinder. How could I talk about a literary crisis, when all I had to do was grab the crank and give it a spin?

He did write like an angel most of the time, but he is never more Chatwinesque than when he is yielding to his conceit. In *The Songlines* he mentions being in Vienna speaking with Konrad Lorenz (in itself something of a boast) on the subject of aggression. Considering that Lorenz is the author of *On Aggression*, this was audacious of Bruce, but he was unfazed in the presence of the master, and went further, cheerfully adumbrating his own theories of aggression ("But surely," he asked pointedly, "haven't we got the concepts of 'aggression' and 'defense' mixed up?"), implying that Konrad Lorenz had been barking up the wrong tree in sixty-odd years of scientific research. Bruce then sketches his Beast Theory: mankind needing to see his enemy as a beast in order to overcome him; or needing to be a "surrogate beast" in order to see men as prey.

It seems astonishing that the renowned zoologist and philosopher did not find Bruce's theory conventional and obvious (as it sounds to me). Instead, "Lorenz tugged at his beard, gave me a searching look and said, ironically or not I'll never know: 'What you have just said is totally new.'."

Chatwin claimed to have the usual English disdain for flattery and praise, which is odd, because he adored it, and of course—praise is cheap and plentiful—it was lavished upon him. To need praise is human enough. Bruce solicited it by circulating to his friends bound proof copies of his books. We would read them and scribble remarks in the margin. I remember the scribbled-over copy of *The Viceroy of Ouidah*. My remarks were anodyne, but some other snippets of marginalia were shrieks of derision: "Ha! Ha!" or "Rubbish" or "Impossible!" He said he didn't care.

Here he is in Dahomey, speaking to an African soldier, in his sketch "A Coup":

> "You are English?"
> "Yes."
> "But you speak excellent French."
> "Passable," I said.
> "With a Parisian accent I should have said."
> "I have lived in Paris."

Much of his reading was in French, usually obscure books. It would be something like *Rousseau's Des rêveries du promeneur solitaire*, Gide's

Nourritures terrestres, Rimbaud's *Les Illuminations* or—one of the strangest travel books ever written—*Voyage au tour de ma chambre*. When he found a book that few other people had read he tended to overpraise it. He might dismiss a book precisely because it was popular.

His ability to speak French well was of course part of his gift for mimicry, and it delighted me, though it irritated many who felt Bruce was showing off. When he appeared on the Parisian literary television show *Apostrophe*, he was interviewed in French and he replied with complete fluency, talking a mile a minute.

He was full of theories. One was highly complex and concerned the origin of the color red as the official color of Marxism. This theory took you across the ocean to Uruguay. It involved butchers in Montevideo, peasants on horseback, Garibaldi and the Colorado Party. I think I've got that right. The theory then whisked you back to Europe, to Italy, to Germany, to Russia, and to the adoption of—was it an apron? was it a flag? It was all very confusing, though Chatwin told the story with precision, and always the same way. I know this because I heard him explain the theory at least four times. He told it to everyone. It was tiresome to hear this theory repeated, but it was even more annoying to realize that he had not remembered that he had told you before.

That was something his friends had to endure. If he couldn't recall that he was repeating something to you verbatim—shrieking each predictable thing and looking eager and hopeful—that seemed to indicate that he cared more about the monologuing itself than about you. The worst aspect of bores—even part-timers like Bruce—is their impartiality, their utter lack of interest in whoever they happen to be drilling into. Because it hardly matters who they are with, they victimize everyone, great and small.

Bruce was a fairly bad listener. If you told him something he would quickly say that he knew it already; and he would go on talking. Usually he was such a good talker that it hardly mattered.

But while most of us knew his stories, there were always great gaps in between them. There is an English saying which expresses befuddlement, *Who's he when he's at home?* Exactly. Everyone knew Bruce was married—we had met his wife, Elizabeth. But what sort of marriage was this? "*A marriage blanc*," a friend once said to me, pursing his lips. Bruce was in his way devoted to his wife, but the very fact of Bruce having a wife was so improbable that no one quite believed it.

One night at dinner, just before he left the table, I heard Bruce distinctly speak of his plans for the near future and say, "I'm going to meet my wife in Tibet." Afterwards, one of the people present said, "Did he say his wife was dead?" and another replied, "No. He said his wife's in bed."

He kept so much to himself. We heard the colorful stories of a born raconteur. But what of the rest of it? We wondered what his private life was really like, and sometimes we speculated. His first book, *In Patagonia*, embodied all his faults and virtues. It was highly original, courageous, and vividly written. He inscribed a copy to me, writing generously, *To Paul Theroux, who unwittingly triggered this off* (and he explained that a book of mine had inspired him). But his book was full of gaps. How had he traveled from here to there? How had he met this or that person? Life was never so neat as Bruce made out. What of the other, small, telling details, which to me give a book reality?

I used to look for links between the chapters, and between two conversations or pieces of geography. Why hadn't he put them in?

"Why do you think it matters?" he said to me.

"Because it's interesting," I said. "And because I think when you're writing a travel book you have to come clean."

This made him laugh, and then he said something that I have always taken to be a pronouncement that was very near to being his motto. He said—he screeched—"I don't believe in coming clean!"

We had a mutual friend, an older and distinguished writer who felt that Bruce was trying to live down the shame of being the son of a Birmingham lawyer. I challenged this.

The man said, "No. You're wrong. Look at Noel Coward. His mother kept a lodging house. And he pretended to be so grand—that theatrical English accent. All that posturing. He knew he was common. It was all a pretense. Think of his pain."

This might have been true in a small way of Bruce, but I think that he was secretive by nature. It kept him aloof. It helped him in his flitting around. He never revealed himself totally to anyone, as far as I know, and in this way he kept his personality intact. In any case, he never struck me as being thoroughly English. He was more cosmopolitan—liking France, feeling liberated in America, being fascinated by Russia and China, something of a cultural exile.

I am skirting the subject of his sexual preference because it does not seem to me that it should matter. Yet it was obvious to anyone who knew him that in speaking tenderly of marital bliss he was always suppressing a secret and more lively belief in homosexuality. That he was homosexual bothered no one; that he never spoke about it was rather disturbing.

In an ungracious memoir, the writer David Plante refused to see Bruce's sense of fun and perhaps even deeper sense of insecurity. Plante wrote at length about how they had gone to a gay disco in London called Heaven, but it is characteristic of the memoir's dark hints and hypocrisy that Bruce's behavior is regarded as sneaky and insincere, while Plante himself never discloses his own motive for going to the gay hangout.

I wanted to know more about his homosexual life, not because I am prurient but because if I like someone I want to know everything. And while Bruce was exasperated by others who kept their secrets, he was secretive himself. He never wrote about his sexuality, and some of us have laid our souls bare.

When he called me he always did so out of the blue. I liked that. I liked the suddenness of it—it suited my life and my writing. I hated making plans for the future. I might not be in the mood that far-off day; I might be trying to write something. If he called in the morning, it was always a proposal to meet that afternoon or evening. And then I might not hear from him for six months or a year.

It surprised me that he had agreed to give a lecture for the Royal Geographical Society, but he had done it on one condition—that it be a duet. Would I agree? I said O.K., and I quickly realized we were both doing it so as to seem respectable among all these distinguished explorers and travelers.

Working together with him to prepare the lecture, I realized how little I knew him and what an odd fish he was. He was insecure, I knew that, and it had the effect of making him seem domineering. "I can't believe you haven't read Pigafetta," he would say, and he would put the book in my hand and insist I read it by tomorrow; and the next day he would say, "Our talk's going to be awful, it's hopeless, I don't know why we agreed to do this"; and later on would say, "By the way, I've invited Sally, Duchess of Westminster."

I found this maddening. I felt it was a task we had to perform, and that we would do it well if we were decently prepared. Bruce's moods ranged from rather tiresome high spirits to days of belittling gloom. "No one's going to come," he said. "I'm certainly not inviting anyone."

We got in touch with a dozen members of the RGS who had photographs of Patagonia, and we assembled eighty or a hundred beautiful pictures of the plains, of glaciers, of penguins, of snow and storms.

When the day came it turned out that Bruce had invited many people, including his parents—his big beefy-faced father had the look of a Dickensian solicitor—and he was miffed that the duchess hadn't been able to make it. The lecture itself I thought was splendid—not so much for the text but for the atmosphere, the oddity. We gave it in the wooden amphitheater, where so many distinguished explorers had reported back to the society; and we stood in the dark—a little light shining on our notes, while big beautiful pictures of Patagonia flashed on the screen behind us. This was thrilling—just our voices and these vivid Patagonian sights.

There was loud applause afterwards. Bruce, who would have been a wonderful actor, was flushed with pleasure. He had been brilliant, and I realized that he had needed me to encourage him and get him through it.

And when I heard him at dinner regaling Lord Hunt and Chris Bonington with his mountaineering exploits I thought: He's flying!

He traveled. We ran into each other in various places—in America, in Amsterdam. When he wanted to meet someone I knew well he simply asked me to introduce him. Graham Greene he particularly wanted to meet. But Bruce was disappointed. He thought Greene was gaga. He could not understand the mystique. He loved Borges. Later he needed glamour. He let himself be courted by Robert Mapplethorpe. He liked the thought of his portrait appearing in Mapplethorpe's notorious exhibition, along with photographs of women weightlifters and strange flowers and even stranger sexual practices.

He went to China—just a magazine assignment, but Bruce made it seem as though he had been sent on an expedition by the Royal Geographical Society. I admired that in him. He took his writing assignments seriously, no matter who he was writing for. He was the opposite of a hack, which is to say something of a pedant, but a likeable one, who was fastidious and truly knowledgeable.

When he fell deathly ill soon after his China trip, the word spread that he had been bitten by a fruit bat in Yunnan and contracted a rare blood disease. Only two other people in the entire world had ever had it, so the story went, and both had died. Bruce was near death, but he fought back and survived. And he had another story to tell at dinner parties—of being bitten by a Chinese bat. He recovered. A friend said to me, "I just saw Bruce walking through Eaton Square carrying a white truffle."

But the blood disease returned. "I was warned that it might pop up again," Bruce explained. What kind of bat was this exactly? Bruce was vague, and he became very ill. Seeing him was like looking at the sunken cheeks and wasted flesh of a castaway. That image came to me again and again, the image of an abandoned traveler—the worst fate for travelers is that they become lost, and instead of reveling in oblivion, they fret and fall ill.

When I visited his bedroom in Oxfordshire—a pretty, homely farmhouse that Elizabeth kept ticking over—his hands would fly to his face, covering his hollow cheeks.

"God, you're healthy," he would say sadly. But later he would cheer up, making plans. "I'm going to California to see Lisa Lyon. She's fabulous. The woman weightlifter? You'd love her." And when I prepared to go, he would say, "I'm not ready for *The Tibetan Book of the Dead* yet."

"He expected to get better, and when he got worse he was demoralized and just let go," Elizabeth told me. "He was in terrible pain, but at the height of it he lapsed into a coma, and that was almost a blessing."

Hovering in this fragile state of health he died suddenly. He had been handsome, calculating, and demanding; he was famous for his disappearances. His death was like that, just as sudden, like Bruce on another journey. We were used to his vanishings—his silences could be as conspicuous as his talk. It seems strange, but not unlike him, that he has been gone so long.

Reflections on Theroux's Style

Theroux begins by reminding us that Bruce Chatwin was a friend. This observation prepares us to listen closely and to respect Theroux's views because they are those of an "insider." Bruce Chatwin was a well-known writer with many friends, as Theroux tells us, and each of them had a different story to tell about Chatwin. Theroux implies that Chatwin may have consciously projected himself differently to each.

Theroux brings us in the second line of the essay to "a particular night" at an important dinner in the presence of well-known explorers. Chatwin is talking, and rather loudly, about his adventures as a mountaineer, but Theroux knew he had never been much of a mountain climber. Theroux relates his surprise not only at Chatwin's talking about his accomplishments, but at his talking in the presence of world-class climbers. "Chatter, chatter, chatter, Chatwin," one friend reported. The nonstop talking, Theroux tells us, was one of Chatwin's most distinguishing features. Another was his fear of writer's block. But one quality captures most of Theroux's attention: Chatwin's conceit. He had ways of dropping famous names and retelling stories that always ended up as self-congratulation. Theroux is eloquent regarding Chatwin's weaknesses. He describes Chatwin as a sometime bore (a "part-timer") and a "bad listener." He told the same story to the same people interminably. Theroux explores the possibility that Chatwin was trying to live down a humble past—for Chatwin, having a father who is a Birmingham solicitor would be humble.

Chatwin was charismatic. Personal charm is often mysterious. People seem to exude it the way an animal will exude an inviting odor. For the ancients, charisma was a mysterious gift, a benefit from the gods. Apparently Bruce Chatwin was possessed of it, and his ability to charm friends and impress people in two languages strikes Theroux as remarkable. One of the points Theroux makes is that although Chatwin had some accomplishments to brag about, he lacked much that others possessed. Yet people found him fascinating.

Why We Care About Someone's Life Story

When Theroux moves his attention to Chatwin's personal life, his secretiveness, his marriage, and his homosexuality, he reveals a need to know more about Chatwin than Chatwin has volunteered. Theroux tells us: "I wanted to know more about his homosexual life, not because I am prurient but because if I like someone I want to know everything." That may be true about most of us. Why do we wish to probe into the lives of people whom we know only from a distance? It may be for the same reason: the need we have to know everything.

Curiosity motivated Theroux at least in part of his inquiry, but it was not curiosity alone that motivated him to write about Chatwin. The segment of the essay that places him and Chatwin on the same stage together at the Royal Geographical Society may give us some clue, since it is clear that Theroux and Chatwin have much in common. When Chatwin chose Theroux to accompany him on the lecture Theroux realized that Chatwin saw something in him that may have been a reflection of himself. Yet, Theroux soon learned "how little I knew him and what an odd fish he was." If that is true, then it is also possible that Theroux himself is a bit of an odd fish, and part of writing about Chatwin helps him sort out the differences as well as the similarities between them. Yet Theroux is careful to make no conscious comparisons and not to worry the reader over his resemblance to or his distinction from Chatwin. He centers himself instead on his fascination and affection for Chatwin.

Ending as he does with Chatwin's mysterious death naturally touches the reader. Theroux is careful not to make it a sentimental or overdone scene. Yet the extravagant story surrounding his illness—the bite from a rare bat from Yunnan—fits into Chatwin's portrait of himself. Chatwin ends by claiming a death that is as rare as his life.

Theroux's memoir is not designed to praise Chatwin any more

than it is to dispraise him, yet it does both. Without trying to be evenhanded or completely fair, Theroux reveals Chatwin and judges him. He sees his shortcomings and in face of them proclaims his affection and friendship. Somehow this adds up to more than simple praise.

Strategies for Writing About Another Person

As you consider writing about someone other than yourself, you have an enormous range of choices. You can choose a famous person about whom you have always wanted to know, or you can choose someone you already know and explore that person's life. You can include all the important information a reader might want to have, or you may write a brief biography centered on a specific incident revelatory of that person's life or of your relationship with that person. Whichever you choose, you will have to make some important decisions about the structure of your essay.

Structure: Chronology and Its Strengths and Weaknesses

Since time limits the story of everyone's life, chronology supports the structure of any essay about people, but the writer has the ability to mold and shape time. For example, in Theroux's essay, the passage describing Chatwin's talking about his mountain-climbing exploits comes first in the essay, but it came late in the order of events in Chatwin's life as told in the essay. The narrative of the actual Royal Geographical Society meeting picks up again in the middle of the essay, with Chatwin's invitation to talk and his asking Theroux to accompany him. The opening scene in Theroux's memoir takes place after their lecture, but we are not aware of this until we get back to the lecture itself.

Theroux uses a few dates, but not many. We know, for example, that Chatwin died in 1989. We do not know, however, when the two of them lectured to the Royal Society. The funeral, which technically ends the narrative, comes in the middle of the essay—although Chatwin's death dominates the end of the essay. Between the introduction of Chatwin talking at the meeting and Theroux's return to the Royal Society meeting in the middle of the essay come several interesting devices. A recollection of Chatwin's endless talking precedes a friend's complaint after having Chatwin as a house guest for a week. Then come several virtual "snapshots": dropping the name of the painter Francis Bacon; stories about Chatwin's postcards; his writer's block; his "disdain for flattery and praise"; his French; his habits as a writer; his background and marriage; his "sexual preference."

We thus see that the essay is not chronological. Theroux provides a sequence of actions told in the order in which they happen once we return to the meeting of the Royal Society. Until then, however, the material is fragmented and might be told in the order of events or not. We cannot know. Theroux has made these choices for a reason. When you tell the story of someone's life, being absolutely chronological risks boredom. By breaking the story effectively, the writer can maintain our attention. By avoiding absolute and unvaried chronology, the writer will produce flexibility in the narrative and a bit of spice for the reader.

Beginning in the Middle of Things

Theroux uses the strategy called beginning in medias res, which means beginning in the middle of the action. Theroux's primary action is the story of his evening at the Royal Society. He starts his essay right in the middle of that lecture/dinner. The effect of the technique is essentially dramatic: we begin at a moment of tension rather than at a slack moment in a preliminary event. Starting at the height of the action improves the possibility of keeping the audience involved and alert. Furthermore, the audience, once interested, wants to know what happened earlier that brought us to the point of the beginning. Theroux uses this technique flawlessly.

Flashback

Flashback, a technique used in films, works just as well in writing about people. It differs from the use of in medias res in that flashback can be used anywhere in an essay. When you feel more explanation is necessary, all you need do is point to what happened in a time earlier than the beginning of your narrative. When Theroux interrupts himself to present Chatwin's very brief conversation "in Dahomey, speaking to an African soldier," he uses flashback. Very brief—only six lines long—it sets a scene with great economy.

Theroux uses many interruptions in his narrative and gives them the force of the flashback. Oddly enough, though, Theroux reveals his impatience with gaps in other people's narratives. He says about Chatwin's *In Patagonia*, "his book was full of gaps. . . . I used to look for links between chapters . . . . Why hadn't he put them In?" Chatwin's response to that question is: "Why do you think it matters?" Theroux might reply by saying that it provides satisfaction in a narrative to have connective details. Theroux, like most of us, reads out of curiosity. When he reads, he wants to know everything possible. The connective details give the reader the sense that not much is missing: the whole story is being told.

VERBAL SIGNPOSTS

Verbal signposts give order to most essays. When arguing a case, for example, signposts organize the issues: "My first point is . . ."; "Second, I will . . ."; "Third, the evidence . . . ." Using the numbers "one," "two," "three," and "four" can clarify the information you present to a reader. Enumeration keeps information organized, and proceeding from least important to most important helps the reader grasp the significance of each point.

In the story of someone's life, chronological signposts help guide the reader's attention. The structure of Catherine S. Manegold's portrait of Kara S. Hultgreen is only partly chronological, yet it relies on many key signposts. Manegold begins with two paragraphs of reflection on the job of flying jets, then in a one-paragraph flashback describes Hultgreen as a college senior. The fourth paragraph begins a chronological narrative with "Once, after landing on an aircraft carrier . . . ." After four paragraphs, we leap to: "Eighteen months later," followed in the middle of the last paragraph with "Then, on Oct. 25," and the final moments of the failure of her aircraft.

EVENTS AS A GUIDE TO STRUCTURE

If you write a relatively short essay of five to ten pages, you cannot undertake to narrate an entire life, with all the important events revealed to the reader. Even massive biographies have a difficult time including all the important events and must therefore choose those that are essential to retell. On the other hand, conventional writing about people usually demands that certain events guide the discussion. Georgia O'Keeffe, the subject of Joan Didion's short essay that follows, assumed as much when she wrote, "Where I was born and where and how I lived is unimportant." She reacted to the likelihood that those who would write about her would concentrate on the factual details of her life: birth, education, marriage, work, and any important events that clarified these landmark events. O'Keeffe wanted people to concentrate instead on her paintings. To some extent, Joan Didion does just that, but she does not exclude events.

JOAN DIDION

Georgia O'Keeffe

"Where I was born and where and how I have lived is unimportant," Georgia O'Keeffe told us in the book of paintings and words published in her ninetieth year on earth. She seemed to be advising us to forget the beautiful face in the Stieglitz photographs. She appeared to be dismissing the rather condescending romance that had attached to her by then, the romance of extreme good looks and advanced age and deliberate isolation. "It is what I have done with where I have been that should be of interest." I recall an August afternoon in Chicago in 1973 when I took my daughter, then seven, to see what Georgia O'Keeffe had done with where she had been. One of the vast O'Keeffe "Sky Above Clouds" canvases floated over the back stairs in the Chicago Art Institute that day, dominating what seemed to be several stories of empty light, and my daughter looked at it once, ran to the landing, and kept on looking. "Who drew it," she whispered after a while. I told her. "I need to talk to her," she said finally.

My daughter was making, that day in Chicago, an entirely unconscious but quite basic assumption about people and the work they do. She was assuming that the glory she saw in the work reflected a glory in its maker, that the painting was the painter as the poem is the poet, that every choice one made alone—every word chosen or rejected, every brush stroke laid or not laid down—betrayed one's character. *Style is character.* It seemed to me that afternoon that I had rarely seen so instinctive an application of this familiar principle, and I recall being pleased not only that my daughter responded to style as character but that it was Georgia O'Keeffe's particular style to which she responded: this was a hard woman who had imposed her 192 square feet of clouds on Chicago.

"Hardness" has not been in our century a quality much admired in women, nor in the past twenty years has it even been in official favor for men. When hardness surfaces in the very old we tend to transform it into "crustiness" or eccentricity, some tonic pepperiness to be indulged at a distance. On the evidence of her work and what she has said about it, Georgia O'Keeffe is neither "crusty" nor eccentric. She is simply hard, a straight shooter, a woman clean of received wisdom and open to what she sees. This is a woman who could early on dismiss most of her contemporaries as "dreamy," and would later single out one she liked as "a very poor painter." (And then add, apparently by way of softening the judgment: "I guess he wasn't a painter at all. He had no courage and I believe that to create one's own world in any of the arts takes courage.") This is a woman who in 1939 could advise her admirers that they were missing her point, that their appreciation of her famous flowers was merely sentimental. "When I paint a red hill," she observed coolly in the catalogue for an exhibition that year, "you say it is too bad that I don't always paint flowers. A flower touches almost everyone's heart. A red hill doesn't touch everyone's heart." This is a woman who could describe the genesis of one of her most well-known paintings—the "Cow's Skull: Red, White and Blue" owned by the Metropolitan—as an act of quite deliberate and derisive orneriness. "I thought of the city men I had been seeing in the East," she wrote. "They talked so often of writing the Great American Novel—the Great American Play—the Great American Poetry. . . . So as I was painting my cow's head on blue I thought to myself, "I'll make it an American painting. They will not think it great with the red stripes down the sides—Red, White and Blue—but they will notice it.' "

The city men. The men. They. The words crop up again and again as this astonishingly aggressive woman tells us what was on her mind when she was making her astonishingly aggressive paintings. It was those city men who stood accused of sentimentalizing her flowers: "I made you take time to look at what I saw and when you took time to really notice my flower you hung all your associations with flowers on my flower and you write about my flower as if I think and see what you think and see—and I don't." *And I don't.* Imagine those words spoken, and the sound you hear is *don't tread on me.* "The men" believed it impossible to paint New York, so Georgia O'Keeffe painted New York. "The men" didn't think much of her bright color, so she made it brighter. The men yearned toward Europe so she went to Texas, and then New Mexico. The men talked about Cézanne, "long involved remarks about the 'plastic quality' of his form and color," and took one another's long involved remarks, in the view of this angelic rattlesnake in their midst, altogether too seriously. "I can paint one of those dismal-colored paintings like the men," the woman who regarded herself always as an outsider remembers thinking one day in 1922, and she did: a painting of a shed "all low-toned and dreary with the tree beside the door." She called this act of rancor "The Shanty" and hung it in her next show. "The men seemed to approve of it," she reported fifty-four years later, her contempt undimmed. "They seemed to think that maybe I was beginning to paint. That was my only low-toned dismal-colored painting."

Some women fight and others do not. Like so many successful guerrillas in the war between the sexes, Georgia O'Keeffe seems to have been equipped early with an immutable sense of who she was and a fairly clear understanding that she would be required to prove it. On the surface her upbringing was conventional. She was a child on the Wisconsin prairie who played with china dolls and painted watercolors with cloudy skies because sunlight was too hard to paint and, with her brother and sisters, listened every night to her mother read stories of the Wild West, of Texas, of Kit Carson and Billy the Kid. She told adults that she wanted to be an artist and was embarrassed when they asked what kind of artist she wanted to be: she had no idea "what kind." She had no idea what artists did. She had never seen a picture that interested her, other than a pen-and-ink Maid of Athens in one of her mother's books, some Mother Goose illustrations printed on cloth, a tablet cover that showed a little girl with pink roses, and the painting of Arabs on horseback that hung in her grandmother's parlor. At thirteen, in a Dominican convent, she was mortified when the sister corrected her drawing. At Chatham Episcopal Institute in Virginia she painted lilacs and sneaked time alone to walk out to where she could see the line of the Blue Ridge Mountains on the horizon. At the Art Institute in Chicago she was shocked by the presence of live models and wanted to abandon anatomy lessons. At the Art Students League in New York one of her fellow students advised her that, since he would be a great painter and she would end up teaching painting in a girls' school, any work of hers was less important than modeling for him. Another painted over her work to show her how the Impressionists did trees. She had not before heard how the Impressionists did trees and she did not much care.

At twenty-four she left all those opinions behind and went for the first time to live in Texas, where there were no trees to paint and no one to tell her how not to paint them. In Texas there was only the horizon she craved. In Texas she had her sister Claudia with her for a while, and in the late afternoons they would walk away from town and toward the horizon and watch the evening star come out. "That evening star fascinated me," she wrote. "It was in some way very exciting to me. My sister had a gun, and as we walked she would throw bottles into the air and shoot as many as she could before they hit the ground. I had nothing but to walk into nowhere and the wide sunset space with the star. Ten watercolors were made from that star." In a way one's interest is compelled as much by the sister Claudia with the gun as by the painter Georgia with the star, but only the painter left us this shining record. Ten watercolors were made from that star.

1976

Reflections on Joan Didion's Style

Most of us might begin an essay with obvious events, listing the important dates and what happened when. But we must also realize that doing so will add up to dullness. That approach narrates a sequence of external events instead of narrating a life. It avoids the psychology of the person and genuine examination of a life. We learn what happened, but not why, not what the person was like, not what emotions guided the person or helped the person change and develop. To be successful, writing about another person needs to involve the writer as much as the subject.

Joan Didion offers us a vision of Georgia O'Keeffe as well as an evaluation of Georgia O'Keeffe. Didion's problem before writing is the same as that of most writers: What can she tell us that will keep our attention, and how much detail will be necessary to communicate the essence of O'Keeffe's life? Didion begins by reminding us that "*Style is character.*" Didion's reader believes that Didion means what she says, and therefore it is logical to think that by examining style—even Didion's own style—we will derive some insight into character.

ENCYCLOPEDIA STYLE

Encyclopedia entries on an individual give us a great deal of information very rapidly. The following entry from *Collier's Encyclopedia* gives the reader a quick overview of Georgia O'Keeffe. We know the dates of her birth, marriage, and death. We know many of the chief events of her life, and we know where she lived. For the researcher, an entry of this kind is a good beginning.

> O'KEEFFE, GEORGIA [oki'f] (1887–1986), American painter, famous for her lucid, geometrically composed desert landscapes and flower studies. She was born in Sun Prairie, Wis., Nov. 15, 1887. Her parents moved to Williamsburg, Va., in 1901, and there she received training in accurately delineating flowers. At the age of 17 she attended the Chicago Art Institute, and at 18, the Art Students' League in New York. In 1909 she worked for a Chicago advertising agency, but in 1912–1914 resumed art studies at the University of Virginia and Teachers College, Columbia. Her first exhibition was at Alfred Stieglitz' "291" gallery in 1916; she married Stieglitz in 1924. As the result of O'Keeffe's visit to New Mexico in 1929, its desert landscape became the main theme of her art. She was given a one-woman show at the Museum of Modern Art in New York in 1946, the year her husband died, and at that time critics commented that her work still showed that immaculate individuality first discernible in her original flower pieces. In the same year she settled permanently in New Mexico, whose landscape continued to be her main inspiration. She died Mar. 6, 1986, in Santa Fe, N.M. For further information consult *Georgia O'Keeffe: A Life* (1990), by Roxana Robinson.
>
>

Useful as this encyclopedia entry is, such an entry cannot impart much about the inner life of its subject, nor can it produce an intimate sense of our relationship with the subject. We know about Georgia O'Keeffe, but we certainly do not know Georgia O'Keeffe.

Didion avoids the temptation to give us all the events: we do not know when or where O'Keeffe was born, although we can figure things out from the fact that O'Keeffe's opening comments were "published in her ninetieth year" and Didion recalls them in a Chicago museum in 1973. But Didion's most interesting stylistic device is one of the most obvious: she narrates an event she witnessed and directs that narration toward revealing the character of her subject, Georgia O'Keeffe. She describes going to an exhibit of O'Keeffe's huge cloud paintings and seeing her daughter so touched by the work that her daughter could only say of O'Keeffe, "I need to talk to her." Didion's choice is to narrate the *effect* of the paintings on one viewer, her daughter. That tells us a great deal about both the paintings and the painter. This brief narration gives us a kind of information that most encyclopedia entries cannot.

Being Concrete

Another of Didion's stylistic triumphs shows up in her choice to begin the discussion of O'Keeffe herself—beginning in paragraph three—with a single word that helps define her as a person: "hardness." Didion reveals the virtue of hardness: a quality of "a straight shooter." This hardness is somewhat masculine, highly determined, and a mark of absolute independence. It revealed itself in O'Keeffe's judgments of other painters: "I guess he wasn't a painter at all." Instead of making generalizations about O'Keeffe, Didion tries to direct our attention to specifics: the comments on individual paintings, the observations on O'Keeffe's intentions in her work, her reactions to others, and her expectations of herself.

Didion lets O'Keeffe speaks in her own voice as much as possible. "I'll make it an American painting," she says of her world famous "Cow's Skull: Red, White, and Blue." Her own words begin the essay: "It is what I have done with where I have been that should be of interest." But Didion does not overload the essay with O'Keeffe quotations, effective though they may be. Eventually, Didion moves on to another level of stylistic discussion: analysis. She not only presents some important commentary by O'Keeffe, but moves to examine it in order to add her own understanding to the issues that concern her about O'Keeffe's life. In paragraph four, Didion gets to one of her most important points: "*The city men. The men.*"

Description

Didion's focus at this point is on O'Keeffe's struggles as a woman artist in a man's world. O'Keeffe constantly concerned herself with what men thought of her work and how men would evaluate it. Didion describes the reactions to men that affected O'Keeffe's work: "The men yearned for Europe so she went to Texas, and then New Mexico." As Didion tells us, "Some women fight and others do not." O'Keeffe was obviously a fighter. Didion emphasizes that she was independent from an early age: "She was a child on the Wisconsin prairie who played with china dolls and painted watercolors with cloudy skies because sunlight was too hard to paint and, with her brother and sisters, listened every night to her mother read stories of the Wild West, of Texas, of Kit Carson and Billy the Kid." The specificity and detail of Didion's writing hold our interest.

Didion's piece is not an encyclopedia entry. But if you examine it for details about O'Keeffe's life, you will see that Didion cites dates, tells us where O'Keeffe came from, where she went, what she did, where she studied, what some of her struggles were, and what values she held. All these details are carefully scattered throughout the essay. We learn a great deal from Didion's piece, despite its brevity. Moreover, we learn, too, that Didion admires O'Keeffe greatly. Just as we know what effect the paintings had on Didion's daughter, we learn as well what effect O'Keeffe's life had on Didion herself. Part of the purpose of this piece seems to be to communicate those feelings to its readers.

Drama: Your Subject in Action

Joan Didion cannot put her subject in action because she has no direct contact with Georgia O'Keeffe. Her contact is with the reputation and the art on display in Chicago. Didion's strategy is clever: instead of putting O'Keeffe into action, she puts her daughter into action and describes the drama of her seeing O'Keeffe's work and responding to it very positively. On the other hand, Paul Theroux takes every opportunity of showing us Bruce Chatwin in action. We hear him talking, worrying, bragging, name-dropping, lamenting. An encyclopedia entry never puts its subject into a dramatic situation or permits its subject to enact a moment of importance.

Description

Writers such as those we have read in this chapter do their best to describe their subject in action if they can. Catherine Manegold says of Kara Hultgreen: "Once, after landing on an aircraft carrier off Key West, she was striding down the deck when the flight bosses noticed her hair tumbling below her helmet." At that point, we want to know what happened. The description of her movement, her hair, and her headgear all work together to establish a sense of drama. Narrating her death, Manegold writes, "The F-14 was only about 150 feet above the water then and Hultgreen slammed into the sea at three times highway speeds." Manegold searches for powerful, suggestive verbs and specific visualizable details.

Theroux's best description is his reference to Chatwin's father: "When the day came it turned out that Bruce had invited many people, including his parents—his big beefy-faced father had the look of a Dickensian solicitor. . . ." Among the few opportunities Theroux takes to describe Chatwin is near the end, when he was dying: "When I visited his bedroom in Oxfordshire—a pretty, homely farmhouse that Elizabeth kept ticking over—his hands would fly to his face, covering his hollow cheeks." In this passage the farmhouse gets almost as much descriptive attention as Chatwin himself, but neither get much.

Dialogue

Instead of description, Theroux gives us dialogue. Most of it is one-sided: the words of Chatwin either responding or holding forth. Occasionally we get both sides of the discussion:

> "YOU ARE ENGLISH?"
> "YES."
> "BUT YOU SPEAK EXCELLENT FRENCH."
> "PASSABLE," I SAID.
> "WITH A PARISIAN ACCENT I SHOULD HAVE SAID."
> "I HAVE LIVED IN PARIS."

Dialogue, in these examples, constitutes important testimony from the subject of the essay. When Chatwin speaks directly, Theroux permits us to make our own observations and draw our own conclusions. Few devices in writing are more dramatic. After all, plays—the essence of drama—normally consist of nothing but dialogue. Consequently, dialogue in the biographical essay represents one of the most important elements essential to creating drama.

Necessary Invention

A careful reader might ask of these essays whether the quotations attributed to subjects Kara Hultgreen and Bruce Chatwin are absolutely true, word for word. In the case of Didion's quoting Georgia O'Keeffe, we know that the text of the exhibition catalog provides the material Didion sets off in quotation marks. Didion, after all, makes no claim to having spoken with O'Keeffe. On the other hand, Theroux was a friend of Chatwin's and spoke with him frequently. Consequently, his strategy of quotation tries to represent the reality of Chatwin's speech in a dramatic form. But is the speech completely authentic and reliable? Well, that question cannot be answered without asking Theroux to explain. But we would guess that unless Theroux had a notebook with him all the time, or unless he knew he would be writing a memoir of his friend, he must have recalled the gist of a conversation, then wrote it down as he remembered it. This method is widely used by writers. Sometimes writers get into trouble if they take too many liberties with the technique (a few recent lawsuits have arisen over authors inventing quotations). But usually, the technique is innocent enough.

When you write about a friend or relative, you are expected to have had enough contact to know generally what he or she might have said in a given context. The more you establish your authority the more the reader will accept your reconstructions of conversations. Theroux is very careful to prepare the reader by describing the amount of time he and Chatwin had spent together on various occasions. They spoke together at the Royal Geographical Society, and therefore we expect that Theroux would have known what Chatwin said. Even if he cannot quote Chatwin verbatim, he ought to be close enough in spirit to be reliable.

The encyclopedia entry does not quote Georgia O'Keeffe (some entries do quote their subjects) because it does not intend to stir readers' emotions. The encyclopedia intends to impart information. Using a dramatic style and quoting your subject heightens the immediacy of your essay, involves the reader's emotions, and intensifies the reader's experience with your text. All of the writers discussed here use dramatic techniques because they wish to be read, and keeping their audience's attention through a dramatic style is one of the best ways of avoiding dullness and boredom.

Reflection and Commentary

Writers who depend on their craft for a living ordinarily emphasize a dramatic portrayal of their subject. Most of us, when writing about someone we think interesting, wish to take time to reflect and comment on our impression of the person. Unfortunately, such a strategy is inherently undramatic. When you evaluate a person directly, with no explicit point of reference in that person's actions, you leave the reader ungrounded. Consider Theroux's opening lines. He tells us that whenever he thinks of Chatwin he remembers a specific dinner. In that first paragraph, you will find that Theroux both reflects upon Chatwin and comments on him: "I knew he had never been much of a mountaineer." But immediately Theroux places both himself and Chatwin in a dramatic situation and narrates the events at the dinner. We then have the chance to qualify Theroux's reflection, and in doing so draw our own conclusions.

Making Your Own Statement

When you write a brief biography, present your own judgment and your own evaluation of the events you narrate. In other words, instead of producing the neutral encyclopedia entry, aim to involve yourself in your subject. Catherine Manegold offers us not just a portrait of Kara S. Hultgreen, but an evaluation of her struggle and a reinforcement of the struggles of women everywhere. Theroux gives us a portrait of Chatwin that includes insights into Theroux as well. Didion does the same when she writes about O'Keeffe. Her emphasis on O'Keeffe's struggles in the art world imply a deep sympathy as a woman. The fact that Didion underscored the presence of her daughter at the exhibition gives more value to her observations.

YOUR SUBJECT'S ACHIEVEMENTS

You may wish to emphasize the achievements of your subject. If so, be sure to describe them in a lively fashion. Be specific and detailed and use appropriate dramatic techniques of dialogue and narration. Avoid rattling off one achievement after another without giving the reader a chance to absorb the implications of what each means. In a short essay of five or ten pages, focus on a single achievement the way Theroux does when he places Chatwin at the Royal Geographical Society dinner. Thoroughness in handling a single achievement will give you a chance to summarize selectively other achievements and fit them into an overall pattern.

DOES THE WORLD PERCEIVE YOUR SUBJECT CORRECTLY?

In addition to recording the important events in a person's life, you may want to examine motive, uncertainties, failures, and complications that shed light on the achievements. You may wish to consider the responses that other people have given—both positive and negative—to the achievements of your subject. If you choose to write about Napoleon, for example, you may want to take into consideration the views of those who see his Egyptian campaign as having been instrumental in creating the modern science of archaeology and igniting the modern world's interest in Egyptian art and culture. On the other hand, you will also want to consider his use of enormous armies to tyrannize many European nations. Napoleon led a nation that had freed itself from the yoke of a despotic aristocratic government, but he did not promote freedom and brotherhood in other nations.

Has Your Subject Earned Your Respect?

One thing comes clear from the essays in this chapter: the subject of most biographical essays has earned the writer's respect. True, at times the respect may verge on fear. Were you to read essays on threatening villains, you would see that respect motivated by fear can degenerate into contempt. But the achievements of the subject must ultimately yield to judgment. There is no doubt in our mind that Hultgreen, Chatwin, and O'Keeffe are well regarded by their biographers. Despite Theroux's criticisms, he considers Chatwin his friend. Despite Hultgreen's early death, Manegold considers her life to have been exemplary.

The likelihood of writing a good essay on another person may depend on the depth of your respect for that person. You may not know whether your respect for your subject will survive research. It may be that you will think less of your subject than you thought you would. If that is the case, make it the focus of your essay. Why have you lost respect? Should your reader share your feelings? What evidence pushes you to your conclusion? Biographers sometimes conclude that their subject is to some degree repugnant. Even in the face of generally positive world opinion, careful research may reveal evidence of unmeritorious behavior. In such cases, a biographer produces a reevaluation of the subject's reputation. Often professional biographers hope to uncover something that will force such a reevaluation and thereby make their biography important.

What Can We Learn from a Biographical Subject?

The encyclopedia entry on Georgia O'Keeffe does not tell us enough about her to help us understand ourselves any better. It does not give us a sense of what we ourselves may be able to achieve in our own lives. It just tells us the facts of O'Keeffe's life. On the other hand, the story of Kara Hultgreen tells us how a person can overcome prejudice. It reassures us that individuals can triumph over difficulties. The same may be said of Didion's essay on Georgia O'Keeffe. Both subjects of those essays faced the problem of being treated as second-class citizens because they were women.

By reflecting on Chatwin's behavior we also learn something

of the way in which people regard each other. Chatwin was a highly accomplished person, but he also had many faults. As we read about him, we can develop a sense of sympathy that might transcend our reaction to him were we to meet him without knowing much about him. His incessant talking might turn us off. His self-promotion might seem insulting and annoying. But Theroux gives us a full picture in such a way as to help us see Chatwin as a person. We ourselves have many of the same faults and may be able to learn from observing Chatwin.

One of your purposes in writing about another person can be to help your reader learn something about the human condition. You may be able to uncover qualities in your subject that will shed light on all of us and give us insight into our behavior. Writer and reader both will profit from such insight.

Suggestions for Interesting Essays About Another Person

First, look around yourself to see if someone you know inspires you to write an essay. Choose from relatives: grandparents, parents, aunts, uncles, siblings, cousins, or other relatives. Consider neighbors, friends of your family, teachers, members of associations to which you belong. If you would like to choose a historical figure, consider those you have heard something about but still do not "know" well. Every history book, every almanac, every reference book is filled with potential subjects. Safe to say, all will reward your research. The box text gives some tips for writing about other people.

TIPS THAT SOMETIMES WORK FOR WRITING ABOUT PEOPLE

1. Choose someone who interests you. That could be someone you know personally or a person about whom you have read who is intriguing enough to stimulate your curiosity.
2. Among your sources include personal interviews, reminiscences of others, letters, diaries, notes, photographs, or autobiographic notes. Where appropriate consult library bibliographic sources such as the *Biography Index*.

3. Choose a critical incident or series of actions around which to center your writing, especially in a short biographical piece. Avoid being encyclopedic.
4. Aim for a dramatic approach—which means to put your subject in action by recording dialogue, behavior, motivation, and responses to circumstances. Make your subject's behavior reveal character.
5. Be concrete: use details, description, quotations.
6. In your early drafts or in revision, decide on the best structural approach. Consider narrative techniques such as flashback.
7. If possible, concentrate as much on your subject's personality as on your subject's achievements.
8. Offer a personal reflection on your subject. Either directly or indirectly reveal your attitude toward your subject.

4

Writing the Argumentative Essay

What Is an Argument and Why Argue?

Arguments develop in situations that admit disagreements. One does not argue about incontrovertible facts, such as: New York City is larger than one's wristwatch; France is wealthier than Iceland; clean air is healthier than polluted air; cancer is a killer. Arguments are rarely settled by marshaling a series of facts that everyone agrees about. Instead, people argue about interpretation of facts: What do they really mean? Are the facts trustable? Which facts are most relevant? For example, the old maxim, "A rolling stone gathers no moss," is designed to convince someone to settle down, but, "A setting hen never lays," is designed to get someone out of a rut. Which is right? Well, that would be the basis of an argument.

The sense in which we will use the term *argument* here implies that it is an instrument of reasoning used to change opinion and create consensus. Arguments are controlled, and in the case of written arguments, they present cases carefully enough to permit a reader to think through a position, absorb key points, and perhaps move to a new opinion or conclusion on an important subject.

One presumption in writing argumentative essays is that your audience will have an open mind and be willing to listen to your views. Of course, one knows that most people, regardless of their experience or expertise, have strong opinions on most issues before they read anyone's arguments. Consequently, a good understanding of one's audience is more important in writing argumentative essays than virtually any other kind of essay. If you know your audience is going to be hostile to your views, then you need to approach readers with a strategy that will be nonthreatening and perhaps even amusing. In the aftermath of the Chernobyl disaster—in which a nuclear plant exploded and dumped radiation over large portions of the Ukraine—you would have a hard time defending nuclear power as the key to future energy needs. But by the same reasoning, you might argue that for the very reason people are frightened by recent events we ought to look all the more carefully at the issues of nuclear power. First, of course, we ought to think about the safeguards essential to making nuclear power acceptable. Second, we ought to reflect on what we have learned from the disaster at Chernobyl as well as from the less serious malfunction at Three Mile Island in Pennsylvania. Nuclear power is dangerous (so is electricity), and the smart approach to argument will weigh the potential risks against the potential gains. The fact that our current population of approximately three billion will increase to more than five billion in the year 2020 may contribute to an argument that admits some risks and hopes to balance them against the absolute needs of the coming population bulge.

Argument and Reasoning

As you can see from the foregoing comments, argumentative writing depends on reasons and reasoning. It presents views and backs them up with a variety of reasons designed to convince a reader that a given position is acceptable and perhaps desirable. However, in some situations reasons are only a part of the dialogue. Many people with a personal stake in a given position do not worry about reasons or reasoning because they are often so deeply involved in their own position that they cannot see beyond it. For example, investors in nuclear technology do not want to hear arguments explaining that nuclear power is so dangerous it should be abandoned. What would happen to their investments? Having a personal stake in a question is called self-interest. It is very difficult to argue with someone whose self-interest will be damaged by accepting your position. The best way to argue is with someone who is disinterested (which means that person has no monetary or policy investment in the issue—is without self-interest). However, that is rarely possible. You may find yourself arguing against nuclear power with someone whose mother works for the Nuclear Regulatory Agency. Where would that person and her mother be if there were nothing to regulate?

A classic case is being made throughout the world—and has been since 1962—for banning or controlling tobacco products because they cause cancer. Tobacco executives, until 1997, protested loudly that no proof of such a causative effect has been found. Now, tobacco companies are paying states billions of dollars to cover the medical expenses of smokers. The U.S. Surgeon General has been powerful enough and respected enough that smoking in the United States has declined by more than 50 percent in the last thirty years or so. But in some other nations, smoking has increased. Any traveler outside the United States notices immediately that smoking bans in public buildings and transportation do not exist. Consequently, the tobacco companies have been thriving in part by diversifying out of tobacco and in part by concentrating tobacco sales overseas, both with great success. Many people in the tobacco industry did not admit that cigarette smoking is addictive because to do so would link it to other addictive substances such as cocaine and heroin. Self-interested individuals conceive the argument from a personal point of view and regard evidence, opinions, reasons, and even facts from an angle that accounts for their personal investment.

Three Appeals in Argument

Everyone has access to at least three appeals to an audience when constructing an argument. Essentially that means you have three strategies—which you can mix together or use separately—by which you may appeal to an audience for its attention. The strategies are based on your presentation of your character to your audience, on your appeal to your audience's emotional response to your views, and on the logical structure of your argument.

THREE APPEALS IN ARGUMENT

Ethical. You appeal to your audience by establishing that you are honest and not personally invested in your position. Your integrity is unquestioned, and you are willing to put your integrity on the line for your position.

Emotional. You appeal to the emotional side of the argument. You express outrage, disappointment, sorrow, or anger and urge your reader to share it. You cite evidence that could result only in your audience's becoming emotional and accepting your views. In some cases it may be impossible or undesirable to omit emotion from an argument. At its best, the emotional appeal asks your audience to imagine the feelings involved in the issues. At its worst, the emotional appeal tries to win the argument without crediting the evidence or its analysis.

Logical. You avoid urging your audience to believe you only because you are honorable and ethical, or to get involved only because of the emotionally charged circumstances. Instead, you present coolly the evidence and its analysis: the logic that convinces people to believe in your position.

Arguing to Win

For many people, including those who write argumentative prose, winning is everything. As a result, they will sometimes stoop to deceptive practices. Withholding evidence contradicting one's position is a deceptive practice. If you were arguing against nuclear power, for example, and held back the estimates of fuel needs in the next fifty years and the extent to which we may fall short of those needs, you might be guilty of deceptive practice. The same would be true if you were arguing in favor of nuclear power and withheld evidence of recent disasters in the industry.

Usually, an exclusive appeal to the emotions is considered deceptive. Once you have your audience riled up, you can get it to believe many things it would not believe in a cooler environment. The terrifying dictatorial governments of the first half of the twentieth century thrived on the emotional appeal: Hitler and the Nazis depended on huge torchlight rallies to stir up anger and resentment against everyone who was not Aryan by birth—which meant most of the world. When Senator McCarthy conducted his scourge of American communists in the 1950s, he used inflammatory language and outrageous charges of a personal nature to defame innocent people. Because he had whipped up anger and passion on his side, he could get away with insult and lies that went almost unquestioned until finally he met his match in the person of Joseph Welch, a lawyer who used facts and reasoning (and a bit of emotion) to dismantle McCarthy's attacks. Unfortunately, it is not always true that the liar and tyrant can be exposed. Sometimes wars, riots, and reigns of terror last for a generation or more without exposure of the treachery that causes them.

One important result of mastering the art of argument is that you will be able to see through the fake, establish your own position, and perhaps make your own reasonable views known with enough force to forestall the kind of tyranny that the world has witnessed in the twentieth century. Democracy depends in part on the willingness of a citizenry to take stands on issues that affect the commonweal. Arguing a position is the way of doing business in Congress, local council meetings, and industrial boardrooms.

The Parts of an Argument

Not all argumentative prose looks alike. Most people arguing a position resist the impulse to declare that they are arguing or to make it totally clear to the reader that the piece is argumentative. Many writers insist that in one way or another every piece of writing argues one position or another. Why write, they say, if you are not trying to convince someone of a truth? There is a great deal to this position, since it is clear that most of us write in order to get something for ourselves (that we believe we deserve), to explain something (that we feel is true), to hide something (convince people it is not there), to defend something (that we believe is worthwhile), to attack something (that we believe is not worthwhile), to get people to do something (that we feel will benefit them and may also benefit us), and so on. In our personal essays—autobiography—we argue that our story is of value, that it can give insight into the human condition and benefit those who read it. Even this paragraph has been nothing but a tissue of argument defending argument as basic to writing.

To say, for example, that there are a given number of parts to an argument is much too simple to account for real-life arguments. An examination of some argumentative essays can help you see how to refine your own approach to argument. As we proceed to analyze representative arguments, you will further appreciate the subtlety and complexity that writers bring to the skills of argument.

Part I Your Position: What You Think You Can Prove

Every argument offers certain choices: you can argue in favor of a position or against another position, or examine a number of positions in order to arrive at the best of them. When you argue in favor of a position, you usually have a reason for having accepted it in the first place. Ideally, this reason is developed from a review of the circumstances, evidence, and other testimony that convinces you. When you argue against a position you usually have a clear-cut target. For instance, the position you attack may hold that nuclear energy is too dangerous because the waste material will last for hundreds of thousands of years. When arguing against such a position, you will need to propose evidence that science will somehow learn how to hasten radioactive decay or learn how to make it harmless. Finally, when you argue from a neutral position, you review the major arguments until you prove that one or another of them is plausible and desirable. Since the scientific evidence is not all in on nuclear energy, it may not be possible to be totally conclusive on either side of the argument.

Claire Sterling, in "Redfellas," a study of the Russian mafia that follows, presents an argument that has as its purpose the providing of information regarding organized crime in the new Russia. Her appeal is not ethical—we know little about her from what she writes. It is not superficially emotional, although the upshot of what she says may strike you as a bit frightening. Its basic appeal is logical: she holds to the position that the Russian mafia is large, powerful, ruthless, and threatening. Her reasons are primarily couched in terms of information: statistics and reports.

Part II Your Claims: What Seems to Follow from Your Position

If you hold to a given position in an argument, you must have some reasons that support your claims. Take, for example, the task of constructing the argument that John F. Kennedy was killed by a conspiracy rather than by a lone assassin. Here is the claim you would have to make along with the reasons that would back up that claim.

Claim Oswald did not kill Kennedy, or if he did, he was not alone.

Reason 1: Oswald was a mediocre shot with an outmoded Italian rifle.

Reason 2: Kennedy was shot from in front as well as from in back.

Reason 3: Oswald was involved in a Cuban political group and Fidel Castro was angry at Kennedy's having planned the invasion of Cuba.

Reason 4: The CIA, humiliated by the Bay of Pigs fiasco—the attempted invasion of Cuba—had reason to permit Kennedy to be hit; and there was a connection with Oswald and the CIA.

Reason 5: Only a high-level organization could have gotten to the president, given his security.

Reason 6: Who was to benefit from the assassination? The Johnson administration, which succeeded Kennedy.

You can easily add to this list if you are an assassination buff, but working with these six alone would produce an interesting argument. To defend the first reason you would have to marshall evidence to show that Oswald's training in the marines proved he was a mediocre shot and that his Mannlicher Carcano military rifle was not capable of the assassination shots. If you could prove this definitively, the argument would be over.

Claire Sterling's first claim lies in the first sentence of her second paragraph: "The Russian mafia is a union of racketeers without equal." That paragraph makes a number of further claims that will need to be substantiated by reasons later in the essay. After a brief pause to give some historical background, she presents her reasons, beginning with the mafia's share of the gross national product of Russia and its growing "kill rate" having reached a world record. Her reasons consist mainly of statistics, comparisons, and a few reports from Russia.

Part III Reasons Back Up Your Claims

The reasons that back up your claims are often facts and opinions. But often they are set in a context of analysis that includes and interprets evidence. For example, take Sterling's observation that the kill rate of Russia's mafia has risen. She compares the U.S. kill rate of "sixty-odd murders" a day with Russia's "more than eighty per day." But she also points to the fact that between 1989 and 1992 in Russia almost one thousand policemen were killed. There were fifteen hundred contract killings in 1992. When Sterling presents reasons for accepting her claim that the Russian mafia is without equal she presents facts, opinions, statistics, and elaborate background information to help us understand how Russia has made the transition from a communist to a capitalist system.

Argument as Information

The argumentative essay aims to persuade, but it often does so by providing crucial information that, added together, persuades the reader without the writer having to reveal that an argument is in progress. Claire Sterling's essay is such a performance. She does not seem at first to be constructing an argument, but by the time we reach the end of the essay, we know that all the details, facts, numbers, and anecdotes have a single goal: to convince us to take the Russian mafia very seriously.

The advantages of constructing an argument in such a way as to concentrate on information are shown in the box.

ARGUMENT AS INFORMATION

1. The reader benefits from being given important information, including background, facts, opinions, personal stories, and statistics.
2. The writer presents the information in such a way as to help the reader draw a logical conclusion and therefore need not constantly remind the reader of the argument's claims.
4. Most informative arguments are nonthreatening because they do not seem to be taking a stand on a controversial subject.
5. Informative arguments persuade by the weight and quality of the information.
6. The responsibility of the writer is to make sure the information in the argument is reliable and complete. If the reader is made to feel that it is complete, the argument is usually won.

CLAIRE STERLING

Redfellas

There are fifty ways of saying "to steal" in Russian, and the Russian mafia uses them all. It is the world's largest, busiest and possibly meanest collection of organized hoods, consisting of 5,000 gangs and 3 million people who work for or with them. Its reach extends into all fifteen of the former Soviet republics, across eleven time zones and one-sixth of the earth's land mass. It intrudes into every field of Western concern: the nascent free market, privatization, disarmament, military conversion, foreign humanitarian relief and financial aid, even state reserves of currency and gold. And it has begun to creep toward the rest of Europe and the United States—"looking at the West as a wolf looks at sheep," a Russian crime specialist told me.

The Russian mafia is a union of racketeers without equal. Unlike the mafia in Sicily, which it admires and copies as a standard of excellence, it has no home seat or central command. There are no ancestral memories or common bloodlines. Nevertheless, its proliferating clans are invading every sphere of life, usurping political power, taking over state enterprises and fleecing natural resources. They are engaged in extortion, theft, forgery, armed assault, contract killing, swindling, drug running, arms smuggling, prostitution, gambling, loan sharking, embezzling, money laundering and black marketing—all on a monumental and increasingly international scale.

Rising from the ruins of the Soviet empire, the new mafia has far outclassed the one that flourished under Leonid Brezhnev. The mafia was Brezhnev's solution for a stifling centralized economy; it provided illicit goods and services by stealing from the state, buying protection, smuggling, cheating, bullying and bribing its way into the Kremlin. It was *korruptsiya* Communist-style, a shared monopoly of power between politicians and crooks. Liberated Russia deserved better. But the old politicians are still largely in place, yesterday's crooks are today's free entrepreneurs and *korruptsiya*, spreading uncontrollably as things fall apart, has become the curse of a stricken nation. "Corruption," Boris Yeltsin exclaimed last year, "is devouring the state from top to bottom."

In 1991, the year the Communists fell, the All-Union Research Institute of the Soviet Interior Ministry estimated that half the income of an average government functionary was coming from bribes, compared with only 30 percent before 1985. During the late 1980s the Soviet prosecutor-general's office indicted 225,000 state officials for embezzlement, including eighteen who worked for the government's Department to Combat Embezzlement. By 1991, 20,000 police officers were being fired yearly for collusion with the mafia—double the rate under Brezhnev. That same year, Alexander Gurov, head of the Soviet Interior Ministry's Sixth Department to Combat Organized Crime, estimated that four out of five agents in the ministry's militia were on the take.

These were merely symptoms of a malignant growth pervading the economy, the banking system and the body politic. It is common knowledge that millions of ordinary citizens steal state property, trade on the black market, swindle each other and buy or sell protection. Obviously they aren't all tied to the mob: Russia is so chaotic and broke that few people can stay honest and survive. Yet if not all lawbreakers are mafiosi, the mafia swims among them like a great predatory shark, recruiting some, exacting payoffs from others, frightening away rivals. Insatiable and seemingly invulnerable, it swallows factories, co-ops, private enterprises, real estate, raw materials, currency and gold: one-quarter of Russia's economy in 1991, between one-third and one-half by 1992.

Between 1989 and 1991, communism's twilight years, the mafia's take shot up from less than 1 billion rubles to 130 billion—the size of the Soviet national deficit. "In the next few years, its [gross] will reach 200 billion rubles," Gurov said in 1991. "Organized crime will then control 30 to 40 percent of the country's GNP."

Meanwhile, the mafia's kill rate has climbed to a world record. Once, Soviet leaders taunted America for its sixty-odd murders per day—a mark of capitalist depravity. By 1993 murders in the Russian republic alone ran to more than eighty per day. Many of the dead were victims of drunken brawls, armed robbery and gang warfare, but contract killings were increasingly popular: there were 1,500 in 1992. In 1993 ten directors of the country's largest commercial banks were murdered, presumably for failing to extend still more outrageous loans than those they had granted already. And a disturbing number of victims were policemen: nearly 1,000 between 1989 and 1992, according to Interpol Moscow.

By the start of 1992, soon after the Soviet Union's borders opened up, all of its institutions were gone, including those for law enforcement. The Soviet-wide Sixth Department, created by Mikhail Gorbachev three years earlier to fight organized crime, was dismantled along with all other nationwide bodies. No central authority remained to coordinate police intelligence, order arrests, control 36,000 miles of border or oversee the movement of people, money and goods. The only organization fully operational in the new Commonwealth of Independent States was the mafia.

The Russian mafia is richer by far than the forces of the law and much better equipped in weapons, communications systems and transport. Members are admitted only with a sponsor, and only after proving their valor by killing somebody on order, preferably a friend or relative—exactly like their Sicilian counterparts. Once in, they risk its death penalties, communicate in a private jargon and flout the tattoos marking their eternal membership: a spider web for drug traffickers, an eight-point star for robbers, a broken heart for district bosses.

The mafia is organized in something like a classic criminal pyramid. First, at the base, are common street hoods, under gang leaders who run their territory like military boot camps. Moscow, for instance, is controlled by twenty criminal "brigades"—some tribal, others regional, others specialized by trade—totaling more than 6,000 armed thugs. Everybody in the city in some kind of business (restaurants, foods markets, gas stations, flower stalls, newsstands, casinos, beggars' corners at the Kremlin) is "under somebody" who collects a monthly payoff. The *Dolgoprudnaya*, who drive around in Volvos with heated seats, control the best protection rackets. The *Lyubertsy* run prostitution. The *Solntsevo* run slot machines. The *Ingushy* smuggle contraband leather and skins to Italy. The Azerbaijanis control the drug trade. Then there are the Chechen, with their own army of 600 killers in Moscow. Natives of a self-proclaimed sovereign enclave in the northern Caucasus, the Chechen are the most notorious and versatile of Russia's mafiosi. They will do almost anything imaginable that is illegal.

A level up from the gangs are a "supply" group and a "security" group. The supply group serves as a conduit, ensuring that directives from above are carried out below. The security group is comprised of respectable citizens—journalists, bankers, artists, athletes, politicians—who provide intelligence, legal aid, social prestige and political cover.

On top of the pyramid are the godfathers, the indomitable *vory v zakone* (thieves-within-the-code); they preserve a "thieves' ideology," administer justice and plot strategy. There are 700 known godfathers at large or in prison. Guiding rather than governing, they provide most of the brains for their subalterns. They are not absolute rulers over violently unruly and fiercely competitive gangs. Rather, "each sphere of influence is under their control," according to I. Pavlovich, deputy chief of the Russian Interior Ministry's Sixth Department. Pavlovich says they meet periodically, settle territorial disputes, decide on operations and make policy. Their power inevitably surpasses the fragile Russian government's. Their edicts are instantly transmitted, unmistakably enforceable and almost universally obeyed.

Two stories illustrate how the mafia has of late transformed itself into a formidable force. First, in January 1991 the most powerful thieves-within-the-code gathered from all over the country to discuss a financial emergency. Valentin Pavlov, premier of the crumbling Soviet empire, had suddenly withdrawn all 50- and 100-ruble notes from circulation. His plan, he said, was to stop the illegal flow of rubles out of the country and prevent "a river of dirty money" from coming in. Everybody in the mafia kept illicit cash reserves in these notes, which at the time were the largest denominations issued.

"My operational report showed that these thieves-within-the-code—the supermen, the big-time mafiosi—got together to discuss ways of selling off or exchanging the banknotes for new ones or getting them out of the country," Gurov later said on national T.V. "The thieves-within-the-code decided where the rubles had to be exchanged or smuggled out. Then they gave permission to set aside a quarter of the entire sum for bribing the administration."

The underworld mobilized overnight. "Black-market currency sharks vanished from Moscow," Gurov declared. The ruble notes were rushed to corruptible state factories and banks in remote regions to be exchanged under the counter. The Konkuret co-op, with only 1,000 rubles in its account, changed 190,000 rubles in 50s and 100s into smaller denominations at the local bank. A Novosibirsk shop taking in 10,000 rubles per day "contrived to hand in" 240,000 rubles. Hundreds of millions of rubles were washed with little trouble. Unlike the poor, who lost their lifetime savings because they had been hiding their rubles under their mattresses to dodge the tax collectors, the mafia came out very well.

Then, a few months later the godfathers met again to consider Gorbachev's 500-day program for transition to a free market. They liked it. A free market in the USSR meant not only mobility, relaxed borders and dollars from abroad, but a chance to mount the most colossal criminal buyout in history. For all the wreckage of Russia's economy, it still had the world's richest natural resources. Once privatization got under way, according to Tatjana Kurjaghina, then the Interior Ministry's top social economist, the whole country would be up for sale.

Though few realized it at the time, the Russian mafia was about to make a big strategic leap: from merely feeding off the economy to owning it. To prepare for privatization, however, the godfathers needed to stall the entire government program until January 1992, and they had to impose a new peace among Moscow's eternally warring clans. A truce that they had worked out in 1988, at Dagomys on the Black Sea, had ended in an orgy of bloodshed after barely a year. But the first stage of privatization was an imperative call to order. The logic of peace was unarguable: once inner harmony was restored, the godfathers divided zones of influence and went after the 6,000 enterprises coming up for auction in Moscow. The rules for privatization were fluid, corrupt officials were easily come by and most Russians had no money to speak of. Within weeks, the Russian news agency *Tass-Krim Press* reported that the mafia had "privatized between 50 percent and 80 percent of all shops, storehouses, depots, hotels and services in Moscow."

Today, according to Yeltsin adviser Piotr Filipov, who heads the Center for Political and Economic Analysis, Russia' mafia controls 40,000 privatized enterprises and collects protection money from 80 percent of the country's banks and private enterprises.

The mafia also controls the drug trade. Nature has endowed Russia and its fellow republics with a prodigal source of narcotics. According to Alexander Sergeev, head of the Interior Ministry's anti-narcotics unit, the ex-USSR produces twenty-five times more hashish than the rest of the world; cannabis grows wild on 7.5 million of its acres—in Kazakhstan, Siberia, the Far Eastern republics, the lower Volga River Basin, the northern Caucasus and southern Ukraine. Luxuriant poppy fields sprawl across Kazakhstan, Uzbekistan, Turkmenistan and Tajikistan.

When Soviet controls were severe, organized crime overlooked this potential bonanza: the chance to create and feed a huge addict population and export for dollars. When communism fell, however, things changed. By 1992 family-sized poppy fields yielding two crops per year were under heavy armed guard. New plantations in Uzbekistan increased by 1,000 percent. Around 200,000 acres were planted in Kyrgyzstan. The number of opium growers in Kazakhstan's Chu Valley tripled. Poppies were planted over 1,000 square kilometers of empty radioactive terrain around Chernobyl. Vladimir Burlaka, St. Petersburg's anti-narcotics chief, estimated that the 1992 crop would be worth $5 billion.

Meanwhile, heroin couriers were moving up from the Golden Crescent through Tajikistan, Uzbekistan and Turkmenistan. They carried forged papers and radio telephones and had paramilitary protection as they crossed the breadth of Soviet territory bound for Odessa, Finland, the Baltic states, Poland, Western Europe and America. The drug mafia was taking over horizontally and vertically, from production and processing to transport, distribution and marketing. Free of centralized surveillance, it moved largely unhindered across the crazy quilt of internal Commonwealth borders, ignoring ethnic tensions.

Underground laboratories were also starting to produce synthetic drugs, such as "Krokodil" and "Chert" (devil), that were 1,000 times stronger than heroin and cheaper than homegrown natural drugs. The most lethal, methyl-fentanyl—diluted in proportions of 1 to 20,000—was made exclusively in Russia.

Soviet cities had always been a drug market of sorts, and it expanded as soldiers got hooked on heroin during the Afghanistan War; but galloping addiction set in only after traffickers mounted their assault around 1985. From then on the addict population doubled yearly. By 1992 Russia had at least 1.5 million addicts and occasional drug users, Sergeev says. (The figure was all the more startling for the carefully preserved fiction that Communist Russia had no addicts whatsoever. In fact, some Russian experts thought the "real" figure was "at least three to four times higher.") Also in 1992 the drug mafia's profits increased nearly fourfold, from 4 billion to 15 billion rubles—this before its first harvest of modernized, commercialized crops.

Sergeev says that Russian mafiosi have been trafficking heroin with Westerners, the Sicilian mafia especially, for nearly a decade. In 1992 they were delivering heroin to Sicilian mafiosi in New York, selling amphetamines elsewhere in the United States and moving cocaine in Vienna, Budapest and Frankfurt. They were said by Interpol Poland to have reached "precise agreements in Warsaw with big German and Dutch cocaine traffickers and Colombia's Cali cartel." That same year a shipment of pure Colombian cocaine shaped into 34,000 pairs of Peruvian-made plastic sandals was spotted in Mowcow, heading for Warsaw.

Despite this, and to avoid Yeltsin's displeasure, the U.S. State Department did not list Russia among forty-eight producer or transit countries in its 1992 International Narcotics Strategy Report. No Western government publication did. In another year, though, they would.

In the summer of 1992 Moscow Interpol's deputy chief, Anatoly Terechov, complained, "Less than half our joint ventures work. Only a quarter deal with their declared activities. Two or three out of five are financed with money of dubious origin. Many . . . are fictitious. Often they're one-man operations to swing hard currency deals. . . . At least 500 of our mafia groups use them to link up with international crime—in the United States, Italy, Germany, Austria, France, Canada, Poland. . . ."

Six months later Yeltsin himself adjusted this estimate upward. "At least 1,000 mafia groups have contacts with international organized crime," he said.

The American and Sicilian mafias were the first in, by way of what was to be the biggest black-market currency swap ever: a plan to trade $7.8 billion for 140 billion rubles, enabling the Westerners to buy Russia's natural resources for rubles and sell them in the West for 300 to 400 times more in dollars. (The plan was aborted in January 1991, but similar dollar-for-ruble scans followed.) With the Americans and the Sicilians entrenched, the Russians are moving out into the rest of the world—and they're heading West.

"It's wonderful that the Iron Curtain is gone," says Boris Uvarov, chief serious crimes investigator for the Russian prosecutor-general, "but it was a shield for the West. Now we've opened the gates, and this is very dangerous for the world. America is getting Russian criminals; Europe is getting Russian criminals. They'll steal everything. They'll *occupy* Europe. Nobody will have the resources to stop them. You people in the West don't know our mafia yet; you will, you will."

Sterling's essay provides a good deal of fundamental information, particularly in reference to the changes that have taken place in Russia since 1991 and the beginnings of massive economic changes aimed at privatizing industry. She has access to a considerable amount of statistical and detailed information that ultimately convinces the reader that the Russian mafia is a force to be reckoned with. She explains that organized crime had always existed in Russia, but that it was controlled by the government in the old days. Today corruption has "devoured the state," and the fate of Russia seems to be in doubt.

After you have read the essay you need to ask yourself whether you are convinced that the Russian mafia is a threat on an international scale, whether you are convinced that the Russian drug trade—expanded overwhelmingly since 1989—represents a threat to the rest of the world, and whether you are convinced that the Russian government is powerless to control the mafia. If your answer is yes to all of these points, then you need to ask what it is that has convinced you. Sterling essentially reports on trends in the new Russia. Crime is up; contract killings are up; corruption is rife; the "take" of crime in Russia is close to a staggering 30 or 40 percent of the gross national product. Everybody who does business in Moscow, she tells us, must pay for protection. These claims are bolstered by occasional quotations from prominent Russians. They are further bolstered by interesting anecdotes, such as the story of how the mafia managed to launder its fifty and one hundred ruble notes by corrupting local collective groups. Meanwhile honest citizens lost their savings.

Since Sterling does not supply a list of sources that the reader can double-check, the question of whether her information is correct remains unanswered. What the reader knows about her is that she is an investigative reporter and that she wrote a book called *Thieves' World*, in which this essay appeared in a slightly different form. The essay itself appeared in a reputable political journal. One may presume that the essay is reliable, but one cannot be sure without checking further. To some extent, the reader must trust the honesty of the writer. The writer's claims are not extravagant—although the final comments, by a Russian crime investigator, are a bit sensational, that the Russian mafia will "*occupy* Europe. Nobody will have the resources to stop them."

Finally, Sterling's comments on the pyramidal structure of the mafia leave certain questions unanswered. For example, is all crime in Russia mafia connected? From some of the statistics that she offers, one might think so. Certainly the observations she makes point to many groups of different ethnic and social origin who act in an organized way as racketeers. The question of whether all these groups belong to a clear organization is still unresolved. On the surface it seems unlikely, if only because there is likely to be a good deal of infighting with such a wide range of groups. Someone interested in arguing against Claire Sterling's position might suggest that the Russian mafia will, by virtue of its predatory nature, control itself by its internal fighting. In crime, competition is not a desirable condition. Competitors in Russia are likely to be dealt with by assassination, just as they are in New York.

Nonetheless, this essay is powerful and generally convincing primarily because of the overwhelming weight of its information. Because the essay appears in a widely read popular journal instead of a scholarly journal, it has no footnotes, no list of sources. The journal in which the article appeared double-checks its articles for authenticity but stops short of supplying the kind of detailed sources that would permit you to check the claims of the argument. This system is not always foolproof, but it is generally reliable and the reader knows that a healthy skepticism should accompany the reading of any such material.

Argument as Inquiry

Argumentative essays can be in the form of an inquiry whose purpose is to present materials, reasons, and evidence to arrive at a conclusion. Instead of defending a single position, the inquiry examines arguments for and against a position. Often the inquiry ends with the reader left to decide the ultimate question. Some people refer to this as Rogerian argument, named after a rhetorician who favors nonthreatening arguments that do not defend a single position. Such arguments attempt to remove controversy so as to avoid knee-jerk reactions from readers convinced of one side of the argument before they begin reading. In fact, the Rogerian strategy is to proceed without appearing to be constructing an argument. For that reason the structure of the inquiry—in which claims and reasons are presented and then carefully reviewed—is extraordinarily effective. It has the advantage of giving the appearance that both writer and reader are working together to arrive at a satisfactory conclusion.

Setting up your argument as an inquiry has many advantages, as shown in the box.

ARGUMENT AS INQUIRY

1. You present yourself as open to believing whatever your investigation proves. In other words, you come to the issue with an open mind and set a good example for your reader. Your reader may feel like a participant with you in the inquiry.
2. You make it possible to examine all the arguments for and against your position, because you have made it clear that you are interested in the truth, not just in defending a position because it is yours.
3. No matter where you begin your inquiry—whether you are inclined to believe a specific position or to question it—honest inquiry has the potential to transform your own attitude toward a question. It has the potential for self-education.
4. If careful inquiry has persuaded you of the truth, you will have a much easier time persuading others.

Evan S. Connell: "Were Custer's Men Brave?"

The following excerpt from a longer study offers a valuable insight into how argumentative prose can help in an investigation. Evan Connell conducts an inquiry into the question of whether the cavalrymen with Custer were brave. As he tells you, some people at the time said yes, and others said no.

EVAN S. CONNELL

"Were Custer's Men Brave?"

Years after the battle a number of Indians claimed that the soldiers became so terrified they dropped their guns. In fact, quite a few did drop their guns or throw them aside, although not necessarily in panic. The guns occasionally jammed because the soft copper shells—unlike hard brass—could be deformed by exploding powder, causing them to stick in the breech. Furthermore, troopers often carried loose ammunition in saddlebags where it was easily damaged. Another possible reason turned up when one of Reno's men talked with an ordnance officer. This officer subsequently wrote to the Chief of Ordnance that Custer's troops used ammunition belts made from scrap leather. The copper shells "thus had become covered with a coating of verdigris and extraneous matter, which had made it difficult to even put them in the chamber before the gun had been discharged at all. Upon discharge the verdigris and extraneous matter formed a cement which held the sides of the cartridge in place against the action of the ejector. . . ."

Whatever the cause, it could take some time to pry a deformed shell out of the breech, or one that had been cemented in place, which explains why troopers under attack occasionally threw aside their rifles. To the Indians it must have appeared that a soldier who did this was terrified—as of course he might have been—but at the same time he might have been enraged.

A letter from Reno to General S. V. Benét, dated July 11, 1876, states that an Indian scout—not identified—was hiding just outside the battle zone, close enough to see troopers working on their guns. Knives with broken blades were found beside several bodies, further proof that the Seventh had to fight more than one enemy.

Such men obviously did not lose their wits. Others did. It is usually assumed that Custer's regiment consisted of blue-jacketed wind-burned agate-eyed tobacco-chewing roosters who could live on sagebrush, alkali, and a little biscuit, who would gallop the field of Armageddon without blinking. Partly this was true. But the Seventh also included unbaptized recruits—perhaps thirty percent—many of whom had not once fired a carbine. Senator Thomas Hart Benton, a Missourian who grew up close to the frontier, referred to these troops as "the sport of Indians." They could not even stay on a horse, he said, but rolled off like pumpkins. Yet such was their faith that most of these innocents thought a yelping mob of Sioux would retreat faster than the Red Sea when old Iron Butt charged. When this did not occur—when, in fact, their intrepid commandant tried to organize a defensive pattern—some of the recruits were bounding over the sagebrush like jackrabbits.

Red Horse, a Miniconjou chief, spoke of whites with contempt. He said many of them asked to be taken prisoner.

An Arapaho named Left Hand rode up to a soldier who simply held out his gun, which Left Hand accepted. Then a Sioux came along and stopped long enough to kill the coward.

"John" is said to have been the name ordinarily used by whites when addressing an Indian. One trooper was heard sobbing this name, as though it might save his life.

John! John! Oh, John!

The plea echoes horribly down a hundred years.

Indians reported many such instances of cowardice among Custer's troops but did not tell similar stories about Reno's battalion. Reno's men must have been terrified when they galloped out of the valley, plunged into the river, and scrambled up the bluff, yet it appears that not one became so crazed with fear that he shot himself or numbly surrendered his weapons.

Quite a few hostiles, among them the Unkpapa war chief Crow King, insisted that all the soldiers, including Custer's men, fought courageously as long as they lived. And the Oglala chief Low Dog said at a conference of government officials in 1881: "They came on us like a thunderbolt. I never before nor since saw men so brave and fearless. . . . No white man or Indian ever fought as bravely as Custer's men."

Perhaps. But it should be kept in mind that for years afterward these Indians told white journalists and politicians what they thought the whites wanted to hear. They believed, correctly or not, that if they said the wrong thing they would be punished; therefore it was advisable to praise Custer and his troops. Being realists, they knew that a wise prisoner does not anger his warden, and nothing infuriated whites more than allegations of cowardice or suicide at the Little Bighorn. Wooden Leg was challenged by another Cheyenne in 1906 to tell a white man—identified only as "Doctor Dixon"—that Custer killed himself. Wooden Leg refused. "Other Indians, at other times, had tried to tell of the soldiers killing themselves, but the white people listening always became angry and said the Indians were liars, so I thought it best to keep quiet."

This dread of punishment persisted for at least two generations. As late as 1926 a half-brother of Sitting Bull refused to attend the semicentennial for fear of being hanged. And several years later Dr. Marquis, whom the Cheyennes liked and trusted, was shown a supply of guns they had kept hidden ever since 1876.

That Custer's elite regiment fell apart in a most unprofessional manner seems to be substantiated by the testimony of whites. The entire battleground was studied by officers from the Terry-Gibbon army and by survivors of the Reno-Benteen command in an effort to learn what happened. Capt. Myles Moylan said he could find no evidence of organized resistance anywhere on the ridge with the exception of Calhoun's L Company. DeRudio was surprised to see so few expended cartridges. Lt. Wallace also noted very few shells: piles of twenty-five or thirty at various places where Calhoun's men fought, otherwise not much indication of a battle.

Calhoun had kept a promise. On April 23, 1871, he wrote to Custer: "I have just received my commission as 1st Lt. in the 7th Cavalry, and it reminds me more vividly than ever how many, many times I am under obligations to you for your very great kindness to me in my troubles. I shall do my best to prove my gratitude. If the time comes you will not find me wanting. . . ."

Benteen could discern no organized line of defense. "You can take a handful of corn and scatter it over the floor. . . ." He said he examined the field carefully in an attempt to see how the battle was fought and concluded it had been a rout.

Custer's problem was compounded by the fact that several of his most experienced officers—among them two majors and four captains—were not with the regiment, having been temporarily assigned elsewhere. Some were in Philadelphia doing one thing or another in connection with the forthcoming centennial festivities. He had tried to get them reassigned to field duty, quite obviously because he suspected he would need dependable officers, but the Washington high command denied his requests.

Just what occurred can be deduced only from battlefield evidence and from what the Indians said later, but there is not much doubt what certain units—such as Calhoun's—fought valiantly and intelligently, others did succumb to panic. This may have been what happened to Lt. Algernon Smith's E Company. It is thought that Indians stampeded most of E Company's horses by yelling and waving blankets. The dismounted troopers then ran downhill and slid into the ravine where their bodies were found.

Some military analysts view the matter differently. A charge by Lame White Man's Cheyennes may have forced Smith's men up the ravine or gully. However they got there, it was the end of the road.

Why Lt. Smith left his men, or they left him, could never be determined.

The hillside above this gully is irregular, spotted with small cactus and sage, and nothing suggests that the slope was forested a century ago. Which is to say, if the cavalrymen did lose their horses at this point they must have felt helplessly exposed and rushed toward the one place that might protect them. Yet the moment they skidded into the gully they were trapped. All they could do was hug the sides or crouch among bushes, look fearfully upward, and wait. A few tried to scramble up the south wall because the earth showed boot marks and furrows probably gouged by their fingers, but none of these tracks reached the surface.

An Unkpapa named Iron Hawk thought these soldiers were scared silly. Just above the ravine he attacked one who had managed to get on a horse. Iron Hawk put an arrow through him.

EVIDENCE

Rather than making any claims, Connell begins with evidence, mostly testimony from those who were at the scene of the massacre of Custer's men. Indians said years later that the soldiers dropped their guns in panic. Red Horse said many of the cavalrymen asked to be taken prisoner. Unkpapa and other Indians said Custer's men fought bravely. Study of the site by Captain Miles Moylan and Benteen indicated "no evidence of organized resistance anywhere on the ridge." Battlefield evidence shows signs of confusion and possible failure to follow orders.

Were you to list these in the form of claims, some of them would be contradictory:

Claim 1: Custer's men were too frightened to shoot.

Reason Indians said the soldiers dropped their guns and ran.

Claim 2: The men were so frightened they surrendered.

Reason Red Horse said many soldiers wanted to be taken prisoner.

Claim 3: Custer's men fought bravely.

Reason Unkpapa and others said Custer's men fought bravely.

Claim 4: Custer's men were panicked and could not organize their defense.

Reason Moylan and Benteen said there was no organized resistance.

Reasoning from Evidence

At the end of this excerpt, Connell says, the matter of Custer's bravery has to be "deduced from battlefield evidence and from what the Indians said later." That being the case, he concentrates on examining the validity of reasons for various claims. Essentially, he determines what can be known from the evidence at hand. He reminds us that evidence must be examined before it can be relied on, since "facts" are not always facts, especially when the facts come from eyewitnesses. First, he examines the claim that dropping their guns meant the soldiers were frightened. He shows that the way equipment was cared for could have made the rifles useless and they may have been thrown away because they were jammed. Eyewitnesses establish that some of the soldiers struggled with their weapons.

Many soldiers were raw recruits who may have been willing to give up. Connell finds evidence that Indians killed some men who disarmed themselves. On the other hand, the fact that Unkpapa and others claimed Custer's men were brave does not make it so, since they gave testimony in a situation that made them feel they should say what white people wanted to hear. Their fears may have distorted their testimony.

That the "regiment fell apart" seems clear from the examination of the battle scene, which is disorganized. But as Connell says, key experienced officers who might have contributed to effective organization were not present at the battle. Fear may have had a large part in the disorganization, but so did inexperience.

Reasoning from Probability

Connell's position at the end of the inquiry is that some of the men were probably brave and some probably not. His examination of the reasons supporting both sides of the argument show that it is not possible to make an absolutely secure claim either way. Even eyewitnesses may have been mistaken about the meaning of what they saw.

Probability is not conclusive proof of anything. However, conclusive arguments respect probability. For example, Custer's Seventh Cavalry has been made into an icon of heroism by films and posters and legend. Many people hold the image of Custer standing in the middle of a small body of men with his sidearm blazing while thousands of Indians pour down on him. Custer's bravery would never be called into question by anyone who has "bought" that view of the battle at the Little Bighorn. However, it is probable that all the men with him were frightened when they saw how outnumbered they were. It is probable that many of them panicked: they must have feared they would all be massacred. It is also probable that some of them were brave fighters, especially those who were experienced soldiers. The probability that they were not all brave or all cowards is easy to accept. Consequently, an argument from probability, such as Connell mounts, appears reasonable on the surface. Connell backs it up with careful analysis of evidence.

Connell does what most writers of good argument always do: he isolates the evidence and then decides how reliable it is and which conclusions can be reasonably drawn. In each of the instances noted above, some kind of claim had been made based on examination of evidence. As he tells us, the testimony of those involved is one kind of evidence, but like all evidence, it must be interpreted and analyzed. If Connell accepted any of the evidence without analysis, he would probably come to an unwarranted conclusion.

Persuasion Through Argument

The basic purpose of an argument is to persuade. Claire Sterling wishes to persuade us that the Russian mafia is a serious threat to Russia and to the rest of the world. Evan Connell's argument ends up persuading us about the behavior of Custer's men.

Being Consistent and Fair

One obligation of a writer of argument is to be consistent in treating the evidence and any other important aspect of the inquiry. Sterling presents the information in her essay in a straightforward manner, as if the numbers she quotes are in the public record, which they probably are. She also confirms her statistics with direct quotations from prominent Russian government and police officials. On the other hand, Connell calls every claim into question, not just some of them. He accepts no one's testimony without qualification. He searches the historical record as well as the record of testimony. He consistently questions Indian testimony that Custer's men were brave, just as he questions the Indians' observation of soldiers casting down their rifles.

Connell maintains a healthy skepticism throughout his article. He deals critically with each claim he makes and examines critically every claim others have made that may argue against his position. Skepticism in argument is healthy. The skeptic basically says, "Show me. Prove it to me." The skeptic will examine a claim, its reasons, and all the evidence amassed in favor of it until a conclusion appears inevitable. At that point, the argument is either won or lost.

The Tone of an Argument

As with any other essay, style can make a great difference in constructing an argument. A writer's tone is expressed in his or her attitude toward the audience. When presenting or defending an argument, the writer has a wide choice of tone. One can be cool and reserved or aggressive and alarmed. One can be abusive or conciliatory toward an audience. One can argue from a perceived position of absolute superiority, or one can assume a humble position of simple inquiry. The range of possible tone is enormous. The box material covers some of the pros and cons of various tones.

ARGUMENTATIVE TONE

1. With an argument, an aggressive tone can backfire. The intended audience will not read your argument, or if it does, it will discount it as diatribe.
2. If you address only those who agree with you, your tone can be witty, even abusive to the opposition. It is not good advice to suggest being abusive; however, you will see and hear such arguments and wonder how the writer can adopt such a tone. The writer who adopts an abusive tone will not be likely to convince an audience of anything it does not already believe.
3. When your audience disagrees with you, your argumentative strategies must be careful and your tone restrained. An abusive tone will get you nowhere with a hostile audience. The best approach is to use a tone appropriate to inquiry. In other words, act as if you

assume you and your audience are equally interested in getting to the truth and that you are both anxious to examine the facts and the evidence fairly. Being amusing or funny can help, too.

4. If your audience is undecided about something on which you hold a firm position, you have a choice of tones to adopt. One is that of the informed source offering information and evidence to someone who wants it. Another is that of a formerly undecided person who reveals the process by which he or she reached a final decision on the argument. A third is the tone of one who expects the audience not to reach a decision, but to reflect on the issues raised in the argument.

Evan Connell's tone is that of the matter of-fact historian. Until you have read through his argument you do not know whether he thinks Custer's men were brave or cowardly. You may still not be sure at the end. He presents the main bodies of evidence, testimony of witnesses, examination of the field of battle, and a reflection on equipment and other mitigating factors. His tone is not condescending: he assumes his audience is as equipped to reach an understanding of the situation as he is. He is also not aggressive or abusive. He explains why Indians who testified in white courts might be likely not to tell the entire truth, but he is not abusive of them or of people who might take their testimony at face value.

Claire Sterling depends on the power of her information to carry the argument. Given her material, she could have produced an alarmist essay designed to frighten her audience. However, she remains cool and presumes her audience follows the points carefully and considers their ultimate impact. Her tone—that of the reporter, the information gatherer who highlights the important details—helps the reader digest the impact of her material. On the other hand, she quotes a number of Russian sources who make alarming pronouncements designed to frighten an audience. For example, she quotes Alexander Gurov saying that "Organized crime will then control 30 to 40 percent of the country's GNP." She also quotes an unnamed "Russian crime specialist" as saying the Russian mafia is "looking at the West as a wolf looks at sheep." These are alarming statements which, if completely true, should evoke fear in most readers. Sterling balances such statements with her own calm tone. On the other hand, her very calm in the face of the threat she describes is quite chilling.

Argument as Debate

Probably many people think of argumentation as taking a stand on an issue and developing every possible point to prove the validity of the argument. Such arguments can resemble one half of a debate. We sometimes think of a debater as limiting the argument to only one side of the issue rather than being fair and examining all sides without prejudice. Occasionally, in the popular press we see an argument that takes only one side followed by a response that takes issue with the original and offers the other side. These situations test the limits of argument. The following is an exchange between two thinkers on the question of welfare mothers. The first writer, Katha Pollitt, is a poet who writes a regular column for a political journal. Midge Decter is a prominent feminist who writes a column for a different political journal. The essays are presented in three parts: first Pollitt's initial essay on welfare mothers, then Decter's angry response, then a slightly later observation by Pollitt that defines and examines some issues but does not specifically respond to Decter—it is a continuation of Pollitt's argument. Since these articles were published in 1994, laws have been passed that would curtail welfare to the very people Pollitt and Decter describe.

KATHA POLLITT

Subject to Debate

Women have been unfairly blamed for a lot of things over the years—the Fall of Man (*sic*), their own rapes and beatings, autistic children. Male journalists are particularly ingenious at the game of *cherchez la femme*: Kenneth Woodward, religion reporter for *Newsweek*, blames women for the impending collapse of the Church of England (selfish ordination-seekers driving traditionalists to Rome); Murray Kempton playfully suggests that Mafia dons are merely small-time grifters trying to support their layabout-marrying daughters. And, as is well known, behind every serial killer is a bad mother—just ask Jeffrey Dahmer's father, who in his recent memoir points out that Mrs. Dahmer was a reluctant breast-feeder.

But poverty? Women cause *poverty*? That is the emerging bipartisan consensus, subscribed to by players as far apart as Charles Murray and Eleanor Holmes Norton, Dan Quayle and Bill Clinton, *National Review* and *The New York Times*. All agree that unwed mothers, particularly teenagers and, to a lesser extent, divorced moms, are the driving force behind poverty, crime and a host of other ills. If mothers got married and stayed married, children would be provided for, the economy would flourish, crime would go down and your taxes too. "Welfare dependency" would vanish, replaced, as God and nature planned, by husband-dependency.

Opinions differ over how to accomplish this goal. Mickey Kaus wants to force welfare moms into state-funded low-wage employment and, if they balk, put their children in orphanages. Charles Murray wants to skip the preliminaries and get right to the orphanage part. More than thirty states are conducting punitive welfare "experiments": refusing increases for children conceived on welfare, cutting grants to women whose kids skip school, stopping payments after two years (or, if Governor Weld has his way in Massachusetts, sixty days!). Bill Clinton's campaign pledge to "end welfare as we know it" has unleashed forces he cannot control: What defenders claim started out as a way to market poverty spending to resistant suburban voters has become a competition over how to prevent the poor and "illegitimate" from being born in the first place. And since this is America, land of family values and pro-life, this end must be achieved in a way that combines the minimum of money and the maximum of social control. Forcing welfare recipients to use Norplant, as many state legislatures are now considering, has an appeal that, say, simply making all birth control free and accessible does not. As for abortion, forget it. Even as the nation contemplates the mass warehousing of poor toddlers, a New York court ruled 6-to-0 in *Hope v. Perales* that a program that funds all medical care for poor pregnant women above the Medicaid line need not pay for even medically necessary abortions. Feminists for Life, who argue that banning abortion will force the government to support women and children, phone home: We are moving toward a system that will force poor pregnant women to give birth and will then take their babies away.

To say that unwed mothers cause poverty is like saying hungry people cause famine, or sick people cause disease. Out-of-wedlock births do not explain why Donna Karen has her clothes produced in Hong Kong, or why $100 sneakers are made by Malaysian women paid 16 cents an hour. Nor do the sex lives of the poor explain why corporations nationwide are laying off thousands of white-collar workers, or why one out of five college graduates are working at jobs that require no college degree. Imagine for a moment that every teenage girl in West Virginia got married before getting pregnant. How would that create jobs or raise wages? Marriage might benefit individuals (or not), but it can't bring back the coal industry. Family values didn't save the family farm, and they won't save the millions of people who have been rendered superfluous by the New World Economic Order.

It would be closer to the truth to say that poverty causes early and unplanned childbearing. Across the income spectrum, after all—and to an extent that would horrify their parents if they knew about it—young people are having sex and young girls are getting pregnant. Strangely enough, however, you don't find many 15-year-olds dropping out of the Dalton School to have babies. Girls with bright futures—college, jobs, travel—have abortions. It's the ones who have nothing to postpone who become mothers. What none of the men who have dominated the welfare discussion betray any sign of understanding is that babies are the centuries-old way that women have put meaning, love, pleasure, hope and self-respect into their lives.

Unlike some on the left, I don't think teenage motherhood is a great idea, either for mothers or for children, and whether or not marriage is involved. But if impoverishing women were a deterrent, it surely would have worked by now: Those supposedly lavish welfare payments are barely two-thirds what they were twenty years ago. Even the orphanage idea has a long history of failure behind it—which didn't prevent Daniel Patrick Moynihan from reminiscing affectionately about the infamous turn-of-the-century "orphan trains" on *Charlie Rose* a few months ago.

Orphanages for children, and for their mothers, "workfare," jail, the street, the church-basement cot—all in the name of values. Where's William Blake when you need him?

MIDGE DECTER

Welfare Feminism

It is fair to say that the *Nation*, having come out every week for almost 130 years now, is the country's longest-lived and most consistent voice of the Left. Therefore on opening a new issue one might, depending on one's

Midge Decter, "Welfare Feminism," *Commentary*, Vol. 98, #1, July 1994. Reprinted by permission of the author.

outlook, expect to be soothed or stirred to passion, illuminated or infuriated. The one thing one does not usually experience is surprise. A striking exception is the column called "Subject to Debate" in the May 30, 1994 issue. The column's author is the much-prized poet and radical feminist ideologue Katha Pollitt, and on this occasion her subject is welfare mothers.

Pollitt begins by pointing out that women have been unfairly blamed for many things, beginning with the banishment from Eden and on down to the serial murderer Jeffrey Dahmer (whose father, says Pollitt, accused Dahmer's mother of being a reluctant breast-feeder). And now women are being subjected by virtually everyone to the most unfair accusation of all: that they are the cause of poverty.

That women are responsible for poverty, Pollitt informs us, is now a matter of wide and bipartisan consensus, subscribed to by people otherwise as disparate in attitude as Charles Murray and Eleanor Holmes Norton, Dan Quayle and Bill Clinton, the editors of *National Review* and the editorialists of the *New York Times*. All these people agree that unwed mothers, particularly teenagers, are the driving force behind poverty and crime. "If," as she sums up this consensus, "mothers got married and stayed married, children would be provided for, the economy would flourish, crime would go down and your taxes, too."

About how to achieve this blissful state Pollitt finds no consensus. Mickey Kaus, she explains, wants to force welfare moms to take low-paid, state-funded jobs, and, if they balk, put their children in orphanages. Charles Murray, on the other hand, "wants to skip the preliminaries and get right to the orphanage part."

In addition, more than 30 states are engaged in instituting punitive welfare reforms, which involve such policies as refusing any further grants for children conceived by women on welfare—all of which are intended in one way or another to prevent more welfare babies from being born. "And since this is America, land of family values and pro-life, this end must be achieved in a way that combines the minimum of money and the maximum of social control."

For instance, Pollitt contends, forcing welfare recipients to use Norplant has an appeal ("social control") that simply making birth control free and accessible does not—as, to say the least, government-funded abortions for poor pregnant women above the Medicaid line also do not. We are, then, as Pollitt (evidently having forgotten about Norplant) sees it, "moving toward a system that will force poor pregnant women to give birth and will then take their babies away."

But whether we do actually reach this point or not, the idea behind proposals to make good on President Clinton's promise to "end welfare as we know it" is, in Pollitt's view, a noxious one. To say that unwed mothers cause poverty "is like saying hungry people cause famine or sick people cause disease."

The illegitimacy rate, she argues, does not explain why so many American businesses have moved their factories to places like Malaysia, where women are paid sixteen cents an hour; nor why corporations are laying off thousands of white-collar workers; nor why one out of five college graduates is working at a job that requires no degree. "Imagine for a moment that every teenage girl in West Virginia got married before getting pregnant. How would that create jobs or raise wages . . . or bring back the coal industry?

In Pollitt's opinion, it would be closer to the truth to put the case the other way around: that poverty creates early and unplanned childbearing. After all, kids all across the income spectrum are having sex and getting pregnant. The difference is that girls with bright futures—"college, jobs, travel"—have abortions, while the ones who have nothing to postpone become mothers." "What none of the men who have dominated the welfare discussion betray any sign of understanding is that babies are the centuries-old way that women have put meaning, love, pleasure, hope, and self-respect into their lives."

In response to the view that these young mothers would be better off if they could get married and stay married, Pollitt can only muster a sneer: " 'Welfare dependency' would vanish," she writes, "replaced, as God and nature planned, by husband-dependency."

And so to her conclusion about where the present consensus is leading us: "Orphanages for children, and for their mothers, 'workfare,' jail, the street, the church-basement cot—all in the name of values."

What is one to make of this? On the practical side, Pollitt seems to have little more to advocate than free birth control and free abortions. This, of course, is neither a novel nor a surprising bit of advocacy, especially for someone on the Left. Nor is it surprising that Pollitt should grossly caricature a position with which she is taking issue: to wit, characterizing a belief in the need for welfare reform as the belief that women are to blame for poverty. Caricature is a time-honored tradition of radical argumentation.

What is surprising is that Pollitt herself has nothing, not one word, to say about welfare, though it is ostensibly a key object of her concern. Since she foresees that reform will lead to dire consequences for welfare mothers—in addition to losing their children, they will be left with nothing but jail, prostitution, and/or homelessness—does she mean by implication to defend the system as it is? Her economic "analysis"—in which, no doubt as the result of a certain unmanageable passion about corporations, she lumps together welfare poverty with white-collar underemployment and unemployment—would suggest that she favors high trade barriers (what then of her poor sisters in the third world?). But this conclusion she does not explicitly draw.

Most surprising of all, she has nothing whatever to say about the children, beyond suggesting that placing them in orphanages would be an injustice to their mothers. Yet it surely cannot have escaped her notice that it is the children who are the real source of the current sense of crisis about the welfare system, with their absconded fathers running a close second.

Clearly, Pollitt's main (or perhaps only) interest in welfare and poverty is to exonerate women from any blame for society's troubles. Ardent feminist though she may be, in a time when gunplay with assault weapons among children has become an ordinary everyday occurrence—as have the deaths of babies and young children from neglect and abuse—to concentrate on the question of whether women are or are not at fault seems . . . well, a trifle light-minded, to say the least.

There ought by now to be some way to get the minds of privileged women off themselves. A woman who can suggest of, say, a sixteen-year-old pregnant girl, blessed or lucky enough to find a young man to marry her and be a father to her baby, that she is merely exchanging one "dependency" for another is someone who, for all her intellectual and political pretensions, has rarely, if ever, looked beyond the end of her own well-cared-for nose.

From time immemorial poets have been granted a license, which, to be sure, not all of them have taken, to be deliberately foolish—*narrenfreiheit*, it was once called, the freedom of fools. But as Katha Pollitt so well illustrates, even this special dispensation is capable of being abused.

KATHA POLLITT

Subject to Debate

Where are the feminist voices in the so-called debate over welfare reform? Since President Clinton's speech last week unveiling his plans to restructure A.F.D.C. [Aid to Families with Dependent Children] as a compulsory work program, I've waded through a small ocean of punditry—well, it's more like a swamp of wet cement, actually—and with a few noticeable ex-

Katha Pollitt, "Subject to Debate." Reprinted with permission from the July 11, 1994, issue of *The Nation* magazine.

ceptions, like welfare-rights activist and author Theresa Funiciello, who called the current welfare debate "misogynist" on *MacNeil/Lehrer*, the speakers and writers and blatherers have been the usual male bean counters and worshipers at the shrine of family values. The "debate" seems to revolve around whether the government should provide compulsory minimum-wage jobs to welfare mothers, who, it is universally agreed, are irresponsible layabouts, or whether that would be socialist coddling and the women should be forced to find jobs on their own. Did I nod off and miss something?

I don't want to single out feminists unfairly. Women raising children on welfare are not exactly a high priority of the other progressive movements upon whom they have a claim: labor, black civil rights groups, children's advocates, like the Clinton-connected Marian Wright Edelman of the Children's Defense Fund. ("She could turn this whole discussion around if she chose," one welfare-rights policy analyst told me sadly.) And what about those child-development experts—Jay Belsky, Robert Karen, T. Berry Brazelton—who have devoted their careers to filling working mothers with guilt for putting their children in daycare? One would expect them to use their considerable media access to decry the prospect of millions of poor children, their lives already stressful, warehoused in full-time daycare that is bound to be vastly inferior to the middle-class arrangements the experts criticize. Have they even spoken out against Charles Murray's mad proposal for the mass orphanaging of "illegitimate" toddlers? Maybe I missed that too.

It's not that feminists have been totally silent. NOW [National Organization of Women], despite its white-professionals image, supports welfare rights and has actively opposed the punitive state measures gaining steam around the country. "Family caps," the denial of grant increases for children conceived on welfare, unites in opposition women on both sides of the abortion debate, from Feminists For Life to NARAL. And yes, I know that women journalists and columnists can be counted on to skewer the more outrageously sexist presumptions of the welfare reformers, beginning with the notion that teenage girls get pregnant through parthenogenesis. But when was the last time you heard a feminist argument for welfare as a positive social program that benefits all women?

Why is welfare a feminist issue? Because when reformers talk about welfare mothers "staying home doing nothing," you can throw away that coffee mug that says "Every mother is a working mother." What is welfare reform, after all, but a massive social denial that A.F.D.C. moms are *already* working? Contrary to popular stereotype, feminists have always maintained that motherhood is socially valuable labor that deserves collective support and recognition. Women's movement campaigns for paid parental leave, flextime, part-time work with benefits, and acknowledgment of women's care-giving role in determining custody and financial settlements in divorce can hardly be helped along if the government officially declares that single mothers are social parasites who ought to be wiping down tables at Wendy's.

Welfare is a feminist issue because it weakens women's dependence on men. It means that pregnant women can choose to give birth and keep their babies even if abandoned by their boyfriends and families; it means that battered women can leave abusive men, and miserable working-class wives, like their middle-class sisters, can get a fresh start without reducing their children to starvation. It protects women at a time when the patriarchal family is disintegrating, and that is why family-values conservatives hate it, even though opposition to welfare forces them to laud employed mothers, whom—in another part of the policy forest—they usually attack.

Admittedly, it will be a hard sell to persuade mothers with jobs, who are now the majority, that they ought to pay taxes so that other women can stay home. Feminists need to point out that it is in the self-interest of most working women to preserve and even expand A.F.D.C. For one thing, they may need those benefits themselves someday (almost half of women on welfare landed there because of divorce). For another, if A.F.D.C. moms are forced into the job market, you can be sure that they're not first going to be trained to drive trucks or do construction. They're going to be channeled into the same handful of job categories—clerical, service, sales—that are already packed with women. They will be competing with mothers who are already employed and—especially if the government subsidizes their hiring—they will depress wages. What chance will there be for unions that try to organize clerical workers, or for the Worthy Wage campaign, which tries to raise the pay and status of daycare workers, if thousands of women are suddenly forced to seek work, particularly in a period of high unemployment? Conversely, the higher welfare benefits are, the higher wages have to be to make work attractive, which is good news for working moms (unless, of course, they happen to be employers). Maybe women should start thinking of welfare as a combination of strike fund and wages for housework.

It's true that welfare rights lacks the cross-party political appeal of abortion rights; certainly it's not as sexy as debates over pornography, sexual harassment and date rape—let alone single-sex education, self-esteem and the Wonderbra. On the other hand, those issues will be around for quite a while—the pornography debate in particular will probably outlast the pyramids—but the fate of millions of single mothers and their children is being settled right now. Let's show them how powerful sisterhood can be.

Emphasis

After reading the first two parts of the welfare debate, we might wonder about the placement of emphasis in each argument. Pollitt emphasizes the blame that women have had to assume through the ages, pointing now to the bipartisan agreement on women contributing to poverty by virtue of their having babies out of wedlock. She is correct in saying that there is a wide base of support for such a view. What remains in doubt is whether Pollitt agrees with that view.

Midge Decter assumes that she does. Decter's early emphasis is on restating Pollitt's argument, and much of what she writes is direct quotation. What she sees as the emphasis in Pollitt's essay may not be what others see. For example, she ends her summary of the position of Pollitt's article by saying, "Nor is it surprising that Pollitt should grossly caricature a position with which she is taking issue: to wit, characterizing a belief in the need for welfare reform as the belief that women are to blame for poverty." For Decter, the emphasis should be on the question of welfare. She complains that Pollitt "herself has nothing, not one word, to say about welfare." Further, she complains that Pollitt "has nothing whatever to say about the children." She summarizes Pollitt's intention in these words: "Clearly, Pollitt's main (or perhaps only) interest in welfare and poverty is to exonerate women from any blame for society's troubles." Decter also complains that Pollitt is being self-centered in suggesting that a woman who marries exchanges one kind of dependence for another.

Interestingly, Decter attacks Pollitt on the level of an ethical appeal—suggesting that Pollitt is a privileged woman responding to things from the position that would be normally expected of the privileged, educated elite. You may or may not agree with Decter's view. Pollitt does drop a few hints as to her social standing, particularly in her judgments regarding education. Of course, it is also obvious that neither Pollitt nor Decter is likely to end up on the welfare rolls, despite Pollitt's pointing out that many women find themselves on welfare because of divorce.

While Pollitt does not respond directly to Decter's attack in the third of these essays, she does address the issue of welfare mothers and their relationship to the ongoing feminist debates of the day.

"Welfare is a feminist issue," she says, "because it weakens women's dependence on men." This is a powerful claim, and one reason backing it is that anything that permits a woman to be independent and not have to depend on the earnings or support of a man is a positive feminist value. The consequence of accepting that claim is that working women should be willing to pay for welfare mothers to stay home with their children. One reason backing this claim is that "motherhood is socially valuable labor." If you accept these claims on the basis of these reasons, then you would accept the argument that feminists ought to "preserve and even expand A.F.D.C."

Writing Argumentative Essays

As a preliminary to beginning your own argumentative and persuasive essay, consider some of the problems that the average writer faces. First, the subject of such an essay, if it does not come to mind immediately as a result of something the writer is working on, may take some thinking. Generally, many writers have a backlog of issues that are important and worth arguing about. Such a list might include the following:

- Bigoted language: is it protected by the first amendment?
- What are the limits of free speech?
- Should assault weapons be banned in the United States?
- Does the Constitution protect individuals' rights to possess weapons of combat, such as tanks and mortars?
- Would it be constitutional to license all gun owners and demand that, like licensed drivers, they pass a test?
- Should Federal grants support artists who criticize the norms of society?
- Should gays be permitted to serve in the military?
- Should gay marriages be legally recognized?
- Are gay and lesbian rights protected by the Constitution?
- The Bible condemns homosexuality. Does that mean homosexual behavior is immoral behavior?

- Is homosexual behavior morally different if it is a matter of choice rather than a matter of biological necessity?
- What are the moral concerns involved in sexual behavior?
- Is racism the controlling feature of American society?
- Which American minorities suffer most from racism?
- There are fewer Episcopalians in America than Muslims. Are the Episcopalians a minority group? Are the Muslims?
- Crime by teenagers has become epidemic. Evening curfews for teenagers reduce crime. Are they desirable and necessary?
- Gang terror dominates many schools and neighborhoods. What should be done about controlling gang influence? Are gangs good or bad?
- Crime is said to be a price we pay for freedom. When will it be too high a price? What freedoms should we be prepared to give up in order to fight crime?
- Drugs have ravaged our society for the last forty years. Would legalizing all currently illegal drugs solve the problem of drug-related crimes?
- Is youth culture an attack on the culture of mainstream America?
- Are MTV and VH-1 subversive?
- Is the culture of mainstream America more vulgar now than when Doris Day and Rock Hudson were romantic stars?
- Should we plan to test everyone for AIDS on an annual basis? What might be the arguments for and against the plan?
- Should people who test positive for HIV be publicly identified so as to help prevent the spread of AIDS?
- Why protect the civil rights of those who carry the AIDS virus?
- Should English be the official language of the United States?

These are only a few suggestions based on current news and concerns that have been at the forefront of the popular imagination.

Each is a potential subject of argument because it admits of different kinds of interpretation. Some of them, such as the question of legalizing drugs, ought to be arguable to the point that rational people could come to agreement. Yet on most of these subjects feelings run high and agreement is hard won if it can be won at all.

Defining Terms

One key point in beginning an argument on any of these subjects is ensuring that the language that defines the question is careful, limiting, and concrete enough that the basis of argument is clear and plausible. For purposes of illustration, let us begin with an argument that is currently popular: Drugs should be decriminalized.

Such a statement is broad, inclusive, and at heart relatively vague. To conduct an intelligent argument, the key terms need to be defined. Here is one way to go about doing so:

Drugs that are currently illegal, such as marijuana, LSD, cocaine, heroin, and even crack cocaine should be decriminalized. Decriminalizing these drugs means that there would be no legal penalty for using them. However, decriminalizing the drugs does not mean that their sale and use would be legal in the same sense that the sale and use of alcohol is legal, in that they could be sold in private stores, as alcohol is in most states. Decriminalizing drugs would mean that the government would make drugs available on demand for a cost that approximates the real value of the commodity. In other words, the current inflation of drug costs—a direct result of their being illegal and of the associated costs of corrupting police, banks, and officials and taking the risk of arrest—would disappear. The profit in drugs would vanish as a result of decriminalization.

Sources for Arguments

This argument has been made often. However, no matter how many times it is made, it is important to think the issue out as clearly as one can. One way to do so is to set up a range of arguments about specific issues. A potential list of such arguments is shown in the box. Reasons for each one of them—along with appropriate evidence and its analysis—can be part of your overall essay. On the other hand, you may find that by going through each of these potential arguments you will want to retain some and dispense with the others.

NINE SOURCES FOR ARGUMENTS

1. Argument from economic benefit
2. Argument from potential social benefit
3. Argument from potential individual benefit
4. Argument from moral grounds
5. Argument from possibility
6. Argument from history
7. Argument from probability
8. Argument from cause and effect
9. Argument by example

Here is a sample list of discussions developed by referring to these nine sources.

1. **Argument from economic benefit**. Currently, illegal drugs are close to a trillion dollar business, and none of the money made is taxed. The cost in terms of lost work, hospitalization, theft, prison maintenance, and premature death may be just as great or greater. The taxpayer must currently support the cost of prisons (whose annual costs average more than Harvard's for each prisoner), a huge law-enforcement agency, an elaborate judicial program aimed specifically at drugs, the cost of abandoned families, and many other such human problems. By decriminalizing drugs the profit will be gone for dealers, and drug rehabilitation centers can replace prisons.

2. **Argument from potential social benefit**. Decriminalizing drugs would rid society of its worst crime wave since the 1920s. The prisons are crowded with drug dealers and drug criminals. Decriminalizing drugs would change that. A reliable source of drugs would also help prevent premature death as a result of overdoses.

3. **Argument from potential individual benefit**. Those who have tried drugs and become addicted could "out" themselves without fear of arrest or public shame and devote themselves to rehabilitation instead of having to hustle the streets and neighborhoods for money to support an expensive habit. Individual drug users would

benefit from lower prices, easy availability, healthy sources, and a regulated product. They would not have to remain part of an underground culture.

4. **Argument from moral grounds**. If drug use is a moral issue, then so is the use of alcohol. The real moral issue in keeping drugs illegal shows up in the resultant corruption of police, judges, bankers, and politicians on an international level. Without their cooperation the drug trade could not continue.

5. **Argument from possibility**. It is possible to decriminalize drugs by legislative act. There is no constitutional or other impediment to making this change.

6. **Argument from history**. Drugs were legal in the United States until 1914. They could be so again. When alcohol was made illegal after World War I, criminals became efficiently organized in order to supply a product that most Americans wanted. In the process, the law prohibiting alcohol made a majority of Americans criminals and—because it was prohibited—alcohol became a fetish in American life.

7. **Argument from probability**. The chief question regarding probability is whether it is probable that drug use would increase if it were decriminalized. If the government supplied drugs to users it could then know what the true scope of drug use is. Once the criminal structure that forces drugs on children and promotes its use through subtle social advertisements breaks down, the government could move toward bringing drug use down to a reasonable level. Probably some people will always want drugs; making them legal may make them less desirable. The probability is that if profit was removed from drugs, there would be few if any pushers trying to hook young people on drugs.

8. **Argument from cause and effect**. The most important effect of decriminalizing drugs would be removing the big profits from street sales. That in turn will affect the nation's economy because it is obvious that drug money has invaded almost every aspect of American life. One short-term effect may be a temporary recession. The long-term effect will be a less criminal society. The effects of the recession may be offset by the fact that muggings, murders, and burglaries would surely decrease. If drug users do not need to steal to get drugs, they will stop stealing.

9. **Argument by example**. One of the most obvious examples

of decriminalizing a popular activity in American life is that of gambling. Gambling was once outlawed in almost every state. Today most states promote it in lotteries and many promote it in casinos and horse tracks. There is still criminal money in gambling, but nothing compared with what there was in 1940. Legalized gambling has not destroyed the moral fiber of the nation. Decriminalizing the use of drugs by a minority of people will not do so either. As it is, the drug empire is so large, its tentacles reaching into almost every walk of life, that the moral fiber of the nation is more damaged by keeping drugs illegal than it could ever be by decriminalizing drugs. One example of a community that has decriminalized drugs, Amsterdam, Holland, demonstrates that decriminalization works. England has also decriminalized drugs and has less drug crime than the United States, but it is still learning how to cope with addicts.

Some of these arguments overlap each other slightly. But they are examples of reasons developed to defend the position that drugs should be decriminalized. If you were defending this view, you would use some of them and reject others. Before you developed arguments relative to Amsterdam or England, you would need to do some basic research to see whether their approach has worked well. You might also find it useful to enumerate three or four of these arguments and concentrate on developing them as the core of your essay. Your job at this point would be to review these arguments, choose the ones that seem most powerful to you, establish your claims and reasons for the main arguments, and then fashion your essay.

Reasons Against Your Position

First, however, you need to consider the reasons against your position. In a debating situation, there are always two sides to every question. In reality, there are often many more than two sides. However, in argumentation it is enough to realize that your own position can be equally defended and attacked, sometimes on the basis of the same evidence. What will differ, often, is interpretation. We can use the very same nine sources for arguments to construct a case against decriminalizing drugs.

1. **Argument from economic benefit**. Decriminalizing drugs would make the government a supplier of a product that is damaging to individuals and society. It would make the government liable to the death by overdose of individuals whose families could sue for large sums. If the government made drugs available at or near cost, a huge specialized bureaucracy would have to be supported across the nation at considerable government expense. Health care costs would skyrocket along with the need for government-supported hospitals and rehabilitation centers. The government would also have to support the growers and processors internationally, all of whom would boost output to take advantage of the open market.

2. **Argument from potential social benefit**. Society will not benefit from having drug use officially supported by the government. Parties with open drug use will then be prevalent instead of, as now, limited to a sector of society. Society will not benefit from approving a behavior that is deadly, psychologically destructive, and physically disabling. Instead of promoting an ambitious, caring, self-improving society, the government will be promoting a wasted, self-involved, egoistic society of pleasure seekers.

3. **Argument from potential individual benefit**. Most individuals are law-abiding, and if drugs became legal, those individuals might think drugs are not destructive because the government approves their use. By removing the stigma and legal penalties, the government might actually lure more individuals into using drugs. The individual does not benefit from using cocaine, heroin, LSD, or crack cocaine on anything but an illusory, short-term basis. Individuals trying to make up their mind about whether to try addictive substances will know that the government will be there to "bail them out" if anything goes wrong. This will create a "drug welfare" program.

4. **Argument from moral grounds**. Drug usage is a moral concern because it blurs the line between acceptable and criminal behavior. People high on drugs not only harm themselves by wasting their lives in apathy and sloth, but often harm or kill others without realizing they are behaving immorally. Drug usage, like alcoholism, is not victimless. Families pay terrible prices for the destructive behavior of drug users—whether they commit explicitly illegal acts or not.

5. **Argument from possibility**. Decriminalizing drugs would

take more than a federal legislative act. The states would not go along with a sweeping edict decriminalizing drugs, since it would rob them of their obligation to preserve the health and well-being of their residents. Nothing short of a constitutional amendment could legalize drugs in the United States, and the resistance to such an amendment in the Congress is absolute. While there may be a great many people who approve of drug use, there are vastly more who do not. Their votes would outweigh the drug-using minority—who, because of drugs, would probably not have the initiative to press their cause anyway.

6. **Argument from history**. When drugs were legal in the United States, widespread addiction was common. The drug of choice in the nineteenth century was opium dissolved in water, called laudanum. Many mothers in the United States were addicts; infants were often dosed with laudanum to make them sleep. Decriminalizing drugs would get us right back there.

7. **Argument from probability**. The probability is that decriminalizing drugs will increase their use and make them acceptable. The model for that is the legalization of alcohol. Alcohol is widely available in bars, restaurants, weddings, parties, and casual get-togethers. It is probable that "recreational" drug use will be as widespread as alcohol if it is decriminalized by the government.

8. **Argument from cause and effect**. If decriminalizing drugs would have the effect of promoting drug use, that, in turn, would make citizens less productive, more tuned out of society, more selfish and uncaring for others. The effect on society would be negative. With the government decriminalizing drugs, there would be no way to promote sanctions against drug usage. Young people especially would have tacit support for "experimenting" with substances that cause irremediable harm and result in addiction and a life-long struggle with self-control.

9. **Argument by example**. Decriminalizing gambling may be similar to decriminalizing drugs. If so, it is not encouraging. Look at the busloads of tourists, many of them senior citizens living on fixed incomes, heading to Atlantic City, Las Vegas, Reno, and local casinos in the south, midwest, and east. People gamble on a larger scale than ever before, and many cannot afford to do so. The growing support groups for compulsive gamblers count their members in the millions. Further, gambling in Nevada, where it was first legal-

ized, attracted the Mafia and mob professionals. Some of them may have gone "legit," but their influence in casinos has never disappeared and it has penetrated to corruption of state and federal governments in order to keep gambling legal. Legitimate or not, the mob is the mob, and its methods are at root criminal. An example of one nation that legalized drugs is not encouraging. Colombia legalized drugs in 1994, but one day after it went into effect the law was rescinded because people were flagrant in their use of drugs in public places. Colombia learned that legalization does not work.

Structuring Your Argument

Now, having a large source of reasons to back up your argument, and having a clear sense of what kinds of reasons might exist against your position, you have some decisions to make. First, having reviewed the pros and cons regarding your original position, you may want to change your views. Certainly, you will want to modify them. Right now, we will make no decisions regarding the argument in favor of decriminalizing drugs. You may wish to distinguish between what you mean by *decriminalization* and *legalization* of drugs. The first takes the crime out of using the drugs, but the second might be construed as making the sale and promotion of drugs legal. There is a difference, and part of your purposes might be to clarify the distinction.

Once you have decided on your position, you can learn a great deal about the possible structure of argument from observing the strategies used by Sterling, Connell, Pollitt, and Decter in their essays. A general, useful structure that has the virtue of simplicity and clarity would include the suggestions given in the following box.

GENERALLY RELIABLE SUGGESTIONS FOR THE STRUCTURE OF AN ARGUMENT

1. Decide on the mix of appeals—ethical, emotional, and logical—to your audience, and aim to put your audience at ease by avoiding a threatening posture. Reveal your position on your subject as much as you feel your audience needs to know. Adopt a position of being informative, conducting an inquiry, or taking sides in a debate.

2. Provide some background and a summary of your position. How did you become interested in the argument, what circumstances make it relevant, and how did you arrive at your position? If you have access to some of the historical background, it might be good to bring that into play early in the essay.
3. Analyze the reasons against your position. Your job in this section is to present the opposing views with as much clarity and strength as someone who truly believes in that position. Then, examine the arguments with an eye toward explaining what their weaknesses may be.
4. Analyze the reasons and evidence in favor of your position. This is the section in which you will be most forceful in establishing and defending your position. Your analyses should be thorough, inclusive, and conclusive. Use of examples, information, or testimony you have collected and a review of alternative interpretations can be helpful in clarifying your argument.
5. Your conclusion will reinforce your original position by permitting your reader to reflect on the strength of your argument and the weaknesses of the arguments against your position.

ENUMERATION

For the sake of this discussion, let us choose four of the arguments developed about decriminalizing drugs for an essay, as follows:

1. *Argument from economic benefit*: By making drugs legal the profit will be gone for dealers and drug rehabilitation centers can replace prisons.
3. *Argument from potential individual benefit*: Those who have tried drugs and become addicted could "out" themselves without fear of arrest or public shame and devote themselves to rehabilitation instead of having to hustle the streets and neighborhoods for money to support an expensive habit.
7. *Argument from probability*: If the government supplied drugs to users it could know what the true scope of drug use is. Then the government could move toward bringing drug use down to a more reasonable level. Probably some people will always want drugs; making them legal may make them less desirable.
9. *Argument by example*: Gambling was once outlawed in almost every state. Today most states promote it in lotteries and many

> promote it in casinos and horse tracks. There is still criminal money in gambling, but nothing compared with what there was in 1940. Legalized gambling has not destroyed the moral fiber of the nation.

How should you order these arguments, and how should you keep them clear in the mind of your reader? You will need to distinguish them from one another, yet remind the reader that they all fit together and form a unity within your essay.

One way of organizing the arguments is to decide which one you wish to begin with, which will follow, and so on, and then list them in your notes, each with a number. Such a technique is called enumeration and would produce an essay that would sound something like:

> First, by decriminalizing drugs we take the profit away from organized crime. . . . Second, those caught in the web of drugs and crime could finally come forth and get help . . . . Third, decriminalizing drugs would help us discover the true extent of drug use in the United States. . . . And fourth, if we decriminalize drugs we could profit from reviewing the example of legalizing gambling.

In the body of your essay, you might refer to each argument by its number, from one to four, or by other signals, such as "next, there is the example of gambling," or something similar.

Enumeration is a simple, effective, and reliable technique. It means what it says: you number each of your arguments and signal your reader when you begin and when you finish with it. You have heard people say, "There are three reasons why I believe we should. . . ." Then they say, "First, we should. . . ." "Next, we should. . . ." "Finally, we should. . . ." Some people even resort to simple numbers: "One, we should. . . ," and so forth. The technique can become mechanical, and if you use it often with the same audience it will be very tiresome. It also has the disadvantage of limiting your imagination because you will not look for ways of linking the arguments together. On the other hand, the advantages are clarity and ease of discussion. Anyone can follow you, and when you enumerate your arguments you give your audience the impression that you have thought things through and that you have reached a reasonable conclusion.

CHRONOLOGICAL ORDER

In the preceding example of enumeration, the arguments are in the order originally listed. But another order that you can give your arguments concerns their relationship in time. If, for instance, one part of your argument needs to be enacted before another, it would be natural to speak of the first part and then explain that if it were enacted, the next argument would follow. If one of your arguments impinges on the past and another on the future, you can use that distinction to organize your essay.

Again, for the sake of the discussion, we will choose five arguments, this time from the case against decriminalizing drugs, and place them in a chronological order. For ease of reference, their original numbers will appear here so you can study their fuller development if you choose:

6. **Argument from history**. When drugs were legal in the United States widespread addiction was common.

4. **Argument from moral grounds**. Drug usage is a moral concern because it blurs the line between acceptable and criminal behavior. Families pay terrible prices for the destructive behavior of drug users—whether they commit explicitly illegal acts or not.

5. **Argument from possibility**. Nothing short of a constitutional amendment could legalize drugs in the United States, and the resistance to such an amendment in the Congress is absolute.

1. **Argument from economic benefit**. Decriminalizing drugs would make the government a supplier of a product that is damaging to individuals and society. Health care costs would skyrocket along with the need for government-supported hospitals and rehabilitation centers.

2. **Argument from potential social benefit**. Instead of promoting an ambitious, caring, self-improving society, the government will be promoting a wasted, self-involved, egoistic society of pleasure seekers.

The chronological order of these arguments follows a simple pattern: the first argument refers to the past, the next two to the present, and the last two to the future: what was, what is, and what will be if drugs are legalized.

The advantage of chronological order is that the relationship of the elements of your essay is easy for the reader to follow. Your arguments are effectively linked, and your reader is given the feeling that the argument unfolds in a reasonable fashion. Sometimes it is desirable to point to the historical connectors, although it is not always necessary. You could use verbal signposts, beginning your discussion with the signal, "In the past. . . ," followed by, "Currently . . . ," and ending with, "In the future . . . ." One virtue of this technique is the fact that your control of the arguments appears clear and forceful to the reader, whose insight into the issues seems deeper for its connections with time.

CAUSE AND EFFECT

An especially powerful structural device in argument is the following of causal links. If A happens, then it will cause B, which naturally produces C, which in turn results in D. Often individual arguments are themselves based on cause and effect, such as the samples immediately below. An argument of the kind under discussion, the decriminalization of drugs, is a natural for using a cause and effect structure. People will want to know what would happen if drugs are decriminalized. Will the effect be positive or negative? If the arguments can be related to one another in terms of how one will cause the next to come into play, the structure will be especially strong. A possible ordering, in terms of cause and effect, of some of the arguments against decriminalizing drugs follows:

8. **Argument from cause and effect**. Decriminalizing drugs would have the effect of promoting drug use. That in turn would make citizens less productive, more tuned out of society, more selfish and uncaring for others. The effect on society would be negative.

3. **Argument from potential individual benefit**. Most individuals are law-abiding, and if drugs became legal, those individuals might think that drugs are not destructive because the government approves of them. By removing the stigma and legal penalties, the government would actually lure more individuals into using drugs.

7. **Argument from probability**. Decriminalizing drugs will probably increase their use and make them acceptable. The model for that is the legalization of alcohol.

4. **Argument from moral grounds.** Drug usage, like alcoholism, is not victimless. Families pay terrible prices for the destructive behavior of drug users—whether they commit explicitly illegal acts or not. Wider usage of drugs will have a negative effect on the nation.

Nestorian Order

Nestorian order depends on your weighting each of the arguments. You decide which one is most important, which is least important, and which ones come in between. You are the judge of which arguments are most effective—usually the most important. You may judge on moral grounds, economic grounds, social grounds, philosophical grounds, or any other. But once you have done so, set your arguments up in the order shown in the box.

NESTORIAN ORDER

1. Second most important argument.
2. Third most important argument.
3. Fourth most important argument.
4. Fifth most important argument.
5. Most important argument.

Using the arguments developed in favor of decriminalizing drugs, one possible structure using Nestorian order would be:

2. **Argument from potential social benefit**. Decriminalizing drugs would rid society of its worst crime wave since the 1920s. The prisons are crowded with drug dealers and drug criminals. Decriminalizing drugs would change that.

7. **Argument from probability**. Once the criminal structure that forces drugs on children and promotes its use through subtle social advertisements breaks down, the government could move toward bringing drug use down to a reasonable level. Probably some people will always want drugs; making them legal may make them less desirable.

3. **Argument from potential individual benefit**. Those who have tried drugs and become addicted could "out" themselves with-

out fear of arrest or public shame and devote themselves to rehabilitation instead of having to hustle the streets and neighborhoods for money to support an expensive habit.

9. **Argument by example**. Gambling was once outlawed in almost every state. Today most states promote it in lotteries and many promote it in casinos and horse tracks. There is still criminal money in gambling, but nothing compared with what there was in 1940. Legalized gambling has not destroyed the moral fiber of the nation. Decriminalizing the use of drugs by a minority of people will not do so either.

1. **Argument from economic benefit**. Currently, illegal drugs are close to a trillion dollar business, and none of the money made is taxed. By making drugs legal the profit will be gone for dealers, and drug rehabilitation centers can replace prisons. Taking the profit out of drugs will help us recover from the current scourge of crime.

As you review these choices you may see things somewhat differently. For example, you may see the moral issues in drug usage as much more powerful than the economic issues, and therefore you will want to organize your arguments differently. That's fine. When you are writing your own essay, you are the one who makes the decisions about which arguments are most effective and what kind of order they should appear in. The most important point is that you recognize that all arguments are not equal. You must make choices and use those choices to organize your position.

Arguments and Counter Arguments

Whichever way you choose to organize your essay, you must remember to pay attention to the arguments against your position. Taking them into account fairly will give your argument strength and purpose. Ignoring them will make your essay unpersuasive to any thoughtful reader. In the case of the arguments for and against decriminalizing drugs, you may not know which side of the question you should be on. The only way to be sure is to take a position, argue it thoroughly—including your analysis of counter arguments against your position—and then see where you are. Should you write an argument that turns out to defeat your original position, change your position. The entire point of argument is to arrive at the truth.

If in the process of writing, you convince yourself of a position different from the one you began with, you have practiced the art of successful argument.

The following box material sums up a procedure for writing an argumentative essay.

TIPS THAT USUALLY WORK FOR WRITING ARGUMENTATIVE ESSAYS

1. Decide whether your argument will inform, will conduct an inquiry, or will take a side in a debate-like controversy.
2. Decide on your position, your most important claims, and the reasons that back those claims.
3. Consider your tone and your most effective attitude toward your audience. Be careful not to antagonize a potentially hostile audience.
4. Decide what combination of appeals is most appropriate to your argument.
5. Use the nine sources of argument to work up strong arguments.
6. When you have lined up your best arguments and have worked out your reasons supporting the arguments, look for evidence and information that will bolster your position.
7. When constructing your arguments, try to account for the strongest arguments against your position and show why they are ineffective.
8. Look for a convincing ordering of your arguments: use enumeration, chronological order, cause and effect, or Nestorian order.
9. Do your best to argue for a position that you truly believe in and for a purpose that you feel is beneficial to people in general.

5

Writing the Familiar Essay

Beginning from Personal Experience

One kind of familiar essay reflects on the details of everyday life. It erupts from a moment of reflection on personal experience, although it is not primarily autobiographical. Instead, it radiates outward into the reader's experience and points to universal truths. This kind of essay aims to provide a deeper insight into daily living. Another kind of familiar essay reflects on an idea or concept that begins in abstraction and ends in concrete experience.

Some writers begin by responding to ordinary objects or places, as does E. M. Forster in "My Wood," which appears in this chapter. Other writers focus on abstractions such as the concept of "the North," as in the case of Cynthia Ozick, or greed, as in the case of Regina Barreca. The act of writing helps these writers sort out their feelings, judgments, and personal values. The familiar essay discovers significance in objects, places, ideas, and experiences. When one has an experience that alters a way of thinking about things, writing about the event helps to piece out its significance.

Analyzing Concrete Details

The abstract and the concrete are sometimes thought to be antagonists. The concrete world is the one we perceive with our five senses. The abstract world can only be contemplated. The airplane in which Cynthia Ozick lands in "North" is concrete, touchable, and therefore describable. Aarhus, Jutland, is a concrete place. The concept she contemplates after she arrives in Denmark is abstract, untouchable: it is the idea of "north." It is not the place, but values associated with it. Ozick arrived in Denmark alone and sensed her aloneness all the more when she checked into her hotel and realized there were no other people quite like her in the vicinity. That feeling excited in her an experience that can only be described as producing an insight into the nature of her circumstances. Writing about the experience later, she came to terms with feelings that might be described as primitive.

CYNTHIA OZICK

North

One dark wet November afternoon a few years ago, I flew in a small plane from Copenhagen to Aarhus, Jutland, and landed in a cold and pelting storm. The wind drove more powerfully than any wind I had ever known before; it struck with a mythic moan, like that of the wind in the nursery rhyme: *The North Wind will blooowww, and soon we'll have snooowww.* Afterward, shivering over tea in the refuge of a snug little hotel, I looked around the dining room, all shining mahogany, and felt myself a desolate stranger. I was traveling alone. The hotel had once been a way station for missionaries heading for foreign parts; no New Yorker, I thought, could be at ease in such a place. I was banished, lost. I ached with forlornness. The people in the dining room seemed enviably at home. They shuffled their newspapers and hardly spoke, and when they did, the alien syllables shut me decisively out.

And suddenly, just then, I found myself assaulted by a brilliant eeriness; enchantment swept me through and through. It was very nearly a kind of seizure: an electrifying pang that shook me to tears of recognition. It was, to choose the palest term for it, a moment of *déjà vu*, but also something vaster, more tumultuous, bottomless. Though I was incontrovertibly new to this wind-ghosted place, it came to me all at once that north was where I had once belonged, north was the uncanny germ of my being.

Northernness—the shrouded poetry of northernness—is why we crave the Scandinavian autumn and winter. It may be that July and August beam down on Copenhagen, Stockholm, Oslo, and Helsinki as attractively as they do elsewhere—who can doubt it? But say it outright: summer in Sweden is for the homebody Swedes. The imagination of a Stockholm-bound traveler is transfixed by a crystal dream of low, cold, tilted light.

We go north "enamored of a season . . . cold, spacious, severe, pale and remote," misted over by "trouble, ecstasy, astonishment"—C. S. Lewis's apparition of Northernness, drawn from childhood susceptibility, and from the icy glimmer of Norse fable. We go north to reclaim something buried, clouded, infiltrating, unsure, or else as sure as instantaneous sensation.

For me, it was, I think, a grain of historical memory in the gleam of that little hotel, a secret idiosyncratic autobiographical Jutland jot: a thousand ancestral years lived to the east, just across the Baltic, along the same latitude, an old Russia's Minsk province. But there are more universal reasons to seek out the north when it is most northern in aspect. The blinding late-October sun-slant on Copenhagen walks; the pewter pavements of Stockholm under a days-long autumn rain—in all of that there lurks a time-before, whirling up from storybooks and pictures and legends, and from some idea that we of our hot inward life set against a rind of frosted light.

Mystically, in sheets of clarified air, the north reminds.

Ozick places us firmly in a foreign environment, one in which everyone else is "enviably at home," while she sits "forlorn" listening to "alien syllables" spoken around her. Her description of the storm and the wind that accompanied her arrival is economical and exact, emphasizing the senses of sound ("it struck with a mythic moan") and touch ("shivering over tea"). When she shifts from the concrete imagery derived from the senses, she tries to describe an abstract and perhaps undescribable feeling: "I found myself assaulted by a brilliant eeriness; enchantment swept me through and through." No reader could know precisely what she means, but from that description and sense of uneasiness, alarm, and mystery we can approximate the experience.

Cynthia Ozick recognized that she as a person is rooted in her deep prehistory in the north. It is not by accident that she reflects on a nursery rhyme when she faces the fierce northern wind. Indeed, "Norse fable" and perhaps the fairy tales of the brothers Grimm connect her childhood imagination with the north. In a sentence that shadows ideas she would like to put in more concrete terms she explains: "We go north to reclaim something buried, clouded, infiltrating, unsure, or else as sure as instantaneous sensation." What could she mean by this? Perhaps she is not sure herself. She is, after all, dealing with vague feelings and impressions excited by her response to being in Jutland on "one dark wet November afternoon." The only way she can make sense of the intense feeling she has is to connect it on a personal level with her own ethnic heritage. As the descendant of Russian Jews whose homeland was "along the same latitude" in "old Russia's Minsk province," she has a deep subconscious resonance that is almost equivalent to a haunting. Indeed, a review of her language reveals it to be like describing the appearance of a ghost.

She does not understand how, but the slanting of the light, the damp, the cold, the wind, all stir in her some deep cultural longings. As she says in her one-sentence ending paragraph: "Mystically, in sheets of clarified air, the north reminds." It reminds her of her roots even though they are roots she never personally experienced.

The impressive aspect of this short essay is the way in which it moves from the exceptionally concrete experience of a given place and a given time to the much more abstract experience of a cultural awareness of a much different and distant place and time experienced by people long dead and far away. Ozick moves from the physically concrete to the almost untellable abstraction of an experience that can be called only an awareness. She uses the word *mystically*, which translates into a simple idea: unexplainable. She has moved, as so many writers do, from the concrete to the abstract, bringing us along with her. Who among us has not had such inexplicable feelings? Who of us has not been in a place that has made us uneasy and led us toward feelings and thoughts that are almost impossible to explain? For Ozick the "north" is not just a place; it is a heritage.

Analyzing an Abstraction

Good writers write about love, happiness, success, despair, and loss, but when they do so, they couch their observations in terms of a specific moment in time and of a specific event. The reason they avoid talking about love or loss in general terms is that they know that without a concrete frame of reference such discourse is boring. Try, for example, to talk about love without referring to someone or some thing that you love. What is love? Or, think of the classic question: What is the meaning of life? Well, who can say? The question is vague. Your reader's attention will wander until you tie the abstraction to a concrete instance or person. Good writers avoid abstraction in their writing even when their subject is abstract.

Some wonderful subjects for familiar essays would be described as abstract ideas:

Love	Optimism
Betrayal	Self-esteem
Hope	Confidence
Success	Uncertainty
Faith	Revenge

The list could go on indefinitely, but these alone would keep a writer at work for quite a long time. However, to write well on these subjects, a writer would have to find concrete experiences to illuminate each of them. These subjects attract the attention of many writers and offer unlimited opportunities for essays.

Techniques for dealing with abstractions are simple and plentiful. The four listed in the box text will always work for any writer. Each is applied here to one individual, Max Pollaner, and to one abstraction: greed.

GENERALLY RELIABLE TIPS FOR DEALING WITH ABSTRACTION

1. Find examples. One of the best ways of dealing with an abstraction is to find an example of behavior that illustrates the abstraction. Behavior concretizes the idea effectively.
2. Analyze cause and effect. Abstractions often cause something to happen, or are the result of an event or series of events. Examining the causes of affection, anger, greed, or lust will help make those abstractions more concrete and meaningful.
3. Examine history and possibility. Every abstraction has some kind

of history. Greed in the Ice Age may have been less possible than greed in the Renaissance (or today)—and the reasons may be worth examining.

4. Consider what others have said about it. Most abstract ideas have been talked about and written about by others. One useful strategy is reviewing what has been said about such abstractions as hope, innocence, fear, loss, or ambition. Whether such statements appear in books, magazines, films, or on television, they have a concrete quality that helps clarify your subject.

RELY ON EXAMPLES

Max Pollaner was a master of watchful waiting. He owned two yachts and the marina they rested in, and people said he had his eyes on another marina up near Del Mar. That marina was owned by Martin Long, a friend of his who was suffering a streak of bad luck. The friend had come for a loan, but instead of giving him some help, Max realized his waiting had paid off with a genuine opportunity, so he convinced his friend to sell him the marina for a fraction of what it was worth. In these difficult times, it was probably his friend's only option.

ANALYZE CAUSE AND EFFECT

More than a few people who had known Max in a casual fashion were puzzled at the contradictions in his behavior. The Max they knew was amusing, witty, and smart. He rallied the local community for a number of important charitable causes, although they noted that he organized other people but rarely gave much money or time to the charities himself. He said his organizing others was contribution enough. Yet, he was clearly thoughtful and concerned as a citizen. The contradictions came in the way he did business. His policy was to take every advantage at his disposal to acquire more and more property and to make it produce more and more income. Whenever he purchased a building or a business, he concentrated on ways to boost the short term income of the property. He seemed unconcerned with the fate of other people. One of his old friends, Stanley Cooper, once explained that Max had suffered terribly in the Great Depression, when he lived with his father, mother, and eight sisters and brothers in a cellar apartment in New York City. There were many days when he went with only one meal, and some days when he went with none. His father's partner had swindled him out of a small interest he had in a business, leaving him to starve, and it was very difficult for Max to trust others. He hardly had time to enjoy his wealth. His most intense fear was becoming poor again.

EXAMINE HISTORY AND POSSIBILITY

Greed is sometimes its own reward. Recently, a prominent hotel owner and mega-millionaire, Leona Helmsley, was said to have been both stingy and greedy. She went to great efforts to avoid paying taxes, saying publicly that "only the little people" paid their taxes. However, her efforts backfired because the government prosecuted her on the grounds that she illegally avoided paying millions in taxes. She spent time in prison contemplating the rewards of her ingenious efforts to boost her already considerable net worth. Max Pollaner read about her case with extraordinary interest and had his accountants examine his books to be sure that, despite his own efforts to reduce his taxes, nothing like that could happen to him.

CONSIDER WHAT PEOPLE HAVE SAID ABOUT IT

Historically, people have shunned and ridiculed the greedy, and they have been treated in literature as objectionable and pitiable. Scrooge, in Charles Dickens's *A Christmas Carol*, has become the stereotype of all callous, greedy people. Max Pollaner was often referred to as a Scrooge by those who disliked him. It was also clear that Max knew what people said about him, but he could not change his behavior. He saw no reason to change, even though he had isolated himself from others and was constantly suspicious of what they said about him. For Max, making more money was the only activity that made sense to him. When people referred to him as money-hungry and greedy, he defended himself by saying that they were envious. Whether he believed that or not—and whether he had any honest apprehensions about his own nature, no one ever knew. Max Pollaner, like Richard Cory in Edward Arlington Robinson's poem, killed himself on New Year's Eve, 1997.

Being Concrete

The following essay, "Greed," by Regina Barreca, is part of a series that appeared in the Sunday Magazine of the *Chicago Tribune*.

It followed her essay on gluttony, and begins with a comparison in order to make the point more concrete.

REGINA BARRECA

Greed

If our fear of Gluttony is the fear of wanting too much, then our fear of Greed is the fear of wanting it all. Even the most enthusiastic of gluttons achieves satiation after the 18th Whopper or the 14th Ring Ding and then falls asleep. Greed never sleeps; the ordinarily Greedy make money in their dreams, and the successfully Greedy make money even *while* they dream.

Greed is like Gluttony—it wants to consume everything around it—but without the possibility of ever having a full belly. This, of course, makes Greed categorically less fun.

Greed is grabbing all the toys and not letting your kid brother have any. Greed spits on the best piece of pizza so that your sister won't want it anymore. Greed steals the answers to the college exam and dares to be proud of its success. Greed steals your hometown boyfriend just to see if she can. Greed wants cash for Christmas instead of homemade socks. At some point Greed has had a nodding acquaintance with us all.

Greed takes pens from hotels without even thinking, "This is the 103rd pen saying 'Sheraton' I have scattered near telephones in my house." Greed is Imelda Marcos' unblinking pronouncement in 1987: "I did not have 3,000 pairs of shoes; I had 1,060." Greed might bring really good wine to the party, but it insists on drinking it immediately; even Greed's gifts come with this sort of price tag. Everything given is really loaned, and everything is loaned with interest. Greed kills deer after deer for the sheer pleasure of making the hit; Greed fishes for the pleasure of the hook and then throws the catch away. Greed sells "We Love the Juice" T-shirts outside the L.A. courthouse as the families of the victims file by. Greed looks astonished when you say that some things aren't worth the price.

Greed wants the best there is and wants it all. Sometimes Greed has to settle, and so we get the joking line about the disgruntled restaurant patron who comes out saying, "The food was absolutely disgusting, absolutely inedible, and besides that, the portions were too small."

These comments, of course, presuppose that most of us still consider Greed a vice; Gluttony was a sure bet in terms of guaranteed disapproval, but Greed is more dangerous. Gluttony remains an essentially personal vice—as in "I'm a glutton for punishment," or "I'm a glutton when it comes to chocolate"—and involves power only insofar as it relates to food itself. But Greed can easily transcend the self. Nobody really cared if Nero ate every roast ox in sight, but it was more problematic when he let Rome burn just because he could. Hermann Goering, as a friend of mine pointed out, may have been a glutton when it came to food, but more significantly he was Greedy when it came to power. We're playing in a different league when it comes to Greed, because Greed does with power what Gluttony does with food—wants it, grabs it, stuffs it away where nobody else can get at it and eventually incorporates it as a natural part of the self. This is why no one wants to be thought of as Greedy; if someone accused any of us of being avaricious, we'd silkily mention "sour grapes" *sotto voce* or we'd simply deny it. *We're* not Greedy, oh no; *he's* Greedy. We're merely comfortable.

"Greed is when other people want more money than you do," declares my friend Hugo. Wendy disagrees, claiming that "Greed is when you're consumed with want for what you already have, whether that's money or attention. Not only can't you get enough of it, you can't even properly enjoy what you've already got. It's like Lynn and her clothes thing." She cites the example of an indubitably Greedy friend who offers to buy garments off other people's backs if she thinks she'll look good in the outfit. This is not an exaggeration; she carries an extra T-shirt in her Coach bag for these occasions, given that she's addicted to blouses and jackets. She has gone up to other women in restaurants and silk has been exchanged for cash. She could clothe all of Finland with what's already in her closets, but that doesn't dampen her appetite. Greed, like this otherwise sane enough woman, always wants more.

Lynn, who would no more call herself Greedy than call herself unfashionable, says that clothes have replaced prey in the hunt of her life and declares that her passion is healthier than being Greedy for either men or money.

Ten years ago Lynn would not have even had to justify herself in certain parts of the world. For a while there, Greed was not a problem. Remember the single most poignant signature line of the '80s, when Gordon Gekko from Oliver Stone's "Wall Street" went into his rapturous aria extolling the virtues of avarice, declaring once and for all "Greed is good"?

You had the feeling that there were men and women in deliberately and delicately crumpled linen suits writing that line down on their cuffs. (It didn't matter if that wasn't the message Stone wanted to send; Greed screens its ideas as diligently as it screens its calls.) Young men in thin yellow ties quoted Andrew Mellon's immortal line, "Gentlemen prefer bonds," and laughed; young women in thin yellow suits and fat white sneakers gave one another needlepointed pillows saying "Nouveau Riche is Better Than No Riche at All."

Greed, after all, is as American as apple pie or baseball—and after this summer's striking of home plate, who would say that baseball isn't about Greed? Only in America do we see bumper stickers saying, "He who dies with the most toys, wins," not because Europeans or Canadians or Africans or Asians are less Greedy, but because they're less fond of broadcasting it; the bumper sticker is, after all, only partially ironic. A friend's husband wryly suggested, after buying his second new Lexus, that if you have enough toys, maybe you don't die at all. "How can you die when you still have a manufacturer's warranty in your hand?" He smiles when he drives. The last 20 years gave us designer jeans, designer drugs, even designer diners, where you could order nouvelle cuisine meat loaf (nouvelle cuisine, as a friend of mine quipped, being the French term for "child's portion"). We heard that you could never be too rich or too thin, and we tried for both, only to discover that if you're rich enough, hey, nobody cares what you weigh, and the rest of us are better off just eating cake.

What's tricky, however, is that Greed is about wanting instead of necessarily about having. You'll be called Greedy if you work overtime and weekends and save obsessively to buy a big house and fill it with antiques, but if you've inherited that big house and the antiques are simply identified as Grampy's set of first editions or Mumsy's matched Degas, then it's OK, and you're not Greedy, you're aristocratic. If you're panting after the stuff, having been denied it at an early age, however, then you're lost to avarice as far as this system is concerned. The only thing worse than not having money in some circles is wanting it. What we all needed, evidently, were Greedy ancestors who could die and leave us without the taint of desire.

What's more unnerving about Greed is the sense of insatiable hunger behind it; where Gluttony was only tangentially about a hunger for food, so Greed is only tangentially about an appetite for possessions. More accurately, Greed is about need. We can never assume we understand somebody else's deepest, most passionate, most authentic needs. We look at a Neiman Marcus-laden lady and wonder why she needs yet another cashmere cardigan; we caustically comment on a coworker's hogging of all the secretary's time. But often we are oblivious to what we ourselves hoard because it never occurs to us that we're stockpiling anything; if questioned, we would explain in all honesty that we take only what we need.

Remember in King Lear when his two mean daughters want to strip him of his last remaining trappings of majesty? He has moved in with them, and they don't think he needs guards. They convince themselves by saying that Lear, used to having everything he has ever wanted, doesn't need a hundred or even a dozen soldiers around him. When they wish to take the final man away from his side, saying "What needs one?" Lear bellows, terrified and suddenly alone, from his innermost depths, "Reason not the need." Lear doesn't need soldiers any more than Scrooge needed silver or Midas needed gold, but it doesn't stop them from wanting it because, in fact, their possessions are the only things that define them. If Gluttony says you are what you eat (to which the character in Nicole Hollander's cartoon Sylvia replies "That makes me a taco chip"), then the Greedy are what they acquire. It makes the driver of a red Porsche first and foremost the driver of a red Porsche if that object is the best, most powerful, most compelling thing about him. (Note: It often is.)

Not even a Greedy character is unsalvageable or even unlovable, as Hollywood has shown. American movies love the Greedy tycoon, the miser, the selfish and powerful manipulator out for his own gain. From 1924 and Erich von Stroheim's "Greed" (a film version of Frank Norris' 1899 novel "McTeague") to Citizen Kane's acquisition of the boxed-up treasures of Europe when all he wanted was paint-peeling Rosebud, to "Wall Street," we get a sense that the Greedy hero is more misguided than anything else. We want to forgive him or, in rare cases, forgive her. These figures are too much like our own dear selves to consider them terminally wicked.

My favorite Greedy film hero is less tragic than his classier peers. When Mel Brooks cast Zero Mostel as Max Bialystock in his 1968 classic, "The Producers," he created a flawless portrait of the Greedy man who nevertheless remains unequivocally heroic throughout. Max, who was once a fabulously successful producer of Broadway hits, is now a gigolo, giving blue-haired ladies one last thrill on their way to the cemetery. He wears a cardboard belt. He is starving for money, and what is most compelling about Max is that he is shamelessly willing to get rich without any hungering after success. Malice plays no role in his endeavors; he just wants the money. He convinces his accountant, Gene Wilder (playing a neurotic Leo Bloom who would make James Joyce proud), to agree to a scheme where they sell 25,000 percent of the profits to a sure-fire flop—a show called "Springtime for Hitler"—with plans to leave town with the leftover cash once the show closes.

Listening to Mostel sing the praises of money to thumb-sucking Wilder is a hysterical presage of Gekko's speech. Mostel sings of "lovely ladies with long legs and lunch at Delmonico's," yelling with joyful envy out his dirty office window, "Flaunt it baby, flaunt it," to a man exiting a Rolls-Royce. Mostel's appetite is catching. When Zero kisses the piles of money he has conned out of willing fools, fondling the fistfuls of cash, saying, "Hello, boys" to all the presidents on the bills, we have Mostel giving voice to the Greedy creature inside all of us. When he screams out in complete abandon, "I Want That Money," we can cheer in a way that we never would have cheered Gekko. Here is Greed we experienced as kids waiting for birthday presents that might or might not come; here's greed with a small "g" that comes out of the hard-won experience of uncertainty. We might grab a little too quickly or hold on a little too long or a little too tightly because we're afraid we'll never see such pleasure again. Too much, as the country song goes, just ain't enough.

This is the kind of Greed we speak of when we think about lovers being Greedy for each other's company or a mother being Greedy for her child's love.

We sense in any deep need the temptation for our desires to boil over, like soup. Every woman I know, including myself, is terrified of appearing Greedy for affection or approval. The question "Do you love me?" is rarely a request for information, as my brother the lawyer once noted, but instead indicates a Greediness of the heart. We pretend to hip aloofness when our scurrying souls are frantically seeking attention. Lovers and mothers, even with a right to their Greedy pleasures of love, risk disaffection even as they seek affection.

Money, however, unlike love, often comes to those who spend all their time hunting for it. The robber barons that made America into the world's wallet—Ford, Rockefeller, the Hunt boys, Getty—didn't get rich by looking sentimentally at pictures of money. They went out and made it—or took it, depending on your point of view and position on the production line—but one way or another, they got it. There isn't a buck that won't lie down for the Greediest man.

But this isn't to say that a certain Greediness isn't a good thing. "Wanting," "desiring," "needing" are the gerunds that make the Western world great. Without the Greed of certain collectors, our museums would be depleted; without the Greed for power located in some of the folks on our side, the Greed for power on the other side would always win. Without a Greed for knowledge, we wouldn't have the discoveries, the vaccinations, the understanding of the world that we take for granted. The process of seeking to attain and secure what your heart wishes for is not a bad impulse, however un-Zen it may be.

Even if our civilization was founded in Greed, for most of us Greed is usually curiously translated into a better impulse, almost despite ourselves. With our desire for cars and clothes, TVs and RVs, rings or even racehorses, few of us can be without this vice. And yet we manage to keep our basic decency. We want to make money, but we don't want to be piggish and wasteful; we want to acquire objects, but most of the time we are more than willing to share with those we love, and even on occasion with those we don't. We want to embrace our heart's desire, and have lots of it, but what's wrong with that?

It might be limiting if what your innermost heart desires can be summed up by the phrase "junk bonds" or can be transcribed numerically, but surely an appetite for getting a lot of what you love has been the cause of much good in the world.

I don't foresee a 12-step program for the Greedy ("Today I will not buy another garment with a Ralph Lauren logo, even at a drastically reduced price," or "Today I will not play Monopoly with real hotels"), but there are no doubt ways to make the lives of the greedy better. Maybe we could take up a collection.

Barreca's comparisons are designed to root greed in our universal experience. Then she begins defining greed through example: "Greed is grabbing all the toys and not letting your kid brother have any." But one of her most effective techniques is personification. She makes greed into a person when she continues with more examples, "Greed takes pens from hotels. . . . Greed kills deer after deer for the sheer pleasure of making the hit." She relates the testimony of friends and authorities, from her "friend Hugo" to the films of Oliver Stone, whose *Wall Street* was a film about greed. She finds examples in literature, from William Shakespeare to James Joyce, and includes a great deal of popular culture, from Nicole Hollander's cartoons to Ralph Lauren to Monopoly.

The entire beginning of the essay consists of examples of greed, especially examples in which greed is personified. When Barreca contrasts greed with gluttony by identifying gluttony as a personal vice, she demonstrates the power of cause and effect: greed has a negative effect on others, which is why most of us do not want to be called greedy. One greedy person will buy clothes "off other people's backs" and carries around an extra tee-shirt to facilitate the exchange. Barreca does not specifically go into the history of greed, but she does treat Shakespeare's *King Lear* as if it were part of the history of greed. It is an example from the past of how greed works. The same is true of her references to Von Stroheim's classic film, *Greed*, and the more recent films *Wall Street* and *The Producers*. They are an important part of the history of greed and they give us insights into the possibilities that we can imagine for greed. Barreca fleshes out her essay by giving us numerous examples of what people say about greed. She begins with real life characters, Hugo and Wendy, and continues with the testimony of numerous fictional characters, such as Gekko, who declares that "greed is good," in Oliver Stone's *Wall Street*.

Each of Barreca's tactics makes greed more explicit, more specific, and more intelligible to us. After reading the essay we will be able to recognize greed when we see it. We will remember that if gluttony says you are what you eat, then as far as the greedy are concerned, you are what you acquire.

Familiar Style

Familiar essays reflect on a condition or situation. They probably have no style distinct from that of other kinds of essays. However, their purposes are especially well served by figurative uses of language, such as analogy, metaphor, simile, imagery, and personification. The familiar essay, by focusing as it often does on an abstract issue, needs a grounding in comparisons and descriptions that invoke sensory representation. Just as it is essential to depend on specific examples wherever possible, it is also important to use a style that is as concrete as possible. Appealing to the five senses, as one does when invoking imagery, or relating something obscure to something familiar, as one does when using analogy, metaphor, and simile, helps the reader have something to hold onto while absorbing the ideas and concerns of the writer. All figurative language is best used to intensify the specificity of the writing.

The same is true of references to other writers, other authorities. Since a writer such as E. M. Forster assumes that his readers will be adults with a background in literature, he feels he can refer liberally to such writers as Shakespeare and such texts as the Bible. These references, even for those who may not know them firsthand, lend authority to his work and help concretize it. Of course, some writers can overdo their use of allusion, but Forster is also aware that not everyone will know the works he cites. Consequently, he is cautious and provides all the information a reader needs to understand his reference. He does not assume any special background of readers.

E. M. Forster's essay, "My Wood," has become a classic. It was written in 1926 and ostensibly describes the effect of his success as a writer. He had taken a royalty check from his popular book, *A Passage to India,* and bought a piece of property, a parcel of land he calls a wood. He is uneasy with the idea that he now owns property and is therefore a person of substance. His personal background was one of privation, not wealth, and this marks a new point in his life. The way he goes about telling us of his experience is both fascinating and practical. He has four points to make, and he gives us useful signposts: "In the first place, . . ." "In the second place," and so on. These are not figures of speech, but rather enumerative guides so that we know where we are when we read.

E. M. FORSTER

My Wood

A few years ago I wrote a book which dealt in part with the difficulties of the English in India. Feeling that they would have had no difficulties in India themselves, the Americans read the book freely. The more they read it the better it made them feel, and a check to the author was the result. I bought a wood with the check. It is not a large wood—it contains scarcely any trees, and it is intersected, blast it, by a public footpath. Still, it is the first property that I have owned, so it is right that other people should participate in my shame, and should ask themselves, in accents that will vary in horror, this very important question: What is the effect of property upon the character? Don't let's touch economics; the effect of private ownership upon the community as a whole is another question—a more important question, perhaps, but another one. Let's keep to psychology. If you own things, what's their effect on you? What's the effect on me of my wood?

In the first place, it makes me feel heavy. Property does have this effect. Property produces men of weight, and it was a man of weight who failed to get into the Kingdom of Heaven. He was not wicked, that unfortunate millionaire in the parable, he was only stout; he stuck out in front, not to mention behind, and as he wedged himself this way and that in the crystalline entrance and bruised his well-fed flanks, he saw beneath him a comparatively slim camel passing through the eye of a needle and being woven into the robe of God. The Gospels all through couple stoutness and slowness. They point out what is perfectly obvious, yet seldom realized: that if you have a lot of things you cannot move about a lot, that furniture requires dusting, dusters require servants, servants require insurance stamps, and the whole tangle of them makes you think twice before you accept an invitation to dinner or go for a bathe in the Jordan. Sometimes the Gospels proceed further and say with Tolstoy that property is sinful; they approach the difficult ground of asceticism here, where I cannot follow them. But as to the immediate effects of property on people, they just show straightforward logic. It produces men of weight. Men of weight cannot, by definition, move like the lightning from the East unto the West, and the ascent of a fourteen-stone bishop into a pulpit is thus the exact antithesis of the coming of the Son of Man. My wood makes me feel heavy.

In the second place, it makes me feel it ought to be larger.

The other day I heard a twig snap in it. I was annoyed at first, for I thought that someone was blackberrying, and depreciating the value of the undergrowth. On coming nearer, I saw it was not a man who had trodden on the twig and snapped it, but a bird, and I felt pleased. My bird. The bird was not equally pleased. Ignoring the relation between us, it took fright as soon as it saw the shape of my face, and flew straight over the boundary hedge into a field, the property of Mrs. Henessy, where it sat down with a loud squawk. It had become Mrs. Henessy's bird. Something seemed grossly amiss here, something that would not have occurred had the wood been larger. I could not afford to buy Mrs. Henessy out, I dared not murder her, and limitations of this sort beset me on every side. Ahab did not want that vineyard—he only needed it to round off his property, preparatory to plotting a new curve—and all the land around my wood has become necessary to me in order to round off the wood. A boundary protects. But—poor little thing—the boundary ought in its turn to be protected. Noises on the edge of it. Children throw stones. A little more, and then a little more, until we reach the sea. Happy Canute! Happier Alexander! And after all, why should even the world be the limit of possession? A rocket containing a Union Jack, will, it is hoped, be shortly fired at the moon. Mars. Sirius. Beyond which . . . But these immensities ended by saddening me. I could not suppose that my wood was the destined nucleus of universal dominion—it is so small and contains no mineral wealth beyond the blackberries. Nor was I comforted when Mrs. Henessy's bird took alarm for the second time and flew clean away from us all, under the belief that it belonged to itself.

In the third place, property makes its owner feel that he ought to do something to it. Yet he isn't sure what. A restlessness comes over him, a vague sense that he has a personality to express—the same sense which, without any vagueness, leads the artist to an act of creation. Sometimes I think I will cut down such trees as remain in the wood, at other times I want to fill up the gaps between them with new trees. Both impulses are pretentious and empty. They are not honest movements towards money-making or beauty. They spring from a foolish desire to express myself and from an inability to enjoy what I have got. Creation, property, enjoyment form a sinister trinity in the human mind. Creation and enjoyment are both very very good, yet they are often unattainable without a material basis, and at such moments property pushes itself in as a substitute, saying, "Accept me instead—I'm good enough for all three." It is not enough. It is, as Shakespeare said of lust, "The expense of spirit in a waste of shame"; it is "Before, a joy proposed; behind, a dream." Yet we don't know how to shun it. It is forced on us by our economic system as the alternative to starvation. It is also forced on us by an internal defect in the soul, by the feeling that in property may lie the germs of self-development and of exquisite or heroic deeds. Our life on earth is, and ought to be, material and carnal. But we have not yet learned to manage our materialism and carnality properly; they are still entangled with the desire for ownership, where (in the words of Dante) "Possession is one with loss."

And this brings us to our fourth and final point: the blackberries.

Blackberries are not plentiful in this meagre grove, but they are easily seen from the public footpath which traverses it, and all too easily gathered. Foxgloves, too—people will pull up the foxgloves, and ladies of an educational tendency even grub for toadstools to show them on the Monday in class. Other ladies, less educated, roll down the bracken in the arms of their gentlemen friends. There is paper, there are tins. Pray, does my wood belong to me or doesn't it? And, if it does, should I not own it best by allowing no one else to walk there? There is a wood near Lyme Regis, also cursed by a public footpath, where the owner has not hesitated on this point. He has built high stone walls each side of the path, and has spanned it by bridges, so that the public circulate like termites while he gorges on the blackberries unseen. He really does own his wood, this able chap. Dives in Hell did pretty well, but the gulf dividing him from Lazarus could be traversed by vision, and nothing traverses it here. And perhaps I shall come to this in time. I shall wall in and fence out until I really taste the sweets of property. Enormously stout, endlessly avaricious, pseudo-creative, intensely selfish, I shall weave upon my forehead the quadruple crown of possession until those nasty Bolshies come and take it off again and thurst me aside into the outer darkness.

Figurative Language

One of the first things to note about Forster's style is his reliance on metaphor and simile. He is also a master of imagery and metonymy (using a part of something to refer to the whole).

METAPHOR: CONCRETIZING THOUGHT

Forster's first use of figurative language comes in the second paragraph when he describes himself as feeling heavy. This entire paragraph is dedicated to examining the effect of ownership in terms of its apparent weightiness. But the weightiness is a figure of speech. Forster has not literally become more weighty because he now owns a wood, but as he says, "Property produces men of weight." This point leads him to reflect on the Biblical parable of the rich man who could not pass through the eye of a needle because he was so stout—or weighty. Owning property makes Forster feel heavy, as if he has somehow accepted the weight of a burden. All of this discussion of weight is figurative: he is metaphorically heavy. In this case the use of metaphor has intensified the significance of Forster's feelings.

IMAGERY: CONCRETIZING EXPERIENCE

Forster's third paragraph is filled with powerful imagery. His appeal to our senses is almost relentless. Having left the abstract notion of his feeling heavy, he gives us a sensory report: "I heard a twig snap in it." It was not a man, but a bird. The bird comes and goes as it will, but Forster reasons that if it is in his wood it is his bird. He describes its "squawk" as it flies to Mrs. Henessy's property.

The paragraph continues some of the pattern of imagery, but then moves to allusion, referring to Shakespeare and ultimately to Dante's searing phrase, "Possession is one with loss." The third paragraph is a miniature analysis of the effects of materialism with an eye to the way in which property can substitute itself for creation and enjoyment, both qualities Forster feels are essential for a happy life. The desire for ownership, he reminds us, can lead us toward greed. He never uses the term (the closest he comes is "lust" in this paragraph and "avarice" in the next), but that is what he means. He understands that greed is a vice, which is to say it is a quality that lessens our humanity.

METONYMY: CONCRETIZING IMAGINATION

The last paragraph depends on a specialized form of language called metonymy: using a part of something to refer to the whole. When we say, "Fifteen hundred rifles marched to the front," we use rifles metonymically: the rifle is the "part" of the soldier that means business, so the expression means that many soldiers went to the front. Metonymy is closely related to metaphor, and it is much more common in usage than its unusual name may imply. When Forster says "this brings us to our fourth and final point: the blackberries," we know that "blackberrries" does not just mean blackberries, but is a figurative term. It is metonymy.

The blackberries stand for all the bounty that the wood may produce, everything of value that might come from it. Consequently, when Forster talks of wanting the blackberries for himself, he describes yet another kind of greed: he wants not to share anything about the property that he now owns. As he says, "Pray, does my wood belong to me or doesn't it?" Well, if it does, then so does everything it produces, and the most essential "rule" about ownership is that the owner has its use. Blackberries are an important element of that use.

Forster ends in something of the same way he begins: by reminding us of his weightiness. He sees himself, if he continues to have the feelings he has become aware of, as "enormously stout, endlessly avaricious." These are the benefits of ownership as he sees it.

We realize after having looked closely at Forster's essay that he, like Regina Barreca, has written a meditation on greed. However, where she has begun with the word itself and explored it as an abstract concept, he has begun with a concrete event and moved us toward an understanding of the concept. Both techniques are extremely effective—both concretize an essentially abstract idea.

Searching for Meaning

One challenge of familiar writing is the search for significance in everyday experience. The familiar essay gives us a chance to explore experiences that we take for granted, things that might go unnoticed in the bustle of everyday life. Many people race through life so rapidly that they do not sense the value of the rich experience that they have. Socrates said that the unexamined life is not worth living. The unexamined life resembles that of a cat or a dog: it happens, but that is about as much as one can say about it. Human beings have a desire to know, which implies a desire to understand. When people need to understand something, they need to establish its meaning in whatever context interests them.

However, with life and experience you do not have the convenience of understanding each context or each action as it happens. That is especially true of complex actions, whose significance may derive from the subconscious and which may therefore require analysis. Most of us know that we would be surprised if we understood the true significance of some of what we do. Sometimes our own actions are understood by other people in a way that shocks us. Either they misunderstand what we did, or we misunderstand our own motives. The very thought that we may misunderstand our own motives is enough to set us on guard and to make us aware of the usefulness of the reflection and the analysis the familiar essay demands.

One way to find meaning in actions is to search for motive. That is not always easy, since motives are ordinarily hidden even from those who possess them. Consequently, a writer needs to be willing to explore possibilities. Take the following passage, which states a condition or situation and then pursues the possible motives for a given behavior. In motive lies meaning.

> For a person who prides himself on resisting anger, I have had to face a surprising realization about myself. I hate those who batter my mailbox each Halloween. Hate. I do not mean dislike. I mean hate. My mailbox, on a rural route, is very large, painted to match the trim of my house, and I visit it everyday in hopes that it will widen the scope of my world. But as I write, I know that this year my new mailbox withstood a terrifying battering with a Louisville Slugger, and its door hardly closes. The rain now seeps in. Soon, the snow will build up inside. The perpetrator is scot-free, a person who hit and ran, someone who struck in the dark of night, for no reason, with no hope of realizing any further pleasure from his action.

The author of this passage understood that hatred is a powerful emotion. Anyone who has read James Baldwin's "Native Son" knows hatred is a passion whose potential for damaging the individual is almost limitless. Consequently, the writer searched for a motive behind his hatred in hope of understanding its meaning.

ANONYMOUS

Coping With Anger

For some reason, battering my mailbox is almost equivalent to battering me. I feel I could defend myself, even against someone with a baseball bat, but my mailbox was defenseless. And it was mine. The act of battering it was an act directed against me by someone who not only had no motive to harm me, but who knew nothing about me at all. It was an irrational act. I imagined scenes in which I nabbed the perpetrator and grilled him for his motives. Those scenes made me grow even more angry as I realized that whoever did this was irrational. Why did he do it? He wouldn't know. He would tell me it was impulse, not something thought out. It was just something to do. And the more I imagined the interrogation and realized that the person who did the deed had no understanding of it, I realized why I hated him so much. He was driven by an impulse that short-circuited his intellectual and moral nature. His acts were as random as a water rat's. They were on the level of animal satisfaction. I hated that person because I could never hope to communicate with him, because he was possessed by a force that I had devoted my life to transcend. Random violence was not part of everyone's life—certainly not a part of the life of one who devoted his attention to ideas and moral reflection. But the terrifying thing is that no matter how refined our moral sense, the animal level remains within us. What I hated, I realized, was the potential for vicious behavior that I am aware of in myself and that I see in the Mischief Night behavior of otherwise sane and normal people. Mischief is a distortion of the soul, and its evidence is all around us, even in such trivial examples as my battered mailbox.

From the Abstract to the Concrete and Back Again

The writer of the familiar essay usually moves from the concrete to the abstract or from the abstract to the concrete. The preceding writer takes hatred and focuses on a battered mailbox. The reader can see or imagine the mailbox, but no one can imagine hatred as anything but a vague personal emotion. Some writers might begin with hatred and go around in circles in an effort to define it or understand it. Hatred is too abstract, even when you try to define it. It is necessary for the writer to look for hatred in action—then the reader has something to address.

However, there is another shift of movement implied here: moving from the concrete to the abstract. The writer takes a mailbox and converts it into an instrument that probes into the subconscious. Why is the concrete mailbox important? Because it points toward an abstract fear. The fear is the writer's sense that within him lies the same potential for irrational behavior that he witnesses in the fact of his battered mailbox. In other words, the damaged mailbox becomes an emblem of irrational destruction and the writer knows that society itself exists as it does because most of its members do not practice random acts of irrational violence. If they did, society would collapse and be replaced with a hierarchy of terror.

The oscillation between the abstract and the concrete moving from an idea to things that, once perceived, somehow embody the idea—is itself powerful. But the opposite is true as well. Any writer who understands the move from the abstract to the concrete will also see that it is equally advanced in thinking to move from the concrete to the abstract. *Things* imply *ideas*. Things can beget ideas, but only when the writer is aware of the process and when the writer makes the effort to respect the reciprocity implied in oscillation from fact to idea, from imagination to the thing itself.

Sensory Experience: The Gate to Awareness

A writer may think that reflection is inward, totally mental, bound only with ideas. But the reality is that the best familiar essays derive from sensory experience. Writers must be in contact with the senses, all of them, and for as much of the time as possible. Forster constantly brings the concrete world of experience before our eyes, either in the form of a Mrs. Henessy or a crop of blackberries. He appeals to eye and ear with the squawk of a bird, to the sense of taste with his berries. Regina Barreca points us toward the concrete world of experience that excites greed in all of us. Without the senses, we could not begin to understand the complexities of these writers' concerns.

The Power of Names

Apart from the observed details that appeal to the senses is another kind of detail: names. Names have a cultural magic. In Asia certain priests cannot reveal their true name. In much science fiction, such as the *Earth Sea* trilogy of Ursula LeGuin, names must be protected. They are not to be revealed casually. For the writer, names have power. The following example from Marianna Torgovnick's "On Being White, Female, and Born in Bensonhurst" uses names to do some of the work of sensory perception:

> Crisscrossing the neighborhood and marking out ethnic zones—Italian, Irish, and Jewish, for the most part, though there are some Asian Americans and some people (usually Protestants) called simply Americans—are the great shopping streets: Eighty-sixth Street, Kings Highway, Bay Parkway, Eighteenth Avenue, each with its own distinctive character.

The common names of groups of people, "Italian, Irish, and Jewish," and the proper names of certain streets, "Kings Highway," all have meaning for every reader. Some readers will know the streets because they have walked across them or driven down them. Other readers will associate a big-city aura to streets with high numbers, "Eighty-sixth Street," just as readers will associate ethnic names with people they have known, or even with their own ethnic group awareness. Naming names is powerful in writing because it invokes associations as powerful as those invoked by imagery. Torgovnick begins with a reference to the mafia, a name feared in many communities. In Bensonhurst, however, it is mentioned because outsiders fear it. As she says, parodying the language of Bensonhurst: "the Mafia protects the neighborhood from 'the coloreds.' " You can see the power of naming in this phrase: "the coloreds" has less power than "the Mafia" because it is less definitive.

Nikki Giovanni also knows the power of names, as she demonstrates in this passage from "Black Is the Noun":

> Like Alex Haley's ancestor, who preserved his past by passing along his name, the slaves told their story through song. Isn't that why we sing "Swing Low, Sweet Chariot"? Isn't that why we know "Pass Me Not, O Gentle Savior"? Isn't that why our legacy is "You Got to Walk This Lonesome Valley"? "Where Were You When They Crucified My Lord?"

Nikki Giovanni knows that people connect through names, and they connect in a major way through family names. If people do not have family names they risk losing part of their identity. In *Roots*, Alex Haley searched for his first ancestor to come to America, and when he finally discovered Kunta Kinte he felt he could rest.

Experience and the Search for Meaning

Because we live our life without feeling the need to write it down or figure it out, we generally do not think about the significance of our actions. However, the writer of familiar prose is different. Most accomplished writers keep journals, diaries, and even notes on the back of dinner napkins in order to remember what happened and who was there when it occurred. The act of writing about these moments helps the writer discover their significance. That means looking for associations and implications and examining the experience from a variety of points of view. Listed in the box are a few ways in which one can begin the process of examining experience for meaning.

GENERALLY RELIABLE TIPS FOR DISCOVERING SIGNIFICANCE IN EVENTS

1. Identify a specific event or experience and connect it with others like it. For instance, if you have helped someone in something important and you wonder why you regret what you did, reflect on other times you had the same feeling. Reflect as well on other instances from the experiences of people either from life or literature or film. Seeing an isolated action in a context of similar actions helps confer meaning on it.
2. Examine the event for its effect on your life or on the life of those who shared the experience. For whom is there more at stake? What exactly is at stake? Were you aware during the event that there was anything at stake? How calculating were you about what you did?
3. Look for connections between your behavior and what you feel

your true character may be. How consistent is your behavior? Does the experience make you feel good about yourself or not? Would others feel good about you?

4. How does the event change things for other people? What is the potential for a good outcome? What is the potential for calamity? In whose life will the event be most significant?
5. What is the long-lasting effect of the experience you have had?
6. What, if any, is the cultural significance of the event? How would your experience reflect your cultural values or change them?

When you reflect on a moment of experience or on a value that arises from an examination of experience, you perform a complex kind of analysis that reveals meaning. As you can see from the examples of writing in this chapter, the process of discovering meaning is not necessarily direct or obvious. It may take some exploration of people and responses to make complete sense of any complex event.

The Structure of the Familiar Essay

Finding a subject for a familiar essay will be easy for some writers, perhaps a bit more difficult for others. However, once you begin to see what kinds of subjects can be appropriate for the familiar essay, you will understand why writers like Cynthia Ozick would never run out of material. It is all around us, all waiting to be examined. Your own special concerns and observations about life grow from within you in response to your environment and your experiences.

There is no set structure for a familiar essay, as you can see from examining the samples in this chapter. A useful guide for beginning the essay is to think in terms of associative details and instances as a way of gathering your material. Then look for a pattern of organization that will lead from *an introduction to your subject,* to the body of the essay, in which you *examine the implications of your subject.* Finally, aim toward the conclusion of the essay, in which you *develop your understanding of the subject.*

You will recognize this as the familiar beginning-middle-end structure. The beginning sets up your subject; the middle explores it; the end refines and perhaps reveals your understanding of it. However, the familiar essay is not a formal essay and there is no regulation that says how it ought to structure itself. The examples you have seen demonstrate that the familiar essay profits from digression. A digression appears to be an unconnected observation, a story or reminiscence, that does not at first seem to apply, but which, on reflection, becomes relevant. When E. M. Forster suddenly brings up blackberries, he seems to be digressing from the subject of the wood. On reflection, however, you see that this digression is relevant and brings us back to the point. Earlier, discussing the work of Virginia Woolf, we made the observation that the structure of some essays is "loose," which is to say that it appears shapeless because the author follows a line of thought until it gives out, then moves on to the next line of thought without worrying about the absolute logic of the connections. The overall subject of the essay—and the fact that some reflection is necessary in the familiar essay—will take care of connecting the material. An experienced writer can digress with the understanding that the digression is temporary and that the main idea or subject will be returned to in due time.

Beginning with Experience

In the following sample we see an approach to writing a familiar essay that begins with experience and practices some of the approaches to the essay that we have described. The writer makes an effort at moving between the abstract and the concrete while searching for the significance of the events that are being described.

ANDRE JAMES

Malls and the Gender Gap

My wife knows that it's no easy feat to get me into the mall, so when we're there I try to approach the experience with the detachment of a philosopher. The first question is: What do you do at the mall? My presumption is that you shop. Since I'm a man, I don't shop when I'm working, and I tend to work a lot. So for me shopping is an event. I don't usually go alone, and when my wife and I go together, we don't always go into the same shops.

Okay, I'll level with you. We almost never go into the same shops. In fact, if it doesn't have food, I probably don't go into many of the shops at all. That point came to me with great clarity only last week when, on a mad impulse, I agreed that we needed something and would probably find it at the mall.

There we were. The interior of this mall is something out of a science fiction movie of the nineteen thirties. On the right are the ever-ascending escalators moving slowly from floor to floor to floor. On the left is a futuristic stainless steel sculpture that raises arms (or are they armatures?) into the heavens and down which trickles water into a pool filled with pennies and a few nickels. Above us is a wire netting that rises about six stories in height and from which dangle stainless steel abstract birds that may have been inspired by Canada geese or the illustrations of M. C. Escher. Small colored lights glisten from these twirling birds and sparkle throughout the entire space. Below us—we are on the level one floor—is a rather large ice-rink with perhaps a hundred young people skating away in gay abandon. On the edges of the rink bright, busy concessions offer ice-cream, candied applies, spun candy, balloons (one just got loose and is rising to the glass ceiling to join a few more floataways), and various other sweetmeats. Obviously, this is not just a shopping experience: the mall is the heart of the surrounding counties. It's the place to be.

So, in the guise of the philosopher I resign myself to the local delights, figuring that I am now one with the community. As we move along the esplanade, I study the community. Its diversity is splendid. The oldsters seem brightly clad, somewhat windburned, clothes a little bleached, but they are uniformly eager. Some of the oldsters stretch their spandex a bit more than one would have thought possible, but then, so do some of the youngsters. And some of both are so skinny one would expect them to make an emergency stop at the nearest burger spot. The youngsters demonstrate a variety of adornment that gives us hope for the future: ten or fifteen earrings climbing up one ear, figurative tattoos in radiant colors, clothes that are either skintight or wadded in blanket style. Some of the young men trudge along in huge sneakers that seem never to need their laces tied. Their trousers bag everywhere but at the ankle, the crotches ride so low as to threaten the tiled pavement. The jackets ride back and off the shoulder as if they were modeling in Paris. And the traditional baseball caps all point backward, sideward, slantward, but never, as their designers hoped, forward. The philosopher in me smiled at such statements of independence.

The Value of Digression

So far the writer has described the mall in enough detail, along with its inhabitants, so that the reader knows what it looks like. Probably, too, the reader has enough experience with large malls to recognize the writer's experience as familiar. But the writer has some personal issues to introduce that not all readers will share. Before arriving at the main issues in this essay—which center on the question of what role a man like the writer plays in a mall in the first place—the writer has digressed to relate some childhood experiences that connect to the experience at hand.

> When I look at the scene with a less than philosophical eye, I recall my early training as a shopper. I grew up when malls existed only in the imaginations of those writers who described cities under glass, with towers connected by ramps and flying ships moving people as if they were commuting from mall to mall. But the reality was quite different. My mother would set out for downtown (or in some New England neighborhoods, "downstreet") with me in tow. Ordinarily I had an agenda of my own, I usually wanted a train track, or something for my chemistry set, or maybe a book—something that spoke to the inner needs of a boy.
>
> The drill was: get up early on Saturday morning, get downtown with plenty of energy. We went to fancy department stores like B. Altman's, and Lord and Taylor, which had plenty of odd looking clothes that my mother would examine in great detail and query me about: "Did I like it?" "Was it smart looking?" Who knew? I always nodded and hoped I'd said the right thing. Then, when the department stores were behind us, it was off to the discount store.

Reaching the End

After filling in some memory gaps, the writer begins to bring the essay to an end. The job now is to aim for some understanding of the modern experience of going to shopping malls—indeed to develop some understanding of malls in general. The experience for the boy is one thing, but for the man it is quite different.

> My mother had her regular areas to shop in: things for her sewing, items for the kitchen. I got to make my way to the toy section and could spend my money any way I wanted to. Sometimes I bought books, sometimes a toy. I would spend my money, clutch my purchase, and then the day would end with a club sandwich at the local Friendly's or McDonalds finished off with an ice-cream soda. How could one be more content? They were hard times where we lived. There were no malls: no escalators, no stainless steel sculpture. No glitz,

either on or off the general public. But a few dollars went a long way, and the excitement of being out of the house and downtown was almost endless.

But then I grew up. Life gets more complicated. Now the mall offers me an assortment of socks, shoes, trousers, shirts, and sweaters. But most men like me have all those in abundance. So when I go to the mall these days it is not usually to buy things, but to see things. I see all the things people think they need. But much more interesting, I also see all the people who think they need those things. For me, that is a much more interesting experience. Somehow, I do not think I am as interesting to them as they are to me, and therein, as Shakespeare said, lies a tale.

The writer of this essay makes some discoveries in the act of writing. One of them is that there are important differences between the way things were when he was a child and the way they are now. Another is that his interest is in people rather than things. The recognition that other people may be more interesting to him than he is to them implies either that he is more curious (more philosophical) or that he simply does not seem to be as stimulating to the world as the world is to him. The implications can be read in several different ways, which the writer well knows. In the process, however, the writer has recovered moments from his youth and placed them in the context of the present, helping him to make sense of one of the most common phenomena of the late twentieth century: malls devoted to shopping.

The following box material sums up suggestions for how to write familiar essays.

TIPS THAT USUALLY HELP IN WRITING FAMILIAR ESSAYS

1. If you begin with a personal experience, describe it carefully with attention to concrete details.
2. Interpret the experience in a manner that makes its relevance understood to your reader.
3. If you begin with an abstract idea, move your essay quickly to concrete experience either through description or figurative language.
4. Whatever your first strategy, be sure to use examples, and cause and effect. Examine history and possibility, and consider what people have said about the experience or idea.
5. Look for opportunities to use metaphor or metonymy.
6. Use the resources of names.
7. Explore your material to discover its significance.

6

Writing the Critical Essay

What Is the Critical Essay?

Generally a critical essay interprets and evaluates another text. That text may be an essay, a poem, a novel, a historical study, a film, a play, or any work of art. Because so many specialized issues are involved in approaching painting, sculpture, film, and drama, this chapter will focus on only two related ways of writing the critical essay. The first centers on evaluation of ideas and thus examines the essay, beginning with an example from Francis Bacon. Such an approach is useful in working with any nonfiction text, and its principles will be useful in all critical writing. It involves establishing what the writer has said, examining the underlying issues for completeness and clarity, and responding to the ideas in light of current knowledge. The second approach centers on the interpretation of a work of literature, with an example of a sonnet by William Wordsworth. Interpretation of literature involves the discovery of meaning and significance that may be hinted at but not stated directly. Because techniques of literary criticism are also specialized, the approach presented here will be based on general principles that may be applied to other literary texts.

Opportunities for Development

One positive critical approach involves finding opportunities to develop ideas that the text has neglected or has treated fleetingly. To discover such opportunities, ask what has been left out, what has been hinted at but ignored, or what has importance for you that has been treated casually by the text. An essay on friendship, for example, may extoll the benefits of old friendships and their superiority to new friendships; or it might praise friendship as a lengthener of one's life. But it might ignore entirely the question of enemies, the opposite of friends. You may feel it is important to consider with equal care the role that enemies have in one's life. Some enemies will make your life complicated, but some may make you rise above your normal limitations and achieve greater things.

Likewise, in an essay on friendship, the distinction between old and new friends may be made in a fashion that seems inappropriate to you. For example, you may feel that the invigorating quality of new friendships will outweigh the sometimes slothful pleasures of old friendships. Older friendships introduce less novelty into one's life and sustain instead the comfortable old patterns. Yet, it is also true that with older friendships one probes deeper into one's own personality while at the same time enjoying a richness of experience with other people. Newer friends will always be less well known, even if they are sometimes more exciting and unpredictable. These issues are subjects appropriate to critical essays.

Thinking Critically About Ideas

In order to write a critical essay we need to place ourselves in a critical frame of mind. For some, this suggests assuming a negative stance, but in our case that is not so. Instead, what is meant here by a critical frame of mind is only that you approach ideas and issues with a questioning attitude. Thinking critically involves a process, some of which was illustrated earlier in this book and some of which is amplified in this chapter. But in essence it implies that as a writer you become an active participant in a dialogue—in the case of this book it is a dialogue between you and a text. As a critic, you are encouraged to ask questions about a text, to discover its essential points, to examine the premises of its statements, to differentiate between fact and opinion, and to decide the truth of conclusions presented to you.

Deciding What Has Been Said

The critic's first job is to decide what the text says. That suggests the ability to summarize the text and then to isolate the ideas that seem most important or most fruitful for discussion. In lengthy texts, this procedure can be difficult because a great many ideas will be introduced and developed. In short texts usually a single issue will be developed, but it will not be equally clear to all readers what that point is.

Stating the main ideas that your essay will cover as well as why you are covering them will help you clarify your own position to your readers. If you have spotted a problem in the text and wish to explore it, your first approach will be to establish the problem and state it clearly, indicating how you intend to approach the problem and what your solution to it might be.

Looking For What Has Been Left Unsaid

Another principle of critical thought is examining texts to see what has been left unsaid. If you can establish the most important points made by a text, then at the same time you should be able to decide what has been left out. All texts are selective, and therefore no text can accommodate everything. All texts omit some very important issues and ideas in an effort to focus clearly on other significant issues. Such practices are normal and essential to writing good prose. Of course, there are times when a writer will intentionally ignore a crucial point that might invalidate a basic view or cast a text's conclusions in doubt. A critical reader will, through a process of questioning and analysis, consider the impact of such an omission. Then, too, a selective or incomplete text will suggest a point to you that needs development and examination. In that case you can take advantage of an opportunity to develop something the original text has neglected.

Analyzing an Essay: Francis Bacon's "Of Studies"

Francis Bacon (1561–1626) was the first English-language essayist, following in 1597 in the footsteps of Michel de Montaigne (1533–1592), whose *Essais* were published in France in 1588. Bacon's essays are very short, usually no more than two pages long. They aim to say everything they can in the briefest possible form, and judging by the way they have been valued and quoted over the years, they achieve that goal. The following is one of Bacon's best known essays.

FRANCIS BACON

Of Studies

Studies serve for delight, for ornament, and for ability. Their chief use for delight, is in privateness and retiring; for ornament, is in discourse; and for ability, is in the judgement and disposition of business. For expert men[a] can execute, and perhaps judge of particulars, one by one; but the general counsels, and the plots and marshaling of affairs, come best from those that are learned. To spend too much time in studies is sloth; to use them too much for ornament is affectation; to make judgement wholly by their rules is the humor of a scholar. They perfect nature, and are perfected by experience; for natural abilities are like natural plants, that need pruning by study; and studies themselves do give forth directions too much at large, except they be bounded in by experience. Crafty men condemn studies, simple men admire them, and wise men use them, for they teach not their own use; but that is a wisdom without them, and above them, won by observation. Read not to contradict and confute, nor to believe and take for granted, nor to find talk and discourse, but to weigh and consider. Some books are to be tasted, others to be swallowed, and some few to be chewed and digested; that is, some books are to be read only in parts; others to be read, but not curiously; and some few to be read wholly and with diligence and attention. Some books also may be read by deputy and extracts made of them by others, but that would be only in the less important arguments and the meaner sort of books; else distilled books are like common distilled waters, flashy things. Reading maketh a full man, conference a ready man, and writing an exact man. And therefore, if a man write little, he had need have a great memory; if he confer little, he had need have a present wit; and if he read little, he had need have much cunning, to seem to know that he doth not. Histories make men wise, poets witty, the mathematics

---

[a]expert men: those who rely on practical experience rather than learning.

subtle; natural philosophy deep; moral grave; logic and rhetoric, better able to contend. *Abeunt studia in mores.*[b] Nay, there is no stond[c] or impediment in the wit but may be wrought out by fit studies, like as diseases of the body may have appropriate exercises. Bowling is good for the stone and reins,[d] shooting[e] for the lungs and breast, gentle walking for the stomach, riding for the head, and the like. So if a man's wit be wandering, let him study the mathematics; for in demonstrations, if his wit be called away never so little, he must begin again. If his wit be not apt to distinguish or find differences, let him study the Schoolmen[f], for they are *cymini sectores.*[g] If he be not apt to beat over matters, and to call up one thing to prove and illustrate another, let him study the lawyers' cases. So every defect of the mind may have a special receipt.[h] 1597; 1625

[b]*Abeunt studia in mores*: Studies lead to manners.

[c]stond: obstacle.

[d]stone and reins: kidney stone and kidneys.

[e]shooting: archery.

[f]Schoolmen: Medieval theologians.

[g]*cymini sectores*: hair splitters.

[h]receipt: recipe or prescription.

A critical approach to this classic essay might begin with establishing what Bacon says in general. He seems to be praising the kind of learning one gets in the schools and universities but also the kind of learning that is characteristic of a curious and inquiring mind. In Bacon's time, all learning would have been in Latin, and very little of it would have had an immediate practical value. We might today call it a liberal education. He warns that learning should be mixed with experience and that it should not be carried to extremes. His opening three-part sentence is the essay in microform: learning gives us personal delight; it permits us to converse with others of similar learning; and it helps us in conducting our business.

Evaluating Bacon's Style

Bacon likes to organize matters into threes, beginning with the opening sentence. He continues:

- "Crafty men condemn studies, simple men admire them, and wise men use them."
- "Read not to contradict and confute, nor to believe and take for granted, nor to find talk and discourse, but to weigh and consider."
- "Some books are to be tasted, others to be swallowed, and some few to be chewed and digested;"
- "Reading maketh a full man, conference a ready man, and writing an exact man."

Bacon's three-part structure permits the reader to grasp his distinctions quickly. A critical approach to this essay might ask why Bacon wishes to write so briskly, without developing his thoughts beyond his declarative statements. One answer is that Bacon assumed he wrote for learned people who could flesh out his statements on their own. Another answer is that his readers were busy people who would not take the time to browse through an expanded version of the essay. A third answer is that in "inventing" the essay form in English, Bacon meant simply to "try" an idea (which is part of what *essai* means) in as few words as possible. This version was published in 1625, but the 1597 version was even shorter.

If Bacon was writing to other educated people, rather than to "expert men," it is also true that he expected them to agree with him. Therefore, one can understand why none of his views are defended by argument. If, indeed, Bacon does argue the case, he does so in the last part of the essay in which he compares study with physical exercise, pointing out that certain exercises benefit certain portions of the body, while certain studies will benefit certain personalities or mental types. In this sense, he seems to argue that studies should continue even after formal schooling.

Evaluating Bacon's Ideas

Bacon alludes to "expert men" and "crafty men" in such a way as to let us know that he realizes there are many intelligent (he would say cunning) men who have no learning but much experience. "Expert men" today might claim that recent college graduates are basically incompetent because all they have is book learning. Bacon has no patience with such a view and demonstrates that "expert men" know their own business well enough, but have not got the wide-ranging knowledge or ability that comes with learning. In other words, they are excellent on a practical level but not on a theoretical level. As he says, "the general counsels, and the plots and marshaling of affairs, come best from those that are learned."

What Bacon Left Unsaid

In one way, "Of Studies" is itself a critical essay because it takes a critical view of the value of experience versus learning, practical knowledge versus theoretical knowledge, and ignorance versus education. Were you to write a critical essay in response to this text, you might examine it for what is missing, such as any allusion to women's learning. The word *man* appears throughout, and it seems to mean man, not all people. You might examine the kinds of learning mentioned in the essay to see if indeed any is relevant to what you feel a woman's education should be. You might also examine it in an effort to see whether he is right when he distinguishes the effects of various studies, as when, for instance, he says "natural philosophy" (what we would call science) really makes a person "deep."

Bacon ignores the question of who ought to be given the gift of learning. The end of studies seems to be to conduct business, which in his day did not necessarily mean running a shop or leading an industry. It meant the running of an estate, the operation of a government bureau, or the like. These were employments for only a few, usually those who were aristocratic or with aristocratic connections. There is no provision in Bacon's scheme for the education of ordinary people, the laboring classes, or the poor. The "expert men" probably would have come from the middle or lower classes and risen to their position through exceptional intelligence and luck. But no matter what they did, they would not have qualified for an education except in unusual situations. William Shakespeare, Christopher Marlowe, and Ben Jonson, great literary figures of Bacon's time, were members of the middle class who benefited from a good general education because they showed exceptional potential or because, as in Shakespeare's case, their parents were successful in business.

How Bacon Stimulates a Critical Response

By approaching this text critically, you can stimulate your own thinking and produce a response that elaborates on or improves on the ideas that Bacon presents us. For example, Bacon assumed that education was appropriate for only some of the people. He does not say as much in the essay, but a knowledge of the historical circumstances combined with the distinctions he makes between the learned and the "crafty" points in that direction. One opportunity you might have as a critical reader would be to examine the basis of his views and decide whether our modern approach in the United States, which assumes that everyone has the right to an education (at least through high school), is more valid than Bacon's. It would be very difficult to imagine Bacon approving universal education, given the views he presents in this essay.

However, one of Bacon's immense strengths is his view that education is of great value. Today you may feel that not everyone will agree with that view. For example, in the United States the proliferation of community colleges, colleges, and universities is such that those who wish to go further than high school in their education can do so. One result is that some people feel too many students go on to college and come out without having benefited very much from their education. Such is not the case in European, African, and Asian nations, where the selection processes are begun early and people are "tracked" into universities beginning at a young age. These other nations agree that education is of great value, but such a view is bolstered by the fact that only the exceptionally talented go to the universities, thus making learning "rarer" and more valuable. It might be interesting to consider the benefits of universal education. Should higher education, what Bacon calls learning, be available to everyone? Or should specialized "crafty" training, such as carpentry, automotive repair, electrical training, and such vocational education be the norm of "further education"? The distinction between training and education in this instance is also of enormous import and offers an opportunity for developing a critical essay.

Thinking Critically About the Arts

Francis Bacon was "artistic" in his essay in the sense that he concerned himself with his style and balanced his sentences carefully.

But he focused sharply on the value of studies in everyday life. Artistic texts, such as poems and fiction, naturally emphasize important ideas, but they do so while responding to special techniques and creating certain illusions. A short story sometimes creates the illusion of reality while presenting to us characters who are pure fiction. A drama, such as *Hamlet*, presents a cast of characters who behave as if they were living through an action that was both real and immediate. In those cases we play close attention to the way the ideas are presented to us. Critical essays on poems or dramas usually interpret the ways in which the ideas are formed and presented. Often, such critical essays search out the subtleties of the form that make the ideas inherent in the text more intelligible and more emphatic. Poets and dramatists write on many levels, sometimes literal in their meaning, sometimes symbolic, sometimes psychological. Usually they write on all these levels and more at the same time. Consequently, it is necessary to approach their texts with circumspection, observing closely and looking for opportunities to make new discoveries about the art by which the texts are created.

Some of the same questions asked about Bacon's essay will be relevant about a poem or piece of fiction. For example, the question, "What has been said?," is certainly relevant, although it is usually not a simple matter to provide a complete answer. Indeed, often every answer will be incomplete because poets especially have a way of saying many things at the same time by implying as much as they say explicitly. Ambiguity is a particular poetic characteristic designed to enrich a text. But an essayist usually wants to avoid ambiguity because the essay is designed to communicate ideas clearly. Clarity and ambiguity do not always go well together. Still, the poet, like most artists, wishes to engage a reader's emotions and deep feelings with the ideas that the poem presents. Bacon is less interested in his reader's feelings than in his reader's understandings. Because the poem combines the two, it offers a special challenge to the writer of a critical essay. When you decide what a poem says, how can you include important information about how the poem makes you feel? And is it not true that the way a work of art makes you feel is important to what it says? There is much debate about this point, but surely the poetry and music we like most impresses us on an emotional level in such a way as to qualify its importance to us. The artist always "says things" in a manner designed to affect our emotional life—perhaps even in a manner designed to change it.

Analyzing a Poem: William Wordsworth's "The Sonnet"

Sonnets are among the most satisfying of poems in part because they have an instantly recognizable form: fourteen lines of iambic pentameter rhymed in a special way. Iambic pentameter refers to a ten-syllable line of verse with the following pattern of accents:

u ´ | u ´ | u ´ | u ´ | u ´
In truth the prison unto which we doom

Usually, the accent falls on the important words or syllables in the line. Sometimes the pattern is varied to avoid monotony, as in the opening words, "Nuns fret not," in which all three syllables are accented. But in the sonnet the general pattern is an unaccented syllable followed by an accented syllable, as in Wordsworth's example. The rhyme scheme for the following poem is: abba abba cdd ccd, which connects it to the Italian form usually favored by Milton, whom Wordsworth praises.

"The Sonnet"

Nuns fret not at their convent's narrow room,
    And hermits are contented with their cells,
    And students with their pensive citadels;
Maids at the wheel, the weaver at his loom,
Sit blithe and happy; bees that soar for bloom,
    High as the highest peak of Furness fells,[a]
    Will murmur by the hour in foxglove bells:
In truth the prison unto which we doom
Ourselves no prison is: and hence for me,
    In sundry moods, 'twas pastime to be bound
    Within the Sonnet's scanty plot of ground;
Pleased if some souls (for some there needs must be)
Who have felt the weight of too much liberty,
    Should find brief solace there, as I have found.

William Wordsworth (1770–1850)

---

[a]Mountains in the Lake District of England.

What Wordsworth Says

Beginning with the question of what this poem says, one early response is that Wordsworth's poem praises the restrictions of the sonnet. For those who are not professional poets, it may seem a special challenge to write a poem that has fourteen iambic pentameter lines that must rhyme in a special, preordained way. Yet this poem celebrates the "prison" that "no prison is" and contrasts it with "too much liberty." His point is that the "prison" of the sonnet provides a form that contrasts with the formlessness of no pattern, and therefore Wordsworth praises form in poetry, and especially praises the form of the sonnet, which provides the poet with "solace" and pleasure.

Wordsworth's Values

Wordsworth reveals important values through several comparisons and metaphors. First, the sonnet is compared with a nun's "narrow room"; second, with a hermit's cell; third, with a student's "pensive citadel"; then with the trades of specialized workers. All these represent positive values. Then Wordsworth uses a paradox when he tells us that the "prison into which we doom / Ourselves no prison is." He tells us that the sonnet (which poets doom themselves to), while it looks like a prison, is actually liberating. He insists that it is fun to write a sonnet when he tells us that " 'twas pastime to be bound / Within the sonnet's scanty plot of ground." Following that paradox to a conclusion, he suggests that there are some "Who have felt the weight of too much liberty" and thus could not write well. The restrictions of the sonnet form produce the inspiration that all poets need.

Wordsworth, Form, and Liberty

The title and the form of "The Sonnet" tell us right away that it is a metapoem, which is to say a poem about poetry. Ordinarily we would assume such a poem to have an interest mainly to other poets. But because Wordsworth praises the sonnet for the very restrictions that make it difficult, we can see that "The Sonnet" spills over into life itself. Sometimes formal restrictions in life, such as a schedule, can make us more productive. Every calling in life, from the nun's to the weaver's, creates a system of formal restriction that is both pleasing and productive. What is not productive is the formlessness of absolute liberty, which we could translate into reference to unemployment and homelessness. This observation is paradoxical at first because our inclination is to assume that the most freeing of experiences is absolute liberty. Wordsworth tells us that restrictions are in their odd way more freeing. Form in the sonnet not only restricts meaning, it contains meaning.

The choices Wordsworth makes in the opening of the poem direct us to contemplate spirituality. The nun is a religious devotee; the hermit is traditionally a religious seeker living plainly; students are traditionally searchers for knowledge, content with little. The spinners ("Maids at the wheel") and weavers perform essential human work, and the bees are tireless natural laborers who pollinate the flowers and provide satisfying sweet refreshment. All this is good, but each of these is dependent on restriction and focus of one kind or another. In this poem, Wordsworth has made sure that the details join to produce a functional whole. He restricts the range of the comparisons and metaphors as carefully as he restricts the range of the line length and the rhymes. The result is that the poem has a spiritual center and involves the idea of the sonnet itself with that center.

Evaluating the Achievement of Wordsworth's Art

Part of the job of a critical essay is evaluative. So far we have simply described what Wordsworth seems to be doing in this poem. We have established "what he says" on a very rudimentary level and have clarified some of the values implicit in the poem. But the question of whether the poem is fully satisfying—whether it is a good sonnet or not—has been left hanging. One reason is that we have not yet established the criteria for excellence in a poem of this kind. In the case of any given poem it is not always simple to agree on the most important criteria. The list of questions to ask, shown in the box, is only a suggestion.

SOME USUALLY RELIABLE QUESTIONS FOR EVALUATING A SONNET

1. Since the form of the sonnet is preestablished, the first question establishes whether the poet has satisfied the requirement of four-

teen lines in iambic pentameter with a consistent rhyme scheme.

2. Are the rhyme-words forced and obvious, or are they natural in the context of the poem? Are they significant to the poem?
3. Is the meaning of the poem clear? Is it appropriate to a short poem?
4. Are the comparisons, metaphors, and images pertinent to the main ideas in the poem? Do they deepen the poem's meaning or are they only ornamental?
5. Do all the details seem to function together to produce a satisfying whole?
6. Does the richness of the poem increase as you examine details more closely?
7. Does the significance of the poem reach into your life and beyond the limits of its restricted form?

Using these questions as a guide (and they are only a guide), we can see that Wordsworth's "The Sonnet" is a successful poem. Its form satisfies the technical requirements of the sonnet and does so without strain or obvious shoe-horning of rhyme words or unnecessary padding to flesh out the ten-syllable line. We can also see that the comparisons, images, and metaphors all help deepen the significance of the poem. Our reading of it suggests that Wordsworth operated on several levels and each is significant to most readers even today.

Naturally, any evaluation will depend on an understanding of what the poem says. However, when trying to decide what a poem says, it is not enough to offer a summary of the literal meaning of the words. For example, if we were to decide that Wordsworth hoped we would see that the restrictions of the sonnet help in writing more interesting poetry, we would be getting only part of what he says. The critical reader will also ask why Wordsworth emphasizes the word *liberty* by using it as a rhyme word near the end of the poem. Liberty is a political term, not a poetic term, and in the age in which Wordsworth lived, with the French revolution one of its most important events, the word *liberty* has special connotations. It reminds the alert reader of the catch phrase of the French revolution: "Liberty, Fraternity, Equality." Unfortunately, the liberty that resulted early in the French revolution was more like a license to kill. In some phases of the revolution the political situation resembled anarchy, the ultimate in political formlessness. The informed critical reader will know from both history and an awareness of Wordsworth's personal disappointment with the revolution that politics, like religion, was a major concern in his life. Therefore, it is no surprise to see it present in a poem that purports to be about something so innocent as poetry.

Such a reading of the poem implies that it is not just a poem about poetry. This reading demonstrates that its significance is wide-ranging and perhaps universal. Its meaning is not at all trivial, but gives us all a great deal to think about. In this sense, then, the poem reaches far beyond its formal bonds and touches all of us. We need to think clearly about the meaning of liberty and the relationship of liberty to the sometimes inconvenient restrictions of responsibility.

Analyzing Texts

No matter what your ultimate critical purpose in writing a critical essay, your process begins with the analysis of a text. The text may be written down, it may be oral, it may be a work of art. Every text excites or implies meaning, which in turn excites or implies values that can be evaluated. In preparation for writing a critical essay, a number of approaches may be brought to bear to help produce a fuller discussion. The box text lists some of them.

SOME GENERALLY USEFUL TIPS FOR ANALYZING TEXTS

1. Establish the major points made by the text, both explicitly and implicitly.
2. Question the text.
3. Examine key definitions.
4. Identify assumptions and potential bias.
5. Separate fact from opinion.
6. Examine the use of evidence as well as the quality of evidence.
7. Examine the style and structure of the text for its effects on the reader.

Niccolo Machiavelli (1469–1527) wrote a book for Lorenzo the Magnificent on the subject of how a prince, or ruler, ought to conduct business in Renaissance Italy. This book was designed to get him preferment in Florence's government, although it failed on that score. On the other hand, it has been read carefully by politicians ever since. It has become a handbook sometimes of tyrants, sometimes of benevolent leaders, but it has been in constant use in politics throughout the world. Machiavelli's personal views, as we know from other, more intimate works, do not necessarily agree with what he says in the brief passage printed here, but the published views have become permanently associated with him.

NICCOLO MACHIAVELLI

The Prince

Of the Things for Which Men, and Especially Princes, Are Praised or Blamed

It now remains to be seen what are the methods and rules for a prince as regards his subjects and friends. And as I know that many have written of this, I fear that my writing about it may be deemed presumptuous, differing as I do, especially in this matter, from the opinions of others. But my intention being to write something of use to those who understand, it appears to me more proper to go to the real truth of the matter than to its imagination; and many have imagined republics and principalities which have never been seen or known to exist in reality; for how we live is so far removed from how we ought to live, that he who abandons what is done for what ought to be done, will rather learn to bring about his own ruin than his preservation. A man who wishes to make a profession of goodness in everything must necessarily come to grief among so many who are not good. Therefore it is necessary for a prince, who wishes to maintain himself, to learn how not to be good, and to use this knowledge and not use it, according to the necessity of the case.

Leaving on one side, then, those things which concern only an imaginary prince, and speaking of those that are real, I state that all men, and especially princes, who are placed at a greater height, are reputed for certain qualities which bring them either praise or blame. Thus one is considered liberal, another *misero* or miserly (using a Tuscan term, seeing that *avaro* with us still means one who is rapaciously acquisitive and *misero* one who makes grudging use of his own); one a free giver, another rapacious; one cruel, another merciful; one a breaker of his word, another trustworthy; one effeminate and pusillanimous, another fierce and high-spirited; one humane, another haughty; one lascivious, another chaste; one frank, another astute; one hard, another easy; one serious, another frivolous; one religious, another an unbeliever, and so on. I know that every one will admit that it would be highly praiseworthy in a prince to possess all the above-named qualities that are reputed good, but as they cannot all be possessed or observed, human conditions not permitting of it, it is necessary that he should be prudent enough to avoid the scandal of those vices which would lose him the state, and guard himself if possible against those which will not lose it him, but if not able to, he can indulge them with less scruple. And yet he must not mind incurring the scandal of those vices, without which it would be difficult to save the state, for if one considers well, it will be found that some things which seem virtues would, if followed, lead to one's ruin, and some others which appear vices result in one's greater security and wellbeing.

Of Cruelty and Clemency, and Whether It Is Better to Be Loved or Feared

Proceeding to the other qualities before named, I say that every prince must desire to be considered merciful and not cruel. He must, however, take care not to misuse this mercifulness. Cesare Borgia was considered cruel, but his cruelty had brought order to the Romagna, united it, and reduced it to peace and fealty. . . .

A prince, therefore, must not mind incurring the charge of cruelty for the purpose of keeping his subjects united and faithful; for, with a very few examples, he will be more merciful than those who, from excess of tenderness, allow disorders to arise, from whence spring bloodshed and rapine; for these as a rule injure the whole community, while the executions carried out by the prince injure only individuals. And of all princes, it is impossible for a new prince to escape the reputation of cruelty, new states being always full of dangers. Wherefore Virgil through the mouth of Dido says: "Hard necessity and the newness of my realm, compel me to do such things and to protect my borders everywhere" (*The Aeneid*).

Nevertheless, he must be cautious in believing and acting, and must not be afraid of his own shadow, and must proceed in a temperate manner with prudence and humanity, so that too much confidence does not render him incautious, and too much diffidence does not render him intolerant.

From this arises the question whether it is better to be loved more than feared, or feared more than loved. The reply is, that one ought to be both feared and loved, but as it is difficult for the two to go together, it is much safer to be feared than loved, if one of the two has to be wanting. For it may be said of men in general that they are ungrateful, voluble, dissemblers, anxious to avoid danger, and covetous of gain; as long as you benefit them, they are entirely yours; they offer you their blood, their goods, their life, and their children, as I have before said, when the necessity is remote; but when it approaches, they revolt. And the prince who has relied solely on their words, without making other preparations, is ruined; for the friendship which is gained by purchase and not through grandeur and nobility of spirit is bought but not secured, and at a pinch is not to be expended in your service. And men have less scruple in offending one who makes himself loved than one who makes himself feared; for love is held by a chain of obligation which, men being selfish, is broken whenever it serves their purpose; but fear is maintained by a dread of punishment which never fails.

Still, a prince should make himself feared in such a way that if he does not gain love, he at any rate avoids hatred; for fear and the absence of hatred may well go together, and will be always attained by one who abstains from interfering with the property of his citizens and subjects or with their women. And when he is obliged to take the life of any one, let him do so when there is a proper justification and manifest reason for it; but above all he must abstain from taking the property of others, for men forget more easily the death of their father than the loss of their patrimony. Then also pretexts for seizing property are never wanting, and one who begins to live by rapine will always find some reason for taking the goods of others, whereas causes for taking life are rarer and more fleeting.

But when the prince is with his army and has a large number of soldiers under his control, then it is extremely necessary that he should not mind being thought cruel; for without his reputation he could not keep an army united or disposed to any duty. Among the noteworthy actions of Hannibal is numbered this, that although he had an enormous army, composed of men of all nations and fighting in foreign countries, there never arose any dissension either among them or against the prince, either in good fortune or in bad. This could not be due to anything but his inhuman cruelty, which together with his infinite other virtues, made him always venerated and terrible in the sight of his soldiers, and without it his other virtues would not have sufficed to produce that effect. Thoughtless writers admire on the one hand his actions, and on the other blame the principal cause of them. . . .

I conclude, therefore, with regard to being feared and loved, that men love at their own free will, but fear at the will of the prince, and that a wise prince must rely on what is in his power and not on what is in the power of others, and he must only contrive to avoid incurring hatred, as has been explained.

MACHIAVELLI'S MAJOR POINTS

In the first section Machiavelli considers aspects of the prince's behavior, especially how he behaves among those who are likely to get to know him. He realizes that there is a distinction between the way we ought to behave and the way we usually behave. We ought to be good, but as he tells us, if the prince is good he is likely to come to grief because there are so many people who are bad. "Therefore," he tells us, "it is necessary for a prince . . . to learn how not to be good." The prince ought to practice the virtues, but "he must not mind incurring the scandal of those vices, without which it would be difficult to save the state."

The second section proposes a question: Is it better that the prince be loved or feared? Machiavelli ultimately decides the prince ought to be both loved and feared, but he also realizes such a paradox is impossible. Therefore, he votes for being feared. He feels that the state will be much safer if the prince is feared because people will not risk rebellion and "disorders." He points out that the love that would bind people to the prince is set aside in times of difficulty, but fear is never set aside. When at the head of an army, the prince must always have a reputation like Hannibal, who was celebrated for "his inhuman cruelty."

When you analyze these passages, you may see the main points somewhat differently. Doubtless few readers would agree on all points in examining such a complex text. However, many readers will agree on the preceding description, perhaps with modifications or different emphases. The differences will most often depend on the sympathy with which one holds Machiavelli and his views.

Questioning Machiavelli

Questioning a text is a key step in developing a critical approach. The uncritical reader will read Machiavelli's text and either fail to understand it or appear to understand it and accept it without question. The critical reader will question the text either in terms of its main ideas themselves or finding the main ideas incomplete. The critical reader asks key questions of the text and demands full understanding. For example, in the first section Machiavelli admits that it is best to be good all the time, and generally his culture praised virtue as our culture does today. However, his practicality shows through when he admits that a leader really cannot be good all the time and indeed probably ought to practice useful vices that will keep him in power. Does Machiavelli then recommend lying, cheating, deceit of many kinds as long as they keep the leader in control? That is a problem for anyone who approves virtuous behavior. Those who agree with Machiavelli accept deceitful politicians. Those who do not reject them. On the other hand, anyone can imagine situations in which a prince may be asked a question the answer to which could compromise people's lives. A covert operation, for example, might qualify in that sense. Should the prince tell the truth and send the undercover agents to their deaths, or should the prince be permitted to lie? Obviously, this is a real-life question for many current politicians. One could respond by suggesting that there should be no covert operations in which people's lives are in danger. Or, one could respond by suggesting that the prince should never be placed in a situation in which such a question could arise. In contemporary terms that would mean we either dismantle the CIA or we make sure the president never permits journalists to ask questions. Either choice is impractical, to say the least.

We can question the second section in several ways. Machiavelli's primary view is that civil order will be maintained better when a leader is feared by the people. They will not commit acts of violence if they know the leader will retaliate quickly, efficiently, mercilessly. If the leader is loved but not feared, then when the people reach a point of dissatisfaction they will not hesitate to cause confusion and rebellion. Thus, Machiavelli recommends that the prince choose fear. The problem with that is that it benefits mostly the prince by keeping the prince in power even when the people may wish a replacement or a different form of government. Moreover, if you can imagine yourself in a nation in which you fear your leader, you can see one major problem with Machiavelli's views: they are scary. Modern tyrants such as Hitler, Stalin, Franco, Peron, and many more, were feared and merciless and made life in their countries miserable for anyone whose views were even slightly opposed to them. Tyranny has been a scourge of the twentieth century, so we may find it difficult to think well of Machiavelli's conclusion.

KEY DEFINITIONS

For a modern reader the first definition that needs clarification is that of the prince. In Machiavelli's time, Florence was a city-state and its leader was known as a prince. Thus, Machiavelli implies that what he recommends would serve for any leader. In our time we can define the prince as a president, a general, an industrial CEO (chief executive officer), or any other leader of any organization. The key issue for Machiavelli was that the prince should be in a position of authority that was envied by others. When that is the case, holding onto the office is of great importance—at least to the prince.

However, Machiavelli does not broaden his definition to include everyone in authority. He seems only to intend his advice for a leader of state. When working critically with this text you would need to establish the range of definition that you are willing to recognize. Further, it would be wise to use the text as your authority for interpretation. If you could justify applying Machiavelli's principles to other than leaders of a state, it would be wise to point to the passages in the text that would validate your interpretation. You can see from this brief discussion that the problem of definitions in critical writing works in two ways. First, there is the necessity to establish what you think the writer means by a given term or expression. And second, you need to establish clearly what you mean yourself by a given term or expression.

Although the expression is not used explicitly in this passage, the idea that "the ends justify the means" is present here. For example, when Machiavelli suggests that cruelty is more effective in governing than clemency, he admits that it is better to be merciful than cruel—at least in general. However, if one wishes to avoid "rapine" and "disorders," then cruelty must be brought into play. Thus, the ends—a peaceful community—justify the means—a cruel government. Not every student of Machiavelli feels he recommends this pattern. Were you to write a critical discussion of this text, you would need to clarify that issue and establish what you feel is a justifiable definition of the ends and means question.

Assumptions and Biases

Establishing Machiavelli's assumptions and his biases might require an essay in itself. But in planning an essay on this portion of *The Prince* you might want to focus on only one or two. You might begin with his assumption that because the general mass of people is not good the prince must "learn how not to be good." Machiavelli implies that people are generally evil and dangerous and that any good prince would meet with a swift and unhappy end.

Examining this assumption is difficult because we cannot validate Machiavelli's assumption for people of his own time in any direct way. Were we to attempt to examine the assumption from our contemporary standpoint we would still have a difficult time, since who is to say that people today are basically good or basically bad? The very fact that we have difficulty with this point also tells us, however, that one would have difficulty with it in any age and probably in any place. What we might take issue with is Machiavelli's certainty. How does he know? How can he be sure?

Machiavelli's distinction between "an imaginary prince" and the realities of everyday politics is worth examining in detail. Machiavelli tells us that there is a difference between the way we ought to live and the way we really live—by which he means that people ought to be honest and good, but that they are not. He prides himself in dealing with realities rather than an imaginary ideal world. That assumption needs examination. Were we to accept it quickly, we could justify all kinds of horrors in the name of effective government. Freedom and liberty are always at risk in every nation, but they would be especially at risk in the government of Machiavelli's prince. What, then, is the reality that Machiavelli praises? Should we praise it?

Fact and Opinion

The question of political reality will always be one of opinion and never one of fact. Even in face of riot and disorder, which are facts, the question of good and evil cannot be decided in terms of what we opine to be reality. This is true, despite the feelings that most of us have about the realities we think we must deal with in government. Realities such as corruption and dissipation exist, and they are not mere opinions, but to decide politicians are corrupt and dissolute as a group is to state an opinion.

In the second passage, Machiavelli makes a curious distinction which he implies is based on fact and not on opinion. He says that the prince should make himself feared, but that he should avoid hatred. Should the prince need to kill someone "when there is a proper justification," then he should do so. But the prince should never take people's property, "for men forget more easily the death of their father than the loss of their patrimony." Their patrimony is their inheritance, their property, and few people wish to lose it. But is it a fact that most people would more easily forget the death of their father than the loss of their inheritance? Are we expected to share this opinion?

EVIDENCE

As you can see from the preceding discussion, there is relatively little evidence in these selections. There is a good deal of opinion. When the discussion requires evidence, however, Machiavelli depends on historical or literary precedent. He excuses cruelty on the evidence of Cesare Borgia, whose cruelty, he asserts, "united Romagna." He also cites Virgil's *Aeneid*, quoting the character Dido, which quotation is evidence that "new states" are "always full of dangers." The example of Hannibal's "inhuman cruelty" demonstrates its effectiveness in keeping an army "in line." One may go through these passages carefully in search of evidence, but little is to be found. Instead, Machiavelli offers his views and his opinions, which he expects his readers to share.

STYLE

Because this is a translation, we can only comment roughly on Machiavelli's style, which is a very direct, almost entirely unadorned style. He does not use metaphor, nor does he use highly balanced sentences (at least in this translation). Instead, he uses a straightforward approach, stating his views directly. At times he depends on a paired structure for his sentences, as in "Still, a prince should make himself feared in such a way that if he does not gain love, he at any rate avoids hatred." In actuality, that sentence continues with another paired consideration, that of property and women. The pairing of opposites is one of Machiavelli's most obvious stylistic devices, as we have seen in his considerations of goodness and badness and of cruelty and mercy. The strength of such oppositions is that they are clear and obvious. The weakness is that they may not be the only alternatives available. Stylistically, however, this is a powerful approach.

The Structure of the Critical Essay

As with all essays, there is no predefined structure that could act as a matrix for the critical essay. However, most critical essays attempt to do similar things and their structures are often recognizably similar. Some of the characteristics of the critical essay are listed in the following:

TIPS OFTEN USEFUL CONCERNING THE STRUCTURE OF THE CRITICAL ESSAY

1. Establish the question. Usually, the critical essay addresses a perceived question and attempts to answer it for the reader. One obligation is to help the reader perceive it as a question worthy of examination.
2. Account for style. Whether approaching a poem, play, essay, painting, or other work of art, the way in which it is created—its style or formal qualities—will need to be discussed. The style of a painting is, as in any written text, of first importance.
3. Account for effect. All texts affect the reader to some degree. Works of art are designed to have a lasting and powerful effect. Consequently, the writer of a critical essay will need to account for the way the text affects the reader's emotions.
4. Account for ideas. Since ideas are often at the center of important texts, no discussion of style or effect can ignore them. One standard critical question concerns the appropriateness of the form for the ideas.
5. Drawing conclusions. The end of a critical essay will benefit from a clarification of the text's conclusions. What is to be gained from an examination of the text using the methods at hand? What does the reader now understand anew?

To illustrate how these tips may be put into action, we will begin by examining a short story by the German writer Heinrich Böll, who won the Nobel Prize for Literature in 1972. The principles that apply to essays and to poetry will apply to this very brief short story as well.

HEINRICH BÖLL

The Laugher

When someone asks me what business I am in, I am seized with embarrassment: I blush and stammer, I who am otherwise known as a man of poise. I envy people who can say: I am a bricklayer. I envy barbers, bookkeepers, and writers the simplicity of their avowal, for all these professions speak for themselves and need no lengthy explanation, while I am constrained to reply to such questions: I am a laugher. An admission of this kind demands another, since I have to answer the second question: "Is that how you make your living?" truthfully with "Yes." I actually do make a living at my laughing, and a good one too, for my laughing is—commercially speaking—much in demand. I am a good laugher, experienced, no one else laughs as well as I do, no one else has such command of the fine points of my art. For a long time, in order to avoid tiresome explanations, I called myself an actor, but my talents in the field of mime and elocution are so meager that I felt this designation to be too far from the truth: I love the truth, and the truth is: I am a laugher. I am neither a clown nor a comedian. I do not make people gay, I portray gaiety: I laugh like a Roman emperor, or like a sensitive schoolboy, I am as much at home in the laughter of the seventeenth century as in that of the nineteenth, and when occasion demands I laugh my way through the centuries, all classes of society, all categories of age: it is simply a skill which I have acquired, like the skill of being able to repair shoes. In my breast I harbor the laughter of America, the laughter of Africa, white, red, yellow laughter—and for the right fee I let it peal out in accordance with the director's requirements.

I have become indispensable; I laugh on records, I laugh on tape, and television directors treat me with respect. I laugh mournfully, moderately, hysterically; I laugh like a streetcar conductor or like an apprentice in the grocery business; laughter in the morning, laughter in the evening, nocturnal laughter, and the laughter of twilight. In short: wherever and however laughter is required—I do it.

It need hardly be pointed out that a profession of this kind is tiring, especially as I have also—this is my specialty—mastered the art of infectious laughter; this has also made me indispensable to third- and fourth-rate comedians, who are scared—and with good reason—that their audiences will miss their punch lines, so I spend most evenings in nightclubs as a kind of discreet claque, my job being to laugh infectiously during the weaker parts of the program. It has to be carefully timed; my hearty, boisterous laughter must not come too soon, but neither must it come too late, it must come just at the right spot: at the prearranged moment I burst out laughing, the whole audience roars with me, and the joke is saved.

But as for me, I drag myself exhausted to the checkroom, put on my overcoat, happy that I can go off duty at last. At home I usually find telegrams waiting for me: "Urgently require your laughter. Recording Tuesday," and a few hours later I am sitting in an overheated express train bemoaning my fate.

I need scarcely say that when I am off duty or on vacation I have little inclination to laugh: the cowhand is glad when he can forget the cow, the bricklayer when he can forget the mortar, and carpenters usually have doors at home which don't work or drawers which are hard to open. Confectioners like sour pickles, butchers like marzipan, and the baker prefers sausage to bread; bullfighters raise pigeons for a hobby, boxers turn pale when their children have nosebleeds: I find all this quite natural, for I never laugh off duty. I am a very solemn person, and people consider me—perhaps rightly so—a pessimist.

During the first years of our married life, my wife would often say to me: "Do laugh!" but since then she has come to realize that I cannot grant her this wish. I am happy when I am free to relax my tense face muscles, my frayed spirit, in profound solemnity. Indeed, even other people's laughter gets on my nerves, since it reminds me too much of my profession. So our marriage is a quiet, peaceful one, because my wife has also forgotten how to laugh: now and again I catch her smiling, and I smile too. We converse in low tones, for I detest the noise of the nightclubs, the noise that sometimes fills the recording studios. People who do not know me think I am taciturn. Perhaps I am, because I have to open my mouth so often to laugh.

I go through life with an impassive expression, from time to time permitting myself a gentle smile, and I often wonder whether I have ever laughed. I think not. My brothers and sisters have always known me for a serious boy.

So I laugh in many different ways, but my own laughter I have never heard.

Establish the Questions

By questioning a text, you clarify the issues that interest you and that will form the basis of a critical essay. As stated in the beginning of this chapter, in the opening section of a critical essay you need to clarify what the text has said and then point out the questions that the text raises for you. This does not necessarily mean the text itself is questionable; it means only that the text suggests questions that arouse concern. The following is one writer's approach:

> The laugher in Heinrich Böll's story of that name is something of a paradox. He laughs professionally, but why in his private life can he never laugh? He stimulates laughter in others, but cannot stimulate it in himself. Yet, there is a complication to what he says about himself. He claims never to have heard his own laughter, but at the same time he also claims to have mastered infectious laughter and to have mastered subtle qualities of laughter that put him at the top of his profession. How, then, can he not have heard his own laughter? Others have heard it and he knows he can affect them powerfully. The answer seems to be that when he complains of not having heard his own laughter he means he has not heard himself laugh honestly or spontaneously. The distinction between professional laughter and amateur laughter, then, is important to the story.

Account for Style

The Laugher tells his own story in a language designed to accommodate the range of his issues and fears. Because the story was translated, any comments on its style will be somewhat limited. Yet certain qualities of style are revealed through translation, which in this case is good enough to make it worthwhile to examine nuances of structure if not of language.

> The story is tightly controlled by the fact that the Laugher is its narrator. Consequently, we really know very little more about the character than he is willing to reveal. The point of view is restricted and as we read we need to look between the lines to see what we can learn about the Laugher that he may not consciously wish to reveal. Böll's most obvious stylistic device is irony. The central irony in the story is the fact that while the Laugher is a gifted professional, he is also a pessimist. This contradiction reveals itself slowly, but once revealed, the reader realizes that the dead-pan seriousness of the prose has worked to validate the Laugher's assessment of himself.
>
> The straight-ahead style has qualities that make it a curious reflection of the person. For example, the Laugher consciously uses "I" frequently, and often in short, snappy phrases or clauses, such as "I have become indispens-

able; I laugh on records, I laugh on tape, and television directors treat me with respect." The Laugher's egoism is apparent in his emphatic references to himself. The string of short clauses using a similar structure is effective when the Laugher discusses other professions than his: "the cowhand is glad when he can forget the cow, the bricklayer when he can forget the mortar, and carpenters usually have doors at home which don't work or drawers which are had to open." This style is convincing because it is so straightforward.

Account for Effect

In the process of writing a critical discussion of this story, it is important to examine the effect it has on the reader. Böll has written the story in such a way as to present a personality that is in some ways bizarre and intriguing. He makes claims that are unusual and quite sweeping, so it is natural to expect that the reader will respond in complex ways to "The Laugher."

When the Laugher begins his story by explaining how much he envies the bricklayer, the barber, and the bookkeeper because they can each explain their profession so simply, we ourselves begin to smile. The very idea of making a living as a laugher is almost ridiculous, and the solemn way in which the Laugher tells about himself intensifies the humor. The premise of the story is laughable, which in turn fits the content of the story perfectly. We imagine the Laugher as a sort of clown, one whose smile is painted on his face in a permanent grin. Yet, conventional lore tells us that the clown is frequently depressed, often downcast, and sometimes very solemn in real life. That is one of the messages of the story. This laugher is a professional whose work resulted from his temperament on one side, but all the while his profession has given him "little inclination to laugh." Instead, his laughter has "frayed" his spirits and made it difficult for him to do anything more than smile. "Even other people's laughter gets on my nerves." Böll is being funny here, and the solemn pleading of his character makes it even more comical.

Account for Ideas

A story of this kind, because it is so brief, cannot be expected to contain great ideas. Yet Böll is certainly interested in making a point. Accounting for the ideas in a story of this kind may be done in any of several ways. One is by discussing what you think the meaning of the story is; another is by discussing the ideas that seem to be part of the meaning of the story; and a third is by excising a single issue that seems important and developing your own thinking on it.

The Laugher is, like many men, deformed by his work. He detests "the noise in nightclubs, the noise that sometimes fills the recording studios." Yet, these are the places in which he must work. He excuses himself on the grounds that all professionals need relief from their professions. He tries to have us believe that the work has somehow made him what he is: "People who do not know me think I am taciturn. Perhaps I am, because I have to open my mouth so often to laugh." Ironically, it is the action of laughing that has made him seem solemn. Yet, he also tells us that "My brothers and sisters have always known me for a serious boy."

All this brings us to a contradiction that is among modernity's chief questions: is the individual formed by environment or disposition? Is the Laugher unable to hear his own laughter because his professional activity has warped him? Or is it that his temperament, as it was understood by his own siblings, has expressed itself in a powerful manner? If it is the latter, then that would explain why in the midst of laughter and as the instigator of infectious laughter, the Laugher cannot laugh.

Drawing Conclusions

The art of drawing a conclusion from critical commentary is subtle and complex. You can follow any of a number of approaches. You may establish the success or failure of the short story. You may qualify the message that Böll seems to impart, or you may suggest that he has left out something of great importance that needs accounting for. Finally, you may point to the ultimate meaning of the story and draw together the lines of thought that lead toward that meaning.

Böll has produced a story that at first resembles straight-faced humor in the style of the burlesque comedians of the early years of the century. Even today, stand up comics will affect a droll seriousness, never breaking a smile as they tell hilarious stories. But the Laugher is not a comedian in the narrow sense of the word. He makes people laugh, as comedians will do, but he does it by being infectious, by acting as a catalyst not to humor but to laughter. The curious thing about the story is that while the entire idea of a professional Laugher seems preposterous when one begins reading, after a while it becomes not only plausible, but almost acceptable.

The idea that one's work can distort one's point of view emerges slowly from a reading of the story. If the Laugher is correct in his analysis of himself, then each of us needs to examine very carefully the work we choose to do. If, on the other hand, one's attitudes and personality are determined by one's inborn temperament, then there is little we can do to avoid whatever our fate in the workplace may be. The Laugher may not have chosen his profession; his profession may have chosen him.

This interpretation also implies an evaluation of Böll's story. The interpretation has pointed to certain strong qualities of the story, the way its style mirrors its content, the ways in which the use of irony enriches the experience of reading, and the way in which the tension between temperament and environment as forces shaping personality merge effectively in one short piece of fiction. Rather than coming out and saying this is a successful story, the writer implies through careful critical interpretation that it succeeds. The closeness of the writer's examination of the text demonstrates that the story is worthwhile and substantial, that it can bear up under the examination, and that it rewards close critical thinking.

The critical essay is useful in many situations. Letters to the Editor of major newspapers often deal critically with issues and events, especially those that have been reported in the newspaper. The effectiveness of such letters will depend on their analysis of the situation and their ability to develop the right questions. Popular criticism, such as the reviews of films and plays that appear in magazines and newspapers, focuses often on performances and specific production details, but even it ultimately deals with the ideas presented by the text and evaluates the success or failure of the production. Formal criticism accounts for many of these issues, and goes further to construct a full interpretation and evaluation of a text as a way of making a personal statement about it. The critical essay can be a creative piece of work to complement the text upon which it operates. Just as a personal essay will center on a moment in time in order to interpret its significance in one's own life, the critical essay serves to interpret a text in a manner that produces insight into the mind and heart of the critic. Like any other essay, the critical essay is an instrument of discovery.

Appendix:

Modern Research Methods

Most writers back their material with research, whether conducted in the field in terms of personal interviews, personal experiences, and memories, or whether developed in libraries and with online services. The more you know, the better you write. Even essays that avoid extensive citations are well researched. The amount of annotation you provide will be a matter of personal style and, in the case of academic essays, a matter of convention. Essays for academic journals have careful annotations. Essays for popular publications include references but rarely offer citations. Today, the resources of the writer are immense, and the opportunities for research make writing in some ways convenient, but in some ways challenging. Today the greatest challenge is in limiting the stunning amount of material a routine search will produce. The following is a brief review of current search methods with suggestions for getting the most out of your efforts at finding information.

Where to Begin

Research begins at home. Most research essays are products of investigation, which means moving from place to place talking with people whose opinions and information may be relevant to the subject at hand. Being on the spot with a tape recorder, camera, or notebook can be very exciting and produce important information. The reader is always interested in knowing about something that the writer has had "hands-on" experience with, and that experience usually shows up in the information acquired by talking with witnesses or people who took part in important events.

Personal Interviews

Interviews have authoritative quality when they come from someone with special knowledge or with a special relationship to your subject. The more authoritative and informed your sources are, the more valuable your interviews will be. By using first-hand investigation, you will produce an essay that no one else can.

Libraries

The library is the place to begin work on most research projects. Books, journals, articles, and other resources in your library can illuminate your subject. High quality publishers—especially University presses—pay experts to read manuscripts and suggest improvements, corrections, and revisions in advance of publication. *Book Review Digest* will provide excerpts from or citations to reviews that can verify the quality of the books.

Your library will have a wide range of journals in specialized fields for you to choose from. More and more journals are now online as well. If you have your own computer account at your university, you may get *The Directory of Electronic Journals and Related Resources* by sending these commands to LISTSERV@ACADVM1.uottawa.ca:

- GET EJOURNL1 DIRECTRY
- GET EJOURNL2 DIRECTRY

If you do not have an account, you may search through gopher or use the web browser at the library. Your library may have back issues as well as current issues of the journals. If you are unfamiliar with web browsers, your library will either assist you or provide written instructions that will help you learn how to use them.

Special Collections

A professional researcher knows that some libraries have exceptional collections of materials that are unavailable elsewhere. For instance, some libraries have unpublished correspondence and papers of people prominent in politics, literature, or science. Libraries will specialize in fields such as Slavic studies, Jewish studies, or religious literature. Some libraries specialize in holdings of obscure literary journals of the twentieth century; African-American, Irish-American, or Italian-American studies; or other areas of special interest. Your college catalog will tell you about your own library's special collections. If your library has a range of special collections, something among those collections may be perfect for a research project. If you are writing about someone well known, use a search engine on the Internet (see below) to locate special collections. Some of them may be near where you live.

Interlibrary Loan

The cost of periodicals is such that many libraries hold a critical number, then rely on interlibrary loan for supplementary materials. Your library will have a department responsible for interlibrary loan, and in some locations the exchange of journals, periodicals, and books will be fairly speedy. However, the key to using the interlibrary loan is planning ahead. You cannot expect your library to secure materials it does not possess unless you provide adequate lead time.

The Reference Collection

A reference librarian is probably your best source of information when you begin a research project. The reference collection does not circulate. It consists of general and specialized encyclopedias, dictionaries, specialized bibliographies, biographies of important people in a wide variety of fields, and various reference texts in many different fields (see box). There will also be a number of electronic resources in every reference collection.

BASIC PRINT REFERENCE SOURCES

Dictionaries
The Oxford English Dictionary
Webster's Third New International Dictionary of the English Language
Encyclopedias
The New Encyclopedia Britannica 15th edition (1997)
Encyclopedia Britannica 11th edition (1910)
Encyclopedia Americana
Biographies
Dictionary of American Biography

Dictionary of National Biography (British)
Special Indexes
New York Times Index
The Reader's Advisor
The Book Review Digest
Guides to Periodicals
Reader's Guide to Periodical Literature
Ulrich's International Periodicals
Art Index
Business Periodicals Index

These resources at best will help you define your subject and provide you with useful bibliography. Restrict your subject as early as possible. You cannot research the history of World War II in five or six weeks, but you can research the details of the air drop at Arnheim during the Battle of the Bulge. The same is true of the American Civil War: it is realistic to research the battle of Gettysburg, but not the entire war. Of course, it is also probably more realistic to research a major battle like Gettysburg and limit yourself to the events of a single episode, such as Pickett's Charge, which was thought to be the turning point of that battle.

Electronic Searches

Many college libraries have removed their card catalogs in favor of an online catalog that gives instant access to books by their author, title, or subject (or keyword). Most online catalogs permit you to search by two or more terms when you approach the problem through the subject. For example, you may search "Gettysburg and Pickett" for books that treat the subject of Pickett's Charge at the battle of Gettysburg. The resultant search will not be complete, but it will be a starting point. Wherever you find a book on the shelf resulting from that search, you may find another on the shelves next to and near that book. It pays to look nearby, since books on the same subject are usually housed together. The online catalog of your library is the best place to begin an electronic search if only because you will know immediately whether your library holds material that you can use. In many libraries you will also be informed whether an item your library holds has been checked out.

SPECIAL ONLINE RESOURCES

Your library may have access to commercial online resources (see box) that will provide you with bibliography and article printouts.

SPECIAL ONLINE RESOURCES

DIALOG (a vendor of general information)
Agricola (Dept. of Agriculture)
America History and Life
Congressional Record
Government Printing Office
Dow Jones News Retrieval Service
Lexis/Nexis (legal, business, and general publications)
National Newspaper Index
Current Index to Nursing and Allied Health
Religion Index
SCISEARCH (scientific material)
SOCIAL SCISEARCH (social sciences)
UPI News
U.S. Political Science Documents
Washington Press Text Full Text
World Affairs Report
Zoological Record

As you can see from this partial list, a great many electronic online data bases exist to serve those who need to do research. These resources cost money, and your library may not subscribe to all of them. But each data base you access will provide you with an amazing amount of information in a very short space of time. Indeed, the problem today is that they provide too much information, and one of your jobs is to navigate so as to select that which is best and most useful. Lilian Biermann Wehmeyer, author of *The Educator's Information Highway*, suggests that you keep a log of your searches so that you can show a reference librarian where you searched, what your keywords were, and what your results are. Such a log could provide very useful information to anyone trying to help you.

CD-ROM ONLINE DATA BASES

Many libraries subscribe to CD-ROM (Compact Disk-Read Only Memory) services that are updated on a regular basis. They often duplicate the same online services mentioned above, but their convenience on CD-ROM is such that libraries make them available on a self-serve basis. Such services are expensive to maintain, but students are not charged for using them. The most important to consult are listed in the box. In the first years of availability, these sources were exceptionally useful because a search would return a reasonable amount of bibliographic sources in an instant.

CD-ROM ONLINE DATABASES

Psychlit
Literature in psychology
ERIC
Education
Infotrac
Indexes a wide range of periodicals
PAIS Public Affairs Information Service
Indexes periodicals, books, government
MLA International Bibliography
Journal articles and books since 1981
Humanities Index
Periodical articles since 1984
Historical Abstracts
History 1450 to present

Today, however, the completeness of these resources has grown so that you are likely to be told about so many books, articles, and references that you will hardly know where to begin. For obvious reasons, you will find yourself encouraged by this process to focus your research in more and more exacting fashion. One important concern is availability. Thirty-five citations will not help you if you cannot get access to more than one of them. Take your online search list and find out which materials are in your library or a neighboring library. Find out which can be obtained through interlibrary loan. That process will help weed out a huge list of citations.

A Lexis-Nexis Electronic Search Sample

Lexis-Nexis can provide you the full text of newspapers, magazines, wire services, broadcast transcripts, government documents, and other sources on your subject. To use the Lexis-Nexis service, request assistance from your librarian and determine the procedure for accessing the service. The computer screens of the service will contain information on the proper procedure for using it at your location. Follow the instructions on the screen for limiting your search by the keywords of your choice. Generally, you will be asked whether you wish to print out the material you have found or to save it. Be sure that you follow the instructions at your location concerning the number of pages you can print out. If you wish to save the material for your use later, bring a three and one-half inch disk with you and save your search with names such as: "a:search1."

Once you have accessed the Lexis-Nexis service you will see a page that offers you a wide range of choices. The first three are news—current, archived, and general:

```
CURNWS 1 Last 2 Years

ARCNWS 1 Beyond 2 years

ALLNWS 1 All News Files
```

The following is a brief excerpt from a search done on CURNWS using "Brady Law" as the keywords. The Brady Law concerns legislation limiting access to handguns. Here are the first items that it found. Any one of these could be called up in its entirety and be read, saved, or printed out.

```
LEVEL 1 - 1543 STORIES

1. U.S. Newswire, December 1, 1994, NATIONAL DESK,
894 words, Justice Department Says All States to
Receive Crime Bill Money to Automate Criminal
History Records, Stu Smith with the U. S.
Department of Justice Office of Justice Programs,
202-307-0784, or 301-983-9354 (after hours),
WASHINGTON, Dec. 1

2. THE DALLAS MORNING NEWS, November 27, 1994,
Sunday, HOME FINAL EDITION, NEWS; Pg. 1A, 1669
words, Paying with pain; States, cities chafe
under unfunded mandates, David Jackson, Staff
Writer of the Dallas Morning News
```

```
3. St. Louis Post-Dispatch, November 25, 1994,
Friday FIVE STAR Edition, EDITORIAL; Pg. 7B, 734
words, CLINTON IS TARGET OF THE ALIENATED, Mary
McGrory Copyright Universal Press Syndicate,
WASHINGTON

4. The MacNeil/Lehrer NewsHour, November 24, 1994,
Thursday, Transcript #5105, 9849 words, House
Divided; Gun Laws; Open Country
```

This represents only a fraction of the entries called up in response to the query, but it demonstrates the value of such an electronic search. First, the articles can be retrieved in their entirety; second, they are absolutely up to date (they were up to date when this search was done); and third, they come from a wide geographic distribution. Most of these entries are from newspapers, but later in the search appear magazine articles and material from other forms of media.

USING THE INTERNET AND THE WORLD WIDE WEB

The World Wide Web offers immense resources to any researcher. The Internet, on which the World Wide Web functions, connects universities, research foundations, businesses, publishers, and the commercial electronic services such as America Online, Compuserve, Prodigy, Genie, Delphi, and more to come. The web must be accessed through your college computer system (mainframe or LAN [Local Area Network]) or through a commercial service that connects you directly from your own computer at your own expense. Once you have connected to the Internet and the World Wide Web, you navigate using a web browser. The most common are Netscape Navigator, Microsoft Explorer, and Mosaic. These permit you to print out and download graphics and print. Lynx is a print-only browser, but it is very useful if your project does not require graphics. Your local online provider or your library will have one or more of these services available.

The web browser offers you a number of choices at each screen. The choices attempt to route you to areas of your interest. Therefore, you need to decide what area your subject belongs in, for example, business, education, science. Once you move from one screen to the next, your choices become more and more specific. When you reach the screen pertaining to your subject, you can download documents, graphics, books, articles, software, and more pertaining to your subject. The browser permits you to move forward easily or to back up to a previous screen, so you cannot get lost. However, it is a good idea to jot down your path so that you can quickly return to the site in which you find your best material.

Web browsers also connect you to high-speed search engines. They can retrieve thousands of documents or links for many subjects. The most popular search engines are Alta Vista (http://altavista.digital.com), Yahoo! (http://www.yahoo.com), Lycos (http://www.lycos.com), HotBot (http://www.HotBot.com), Excite (http://excite.com), Infoseek Guide (http://guide.infoseek.com), Open Text (http://www.opentext.com), Magellan (http://www.mckinley.com), Savvy Search (http://guaraldi.cs.colostate.edu:2000) and WebCrawler (http://webcrawler.com). Each of these search engines is different in approach and in its focus. Therefore it is useful to read the "Help" guide that is available online with each search engine. Different search engines will often retrieve different sites, so it helps to use more than one if they are available to you. The Yahoo! search that is given as an example actually uses Alta Vista to do its searching. Yahoo! offers a slightly different approach from that of Alta Vista in part by listing specific general categories that can sometimes speed a search.

Some of the material you will find on the web will be very large, and downloading it to your computer will take a good long time. Therefore, plan carefully when to use the World Wide Web. Ask your librarian or someone in your computer center the best time to get files from the web. Many of the files are compressed and will need uncompression software such as PKunzip. Check with your computer center or with someone experienced with the software.

Since the World Wide Web is in its infancy, before you begin to use it, be sure to find a reference book, magazine, or library handout that will help you (some suggestions appear at the end of this discussion). Once having begun, however, you will find that the resources are surprising and that the web is fun to use. If enough people are interested in your subject, you may discover a newsgroup on Usenet available for taking part in a discussion of your subject. Some search engines include Usenet as an option. For help accessing Usenet, see your librarian.

Using Yahoo! and Alta Vista Search Engines

The following is a brief excerpt from a search on the World Wide Web. With the web, you click your mouse button on "hyperlink" keywords. Hyperlink means a connection to a distant file with more information. The hyperlink words appear in color on your screen (usually blue). Each links you to another screen until you find the document or documents you need. This search was conducted by connecting to the web browser, then choosing the Yahoo! List, a popular organizing list that establishes a hierarchy of subjects. Yahoo! uses Alta Vista, Digital company's search engine. Here is the first Yahoo! screen:

options

Yellow Pages - People Search - Maps - Classifieds - News - Stock Quotes - Sports Scores

☐ **Arts and Humanities**
Architecture, Photography, Literature...

☐ **Business and Economy** [Xtra!]
Companies, Investing, Employment...

☐ **Computers and Internet** [Xtra!]
Internet, WWW, Software, Multimedia...

☐ **Education**
Universities, K-12, College Entrance...

☐ **Entertainment** [Xtra!]
Cool Links, Movies, Music, Humor...

☐ **Government**
Military, Politics [Xtra!], Law, Taxes...

☐ **Health** [Xtra!]
Medicine, Drugs, Diseases, Fitness...

☐ **News and Media** [Xtra!]
Current Events, Magazines, TV, Newspapers...

☐ **Recreation and Sports** [Xtra!]
Sports, Games, Travel, Autos, Outdoors...

☐ **Reference**
Libraries, Dictionaries, Phone Numbers...

☐ **Regional**
Countries, Regions, U.S. States...

☐ **Science**
CS, Biology, Astronomy, Engineering...

☐ **Social Science**
Anthropology, Sociology, Economics...

☐ **Society and Culture**
People, Environment, Religion...

My Yahoo! - Yahooligans! for Kids - Beatrice's Web Guide - Yahoo! Internet Life
Weekly Picks - Today's Web Events - Chat - Weather Forecasts
Random Yahoo! Link - Yahoo! Shop

National Yahoos **Australia & N.Z.** - Canada - France - Germany - Japan - **Korea** - U.K. & Ireland
Yahoo! Metros Atlanta - Austin - Boston - Chicago - Dallas / Fort Worth - Los Angeles
Get Local Miami - Minneapolis / St. Paul - New York - S.F. Bay - Seattle - Wash D.C.

How to Include Your Site - Company Information - Contributors - Yahoo! to Go

Because the search was interested in gun control and the Brady Bill, the next screen searched "Gun Control Brady Bill" and retrieved a link to Primary Sources:

Search for documents in

Help . Preferences . New Search . Advanced Search

2 documents match your query.

1. **Primary Sources**
   Primary Sources: Statutes. Federal Cases. Resources for Specific Areas of Law Federal Legislative Info. Legislative History. Historical Documents....
   http://www.mdla.org/fed-law.htm - size 8K - 6-Mar-96 - English
   http://www.diamond-link.com/link/fed-law.htm - size 8K - 17-Oct-95 - English

Tip: The **word count**, located below the results, indicates how many times a term appears in the entire Web. Use it as a spelling or usage checker: type in both spellings for a word, and see which one wins.

Word count: Gun Control Brady Bill: 2

Our Network | Add/Remove URL | Feedback | Help
Advertising Info | About AltaVista | Jobs | Text-Only

Digital Equipment Corporation
Disclaimer | Privacy Statement

As it turned out, both the listings on this screen were for the same link, which appears in the following screens:

Primary Sources:

Statutes • Federal Cases • Resources for Specific Areas of Law
Federal Legislative Info • Legislative History • Historical Documents

---

Statutes

- U.S. Constitution
- U.S. Code The general and permanent laws of the United States.

    - U.S. Code (most up to date) (not searchable)
    - U.S. Code (January 4, 1993) (searchable only within individual titles; includes a Table of Popular Names for Acts of Congress)
    - U.S. Code (January 2, 1992) (searchable) (experimental)
    - U.S. Code (January 2, 1991) (each title is a single file)
    - recently adopted statutes (summaries)
- Code of Federal Regulations List of sites with CFR text
    - CFR An experimental WWW site offering full text search of CFR
    - Federal Register
    - State Legal Resources A compendium put together by Congress of state laws on the Internet
    - Statutes

- **Administrative**
    - Federal Court U.S. Federal Court's Home Page - maintained by the Administrative Office of the U.S. Courts on behalf of the U.S. Courts
    - Federal Court Locator "The Home Page for the Federal Courts on the Internet" - Maintained by The Villanova Center for Information Law and Policy
- **United States Supreme Court**
    - Justices of the Supreme Court
    - Supreme Court Decisions searchable by topic or key word, courtesy of Project Hermes and the Legal Information Institute at Cornell Law School.
    - Supreme Court Search - Search 5 years of Supreme Court Decisions.
- **United States Circuit Courts of Appeal**
    - 3rd Circuit 1994 & 1995 Decisions - search capabilities by key word and party to be added in the near future.
    - 4th Circuit 1995 Decisions - searchable by key word and an index by party. Geographic jurisdiction: Maryland, North Carolina, South Carolina, Virginia, and West Virginia
    - 5th Circuit 1992-1995 Decisions - searchable by full text, docket number, party

- 6th Circuit 1995 Decisions - searchable by keyword and party - Geographic jurisdiction: Kentucky, Michigan, Ohio, and Tennessee
- 9th Circuit 1995 Decisions - very new site, under construction
- 11th Circuit 1994 & 1995 Decisions - alphabetical listing, searchable by keyword
- 11th Circuit 1995 Decisions

Resources for Specific Areas of Law

- Copyright: U.S. Copyright Acts
- Consumer Law: Fair Credit Reporting Act
- Disability Law: Americans with Disabilities Act
- Freedom of Information Act Citizens Guide to Using FOIA
- Gun Control: Brady Bill
- Privacy: Privacy Act of 1974
- Trade: EEC: Maastricht Treaty
- Tade: NAFTA

Federal Legislative Information

- House of Representatives World Wide Web Site Lots of general information about the House. Has some good resources for bill tracking: committee and floor schedules.
- Thomas Full text of all versions of all House and Senate bills, the Congressional Record, and other resources from the Library of Congress.
- HIS's Legislation List General list of legislation gathred by House of Representatives Information Services

---

Legislative History

- Congressional Record (excerpts)
- Reports of the House and Senate
- Rules of the House and Senate

Historical Documents

- Declaration of Independence
- Declaration of Independence
  - another copy
  - another copy
  - another copy
  - Articles of Confederation
  - Federalist Papers Nicely put together site offering the full text of the Federalist Papers
  - Jefferson, Works of Thomas
  - Paine, Works of Thomas
  - Several collections of historical legal and political documents from
  - The University of California Santa Barbara
  - The University of Minnesota
  - Queens, New York Library
  - Presidential documents

To Home AccessPage

Last Updated: 16 October 1995

This AccessPage was developed by Diamond Link Business Solutions Group Diamond Link Groups provide Internet Business Solutions and Training Find out more about Diamond Link Group at pberge@diamond-link.com

Copyright © 1995 Peter H. Berge & Diamond Link Group, Inc.

Primary Sources permits you to download U.S. codes and laws so that you can read them in detail. It offers many other documents as well, so it can stand as a useful resource for anyone researching important documents in U.S. law. By searching through U.S. code, you can retrieve the specific language of the Brady Bill. What follows is only a small part of one of the sections:

```
TITLE XI-FIREARMS - Sections 110101-110106
TITLE XI-FIREARMS - Sections 110101-11010
  Subtitle A-Assault Weapons
  SEC. 110101. SHORT TITLE.
```

```
  This subtitle may be cited as the "Public Safety
and Recreational Firearms Use Protection Act".
  SEC. 110102. RESTRICTION ON MANUFACTURE,
TRANSFER, AND POSSESSION OF CERTAIN SEMIAUTOMATIC
ASSAULT WEAPONS.
  (a) Restriction .-Section 922 of title 18,
United States Code, is amended by adding at the
end the following new subsection:
  "(v)(1) It shall be unlawful for a person to
manufacture, transfer, or possess a semiautomatic
assault weapon.
  "(2) Paragraph (1) shall not apply to the
possession or transfer of any semiautomatic
assault weapon otherwise lawfully possessed under
Federal law on the date of the enactment of this
subsection.
  "(3) Paragraph (1) shall not apply to-
  "(A) any of the firearms, or replicas or
duplicates of the firearms, specified in Appendix
A to this section, as such firearms were
manufactured on October 1, 1993;
  "(B) any firearm that-
  "(i) is manually operated by bolt, pump, lever,
or slide action;
  "(ii) has been rendered permanently inoperable;
or
  "(iii) is an antique firearm;
  "(C) any semiautomatic rifle that cannot accept
a detachable magazine that holds more than 5
rounds of ammunition; or
  "(D) any semiautomatic shotgun that cannot hold
more than 5 rounds of ammunition in a fixed or
detachable magazine.
```

This sample is purposely abbreviated, since the information downloaded from this search filled many pages. The Internet is remarkable for the amount of material it provides rapidly. Because every journey on the web is a discovery, one must plan enough time not to rush things. You will find more than you thought was there, and you may change your research plans in light of what you discover. Having the time to make such changes is of great importance. Start your web search early.

You must be prepared for surprises because the Internet changes every day. New search engines appear regularly, and some links are unavailable. The fact that you get a good return on your search will not necessarily mean you will get good information. For that reason it is wise to consult printed directories of reliable Internet resources. Directories such as *The Internet Yellow Pages*, 3rd ed., edited by Hurley Hahn (New York: Osborne McGraw-Hill: 1996) and books such as David Clark's *Student's Guide to the Internet* (Indianapolis: Alpha Books of Prentice-Hall Macmillan, 1995) and Andrew Harnack and Eugene Kleppinger's *Online! A Reference Guide to Using Internet Sources* (New York: St. Martin's Press, 1997) can be indispensable.

Print Resources

Online sources and CD-ROMs have a special cachet because they are quick and easy to use. However, other important print resources should be added to your repertoire when you begin research. *The CQ Researcher*, the *Congressional Quarterly*, published weekly, focuses each issue on a single important topic, such as child sexual abuse, violence against women, or gay rights. Each issue gives a definition and clarification of the topic, a history of important decisions regarding the topic, several articles on the topic from divergent points of view, a debate on the issue, and a current bibliography of important books and articles. It is an excellent place to begin researching any current issue.

Facts on File summarizes current news events and supplies a great many facts about people and events. It has a useful index and covers popular entertainment as well as international news. Its obituaries are useful thumbnail biographies. Some other important print resources are listed in the box.

PRINT RESOURCES

The Black Resource Guide
Guide to Scholarly Journals in Black Studies
Index to Black Periodicals

Latin American and Carribean: A Directory of Resources
Latin American Studies: A Basic Guide to Sources
Index to International Statistics
World Tables
U.N. Demographic Yearbook
Editorials on File
Keesings Record of World Events
Statistical Abstracts of the United States
Biography Index

How Much to Use

No one can tell you in advance how much of your material you have to use in a specific essay. However, several problems in writing research essays are common, and ought to be avoided. One extreme is to refer to every item you have uncovered. The other extreme is to refer to none. The fact that essays in magazines with wide readership have few if any notes or citations tells us simply that audiences are not generally interested in the details. They want to think the writer is authoritative, but they do not want to be bothered with interruptions of the text or see the underpinnings of the work.

Providing citations makes the researcher responsible, one who has mastered the materials that support careful conclusions. The reader should have the chance to check up on your work, but be sure to distill the material until it is refined, and give it to the reader sparingly. In an academic course, full citation is essential. When writing an article for a newspaper, notes are inappropriate.

Choosing an Interesting Research Subject

Your next research essay will probably be for a college course. Your first job is to research something that you know about and will find interesting. This is not to say that looking for totally fresh subjects is not a good idea. It is, but only if you have a fresh subject that will encourage you to do your best. For example, if you plan to be a lawyer and you are writing a paper in a course that covers American history of the Civil War period, you would probably learn a great deal by researching the trial of John Wilkes Booth and the conspirators who assassinated President Lincoln.

Conducting a Search of the Online Catalog

Here, for example, is the result of a brief search of a college library online catalog for information about John Wilkes Booth:

SEARCH REQUEST: S=BOOTH, JOHN WILKES UCAT—UCONN CATALOG

SEARCH RESULTS: 16 ENTRIES FOUND SUBJECT INDEX

BOOTH, JOHN WILKES 1838-1865

1 ASSASSIN ON STAGE BRUTUS HAMLET AND THE DEAT <1991>

2 ASSASSINATION <1979>

3 ASSASSINATION OF PRESIDENT LINCOLN AND THE T <1954>

4 BOOTH <1982>

5 GREAT AMERICAN MYTH <1940>

6 LIFE CRIME AND CAPTURE OF JOHN WILKES BOOTH <1865>

7 LINCOLN MURDER CONSPIRACIES BEING AN ACCOUNT <1983>

8 LUST FOR FAME THE STAGE CAREER OFJOHN WILKE <1982>

9 MYTHS AFTER LINCOLN <1941>

10 TRUE HISTORY OF THE ASSASSINATION OF ABRAHAM <1975>

11 WILKES BOOTH CAME TO WASHINGTON <1976>
BOOTH, JOHN WILKES 1838-1865--DRAMA

12 GETTYSBURG MANTUA ACOMA <1930>

13 MADAME SURRATT A DRAMA IN FIVE ACTS <1968>
microcard

14 MADAME SURRATT A DRAMA IN FIVE ACTS <1970>
microcard
BOOTH, JOHN WILKES 1838-1865--FAMILY

15 AMERICAN GOTHIC THE STORY OF AMERICAS LEGEND
<1992>
BOOTH, JOHN WILKES 1838-1865--FICTION

16 JUDGES OF THE SECRET COURT <1961>

These sixteen entries are all abbreviations for the fuller citation in the catalog, which you find by typing in the number of the entry. Here is one of the above entries as it appears in expanded form:

SEARCH REQUEST: S=BOOTH, JOHN WILKES UCAT–UCONN CATALOG

BOOK - Record 7 of 16 Entries Found Brief View

Author: Hanchett, William, 1922-

Title: The Lincoln murder conspiracies: being an account of the hatred felt by many Americans for President Abraham Lincoln during the Civil War and the first complete examination and refutation of the many theories, hypotheses, and speculations put forward since 1865 concerning those presumed to have aided, abetted, controlled, or directed the murderous act of John Wilkes Booth in Ford's Theater the night of April 14 / William Hanchett.

```
Publisher: Urbana: University of Illinois Press, -
           1983

Subjects:  Lincoln, Abraham, 1809-1865—
           Assassination. Booth, John Wilkes,
           1838-1865. United States—Politics and
           government—Civil War, 1861-1865.
```

Such an entry will tell you whether the book is likely to be of use to you. By examining each of the sixteen items discovered in the catalog, you can hope to have access to a fully rounded discussion of events. A similar search on INFOTRAC—limited to articles dated from 1991 on—produced the following:

```
Database: Expanded Academic Index

Subject: booth, john wilkes

Library: Homer Babbidge Library
```

```
The Booth obsession. (John Wilkes Booth) (Cover
Story) Gene Smith.

 American Heritage, Sept1992 v43 n5
p104(14).Mag.Coll.:65h2511

 —Abstract Available—

 John Wilkes Booth's other victim. (William
Withers Jr.) Richard

 Sloan. American Heritage, Feb-March 1991 v42 n1
p114(3)
```

Each of these articles was in the bound section for periodicals and each provided important information on Booth and his motivations. If you conducted the search in the Expanded Academic Index Backfile, you would have covered the period from 1980 to 1990, with numerous other articles that would help your research. From this point, you will discover that the bibliographies in the articles and books you consult will provide you with many more leads.

Storage and Recovery: Filing Cards and Notesheets

You have probably developed strategies for collecting, storing, and eventually recovering your research materials, but it is worthwhile to consider two methods used by contemporary researchers. First, the time-honored method of using filing cards, either three-by-five or five-by-seven inches, convenient primarily because they can be alphabetized in the early stages of your reading and can be organized in the order in which you intend to use them in the later stages.

The negative side to the card method is that you can place a very limited amount of information on such a small card. Further, if you write down important passages you intend to quote later, you run the risk of making a mistake in the quotation when you transfer it to your own essay. On the other hand, the small size of the cards means you are more likely to avoid overdoing any one source by quoting too much.

A second method involves using notesheets, ordinary typescript pages. The first spaces of the notesheets will have the bibliographic information that will go into your "Works Cited" page (see the discussion below), and the body of the notesheet will have your observations and analyses in note form, as well as the passages that you quote directly from your sources. Always place every quotation from your sources in quotation marks and begin every quotation with the number of the page from which it comes.

This method works best if you enter the information in a computer and save it to disk: you can move the material you have quoted into the appropriate place in the final essay without having to retype it and risk getting it wrong. Typing accurately in the first place, then, is very important. Even if you rely only on handwriting or typing, the larger size of the notesheet should make copying more accurate.

If you use the computer to keep your notes, one important suggestion is that you make a separate directory for the essay you are writing. Call it, say, "Civilwar.997," with the numbers indicating the date, September 1997. Then, in this directory name the essay you are writing as "Draft1" for the first draft, "Draft2" for the second draft, and "Final" for the last draft. In the same directory as your drafts, keep all your research notes, however long or short, in separate files named for each of the authors: Hanchett, Smith, Sloan. Be sure to back up the entire directory on a floppy disk, thus preventing the machine from eating your research.

Here are two samples of keeping records as you do your research:

Three-by-five inch card:

> Brittain, Vera. *Testament of Youth.* London: Gollancz, 1933
>
> Brittain talks about the first Christmas she spent with her mother during the first World War. She sensed a real shock that surprised her when she realized the long-awaited war had actually come.
>
> 113, "That first wartime Christmas seemed a strange and chilling experience to us who had always been accustomed to the exuberant house-decorating and present-giving of the prosperous pre-war years."

Notesheet:

Brittain, Vera. *Testament of Youth.* London: Gollancz, 1933.

(put your name here because these are your notes):

Brittain seems not to have realized the seriousness of the war at first. She talks about visiting Oxford, where she went to college, and about going into London to go Christmas shopping. Things seemed normal for a long time, but she also seemed nervous.

113. "That first wartime Christmas seemed a strange and chilling experience to us who had always been accustomed to the exuberant house-decorating and present-giving of the prosperous pre-war years.

'A good many people,' I observed, 'have

```
decided that they are both too poor and too
miserable to remember their friends, particularly
the rich people who have no one at all in any
danger. The poorer ones, and those who are in
anxiety about something or other, have all made an
effort to do the same as usual. At St. John's. . .
we had the inevitable sermon dwelling on the
obvious incongruity of celebrating the birth of
the Prince of Peace while the world was at war.'"
```

(your name here): She seems to be quoting from a diary that she kept during this period.

In addition to keeping notes on cards or notesheets, you will also want to use the photocopier to copy articles or pages from books that you feel are central to your research. Be certain to write the full name of the author, the full title of the book, the publisher, and the place and date of publication on the photocopy itself.

Richard Worsnop, "Gun Control"

A typically researched essay by Richard Worsnop, "Gun Control: The Issues," appeared in the June 10, 1994, issue of *CQ Researcher.* It is reprinted here. Worsnop made every effort to integrate his research naturally into his own writing. He also worked hard to engage the attention of the reader by being concrete and specific at the very first. Worsnop quickly brings us up to date in the argument over gun control, one of the most volatile of current topics. It is inherently interesting, is important to our culture, and involves us all.

> For gun control advocates, the past six months have seen one dream come true and another move close to realization. First came the passage last November of the Brady law, which requires a five-day waiting period for handgun purchases. Then, on May 5, the House joined the Senate in approving legislation banning 19 assault weapons linked to violent crime. The proposed ban is expected to become part of the omnibus crime bill that Congress will vote on this summer.
>
> Gun control proponents feel confident the tide of opinion is rolling their way. "The lesson of the Brady law and the assault weapons ban is that the American public wants more gun laws, not fewer," says Susan Whitmore, communications director for Handgun Control, Inc., the largest group promoting firearms regulation.

> Groups opposing gun control reject Whitmore's appraisal. John M. Snyder, public affairs director of the Citizens Committee for the Right to Keep and Bear Arms, predicts gun owners will mobilize this fall to trigger a "major change in the makeup of Congress," unseating members "who heretofore have been foursquare on the pro-firearms side of the issue and then switched and voted the wrong way."

Worsnop writes a plain style, with few images or figures of speech—the use of the verb *trigger* in the last paragraph, an exception, is an admissible pun. He clarifies two instances, the Brady Bill and the crime bill; then he clarifies two positions, one in favor of gun control and one opposed. Careful not to take explicit sides in the debate, Worsnop balances the views of each group one after the other. The charts that accompany the article are factual, and you can make of them what you will. The statistics are also factual, but they may need interpretation.

Worsnop cites people in interviews and provides numbered endnotes referring to important published material on gun control. If you were concerned with gun control and wanted to do your own research, the notes provide important information. This essay appeared in an issue of *CQ Researcher* devoted entirely to the question of gun control, with a bibliography of articles, books, and government documents on that subject.

RICHARD L. WORSNOP

Gun Control

THE ISSUES

For gun control advocates, the past six months have seen one dream come true and another move close to realization. First came the passage last November of the Brady law, which requires a five-day waiting period for handgun purchases. Then, on May 5, the House joined the Senate in approving legislation banning 19 assault weapons linked to violent crime. The proposed ban is expected to become part of the omnibus crime bill that Congress will vote on this summer.

Gun control proponents feel confident the tide of opinion is rolling their way. (*See poll, p. 508.*) "The lesson of the Brady law and the assault weapons ban is that the American public wants more gun laws, not fewer," says Susan Whitmore, communications director for Handgun Control Inc., the largest group promoting firearms regulation.*

Groups opposing gun control reject Whitmore's appraisal. John M. Snyder, public affairs director of the Citizens Committee for the Right to Keep and Bear Arms, predicts gun owners will mobilize this fall to trigger a "major change in the makeup of Congress," unseating members "who heretofore have been foursquare on the pro-firearms side of the issue and then switched and voted the wrong way."

In fact, says, Tanya K. Metaksa, chief lobbyist for the National Rifle Association (NRA), passage of the Brady law has prompted former NRA members to rejoin the organization at five times the normal rate. "Our biggest challenge is going to be harnessing the energy of our members," she says.

Gun control experts credit law enforcement groups with their recent successes. "Not every law enforcement official agrees" that certain assault weapons should be outlawed, says Don Cahill, national legislative chairman for the Fraternal Order of Police (FOP), "but the majority of them do." Cahill says he "can understand someone from Utah or Wyoming complaining that this is not a problem, because it's not a problem in their states. But it's a problem in 75 percent of the rest of the country." Without a federal assault-weapons law, he says, "we'll have the same problem we had prior to Brady. That is, if a person can't buy a gun in one state, he'll go to another state."*

In some communities, the Brady law and the proposed assault-weapons ban don't figure to have much impact at all. For instance, Officer Denney Kelley of the Portland (Ore.) Police Bureau's Intelligence Division says Brady will have "virtually no effect on us." That's because Oregon already requires handgun purchasers to wait 15 days. Moreover, Portland and surrounding Multnomah County also have ordinances that

---

*The group is chaired by Sarah Brady, wife of James S. Brady, President Ronald Reagan's first press secretary, who was seriously wounded by a handgun during the attempted assassination of Reagan in March 1981 by John Hinckley. Brady himself is a board member of a sister group, the education oriented Center to Prevent Handgun Violence.

*The Bureau of Alcohol, Tobacco and Firearms (ATF) generally describes assault weapons as copies of military-style firearms or machine guns. They usually have a large ammunition capacity. Many military firearms are automatics, which fire several bullets each time the trigger is pulled. The versions used on the street are semiautomatics. The trigger must be pulled each time to fire a bullet.

"basically say people can't carry a lot of types of assault rifles," notes Sgt. Kathy Ferrell of the Sheriff's Office.

Though experts differ on how to combat gun violence, there's no disputing the problem's existence. In 1992, handguns were used in nearly 931,000 violent crimes—a 21 percent increase over the 1991 total of 772,000.[1]

Such figures could fuel demands for tougher state and federal gun control laws. At the same time, they're likely to stimulate firearms purchases. Experience shows the two trends often move on parallel tracks.

The assassinations of the Rev. Dr. Martin Luther King Jr. and Sen. Robert F. Kennedy, D-N.Y., inspired Congress to pass the Gun Control Act of 1968 (*see p. 512*). But shortly before the law took effect, nationwide handgun sales doubled. Similarly, soon after the House banned assault weapons, gun dealers reported panic buying of those very weapons.

Nowhere is the demand for guns of all kinds stronger than in California. Attorney General Dan Lungren reported in January that Californians bought a record 665,229 firearms in 1993, about two-thirds of them handguns. The previous California gun sales record of 559,608, set the previous year, was attributed at the time to fears generated by the Los Angeles riots. But no single event seems to have sparked the '93 sales surge.

Advocates of stronger firearms laws and their opponents are not necessarily at loggerheads. Rather, they reflect intertwined concerns about gun-related crime on the one hand and appreciation of the Second Amendment "right of the people to keep and bear Arms" on the other.

Significantly reducing firearms violence while respecting the individual right to gun ownership has always been the central challenge facing gun control advocates. As the various parties to the firearms dispute vie for popular and legislative support, there are some of the key questions being asked:

Do gun control laws curb violent crime?

Gun control advocates argue that limiting access to firearms will reduce gun-related crimes and accidental shootings. They feel, in short, that firearms themselves are the key worry.

Gun control opponents, on the other hand, believe the problem with gun-related violence rests with the person holding the gun. As the National Rifle Association puts it, "Guns Don't Kill People—People Do."

Gun fanciers say that if firearms were made hard to obtain, or even outlawed altogether, criminals still would be able to get them by theft or through the black market. But law-abiding citizens would be deprived of an effective means of self-protection against armed criminals.

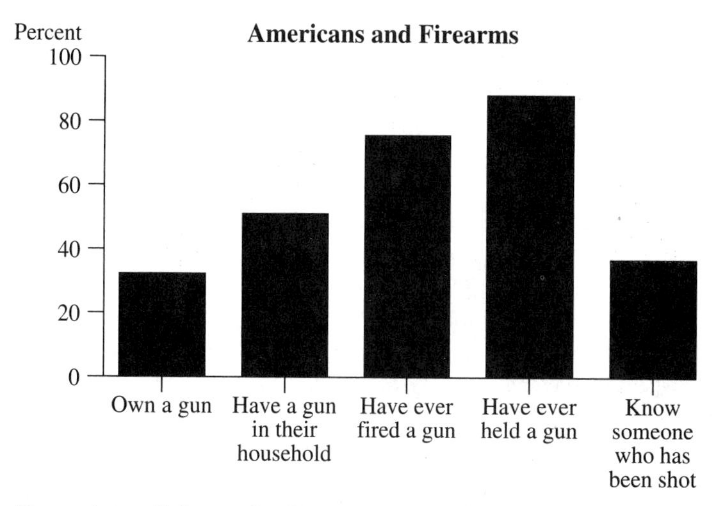

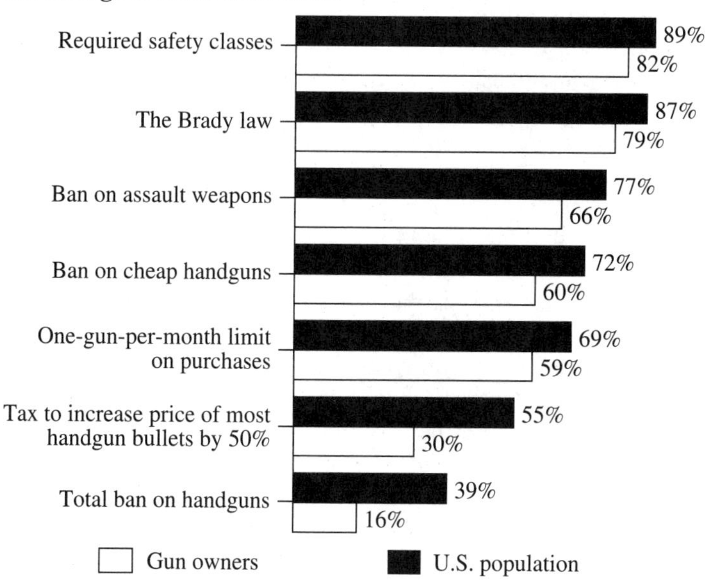

Source: USA Today*/CNN/Gallup Poll. Dec 17–21, 1993*

How Americans Feel About Gun Control. A majority of gun owners and the public at large favor stricter gun controls, including required safety classes, the Brady law and bans on assault weapons and cheap handguns, according to a national poll. But only 39 percent of the public backs a total ban on handguns.

According to Franklin E. Zimring, a law professor at the University of California-Berkeley, available evidence tends to be ambiguous. "Ample data confirm that as guns become more available, people are more likely to die during violent crimes—a connection that opponents of gun control have tried to deny," he wrote. "Research also shows that many laws do not significantly diminish the number of guns used in violence, although many advocates of gun control have assumed they would."[2]

Gun control supporters have the harder case to prove, since it's impossible to count the firearms-related crimes that did not occur because a firearm wasn't available. Still, experience with the Brady law and similar state laws is cited to back the claim that guns can be kept out of criminals' hands. The Brady law's five-day waiting period allows local police to check the prospective buyer's background. During March, the first month Brady was in effect, 375,853 inquiries about gun purchasers were made to the FBI's computerized criminal information network. Of those, 23,610—a little over 6 percent—were identified as possible felons.

Some prospective purchasers who flunked the background check doubtless turned to illegal channels, noted Northwestern University Law Professor Daniel D. Polsby, "but just as surely not all of them did."[3] To the extent that individuals with a criminal record or a history of mental illness or drug abuse are blocked from getting firearms, gun control supporters reason, crime is marginally reduced.

The Brady law "is breathing hope into this battle against crime involving firearms," declared John W. Magaw, director of the Bureau of Alcohol, Tobacco and Firearms (ATF).[4]

Gun control supporters say the proposed federal ban on assault weapons will further energize the fight against gun-related crime—and help save the lives of policemen. Two and a half years ago, Cahill recalls, several police officers were sent to arrest a Dale City, Va., man suspected of killing a policeman. One officer positioned himself behind a portable shield in front of the house. But he was killed when the suspect fired a round from an AK-47 rifle that pierced the shield and hit him in the head.

The AK-47 is one of the assault weapons that would be banned under the legislation pending in Congress. . . . If the ban had been in effect then, says Cahill, "It wouldn't have been an AK-47 that killed that officer. The suspect might have pulled a different kind of gun, and it might not have penetrated" the shield.

Gary D. Kleck, a professor of criminology at Florida State University, dismisses the assault weapons ban. "There's no conceivable way that a federal ban could save a single life or prevent a single injury," he says, "unless you're willing to believe that there are criminals committed solely to using one of these particular 19 models, and not mechanically identical models among the 600 [other] unregulated assault weapons."

Polsby concurs. A partial assault weapons ban "will not affect the crime rate," he says. "Neither will the Brady bill. The crime rate is going to be worse four or five years from now, not better. Nobody will ever credit this kind of regulation with reducing any lawless or socially destructive behavior. It's pure gesture, pure theater."

To NRA Executive Vice President Wayne R. LaPierre Jr., the proposed assault weapons ban is merely "pretend crime control by people that don't want to spend the money to give us real crime control."[5]

Does gun ownership afford protection against violent crime?

Gun enthusiasts argue that weapons kept at home deter crime. In fact, some 8 million gun owners say they have used a gun to defend themselves or their family, according to a recent poll.[6] But gun control advocates contend that household guns often are fired in anger during family fights, causing injury or death. They also note that such guns are involved in numerous suicides and accidental shootings. . . .

To resolve the issue, Arthur L. Kellerman, a physician at the University of Tennessee, and nine associates conducted a study on "Gun Ownership as a Risk Factor for Homicide in the Home." Published last fall in the respected *New England Journal of Medicine*, it concluded that "A gun kept in the home is far more likely to be involved in the death of a member of the household than it is to be used to kill in self-defense."[7]

The study evaluated 388 home homicides (half involving firearms) that occurred in the Cleveland, Memphis and Seattle areas between 1987 and 1992. A second set of 388 households in which no homicide had taken place served as a control group.

Among other things, the researchers found that 51 percent of the homicides "occurred in the context of a quarrel or a romantic triangle"; 77 percent of the victims "were killed by a relative or someone known to them"; and half of the victims died from gunshot wounds. According to the study, "the link between guns and homicide in the home was present among women as well as men, blacks as well as whites and younger as well as older people."[8]

Many gun control supporters hailed the study, saying it confirmed their warnings about the inherent hazards of firearms possession. Before long, though, other firearms experts pointed to what they termed serious flaws in the findings.

Kleck at Florida State University notes that given the study's premise, it will be assumed that "a lot of these people were killed with a gun kept in the victim's household. "But the study doesn't say a word about where the guns involved in the shooting homicides came from. Yet, it's possible the killers used a gun that was in the victim's home. But it's more likely they brought in a gun of their own."

Kleck bases this surmise on the study's finding that 54 percent of the accused killers "were total strangers to the victim or had no known relationship—certainly not a live-in relationship."

What the study actually demonstrated says Kleck is that "people who live in dangerous circumstances are more likely to acquire a gun in response to those circumstances. One of the reasons they got a gun in the first place was because they anticipated being a victim of some kind of violence."[9]

Indeed, Kellerman and his colleagues acknowledge this possibility, noting that "reverse causation" could have "accounted for some of the association we observed between gun ownership and homicide—i.e., in a limited number of cases, people may have acquired a gun in response to a specific threat." To Kleck, the disclaimer is "one of those non-operative caveats [the authors] dropped in for the sake of anticipating criticism. They don't allow it to affect their conclusions."

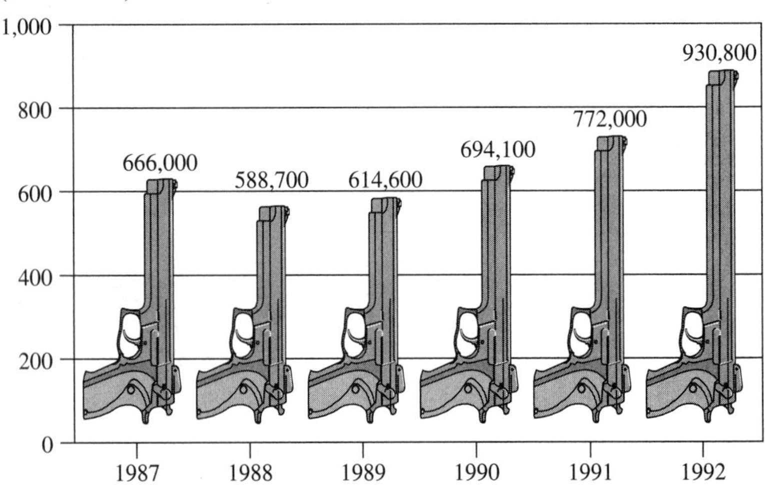

Source: Department of Justice, Bureau of Justice Statistics. May 15, 1994

Handgun Violence on the Rise. Violent crimes involving handguns increased more than 21 percent from 1991 to 1992, according to the latest figures from the Justice Department's Bureau of Justice Statistics. Handguns were used in nearly 931,000 murders, rapes, robberies and assaults in 1992, up from 772,000 in 1991.

Is the gun lobby losing its clout?

Over the years, the NRA and other pro-firearms organizations have built a reputation as one of the strongest pressure groups on Capitol Hill. Their influence stems largely from two sources: their ability to get members to bombard congressional offices with letters, faxes and phone calls demanding the defeat of hostile legislation, and their campaign contributions.

Since the 1992 election, for example, the NRA has given more than $535,000 directly to House members, including $150,000 in March. Handgun Control gave $12,000.[10] Now, though, some gun control advocates say they sense a shift of popular sentiment on firearms issues.

Noting that the NRA has "suffered some serious hits" over the past year, Handgun Control's Whitmore questions whether the nation's largest organization of gun owners "will ever be as strong as it once was." Even some NRA members "are finding fault with their leaders' policy of no compromise," she says.

Josh Sugarmana, executive director of the Violence Policy Center, cautions that "it would be hasty to declare that the witch is dead. Historically, every time it loses, there's a tendency for people to say, 'It's the end of the NRA'. That reaction is actually a testament to the organization's power." At the same time, he says, "the NRA has isolated itself to a great extent outside the mainstream [of public opinion]."

What's different now, says Sugarmann, is that "these losses are starting to accumulate. Every time a Brady bill or assault weapons ban wins approval and the sky doesn't fall, gun violence becomes easier to talk about on Capitol Hill."

According to Polsby, "there's no doubt" that the NRA is losing influence, and that the House ban on assault weapons "is a great political victory for the gun control movement." But the NRA is only part of the story, he feels. "Democracy is working itself out, in the way that it will, bringing together a motley collection of potential armies who didn't previously know of one another's existence." Through this process, Polsby says, the gun control movement has emerged as "an effective counterweight to the NRA."

Since Kleck considers the proposed assault weapons ban "a nothing piece of legislation," he doesn't think its approval by the House says anything about the NRA's influence with Congress. "The only really quantifiable indicator of NRA strength is its membership," says Kleck. "And membership has been growing, not declining. The NRA now has 3.3 million members, each paying $25 or more a year." (Handgun Control claims about 1 million members.)

Moreover, Kleck notes, most legislation concerning guns is passed at the state level, not the federal level. "That's where the NRA gets its quiet victories," he says. "The big trend of the past 20 years, virtually unreported by the national media, and only lightly reported within the respective states, has been pre-emption statutes," which bar localities from regulating firearms more strictly than state laws. . . .

"That's really significant," says Kleck. "It's like getting 100 defeats of gun control bills in each of those states, because each type of local regulation that might have been proposed in effect has been voted down already."

Notes

1. Department of Justice, U.S. Bureau of Justice Statistics, "Guns and Crime," April 1994. For background, see "Reassessing the Nation's Gun Laws," *Editorial Research Reports*, March 22, 1991, pp. 157–172.
2. Franklin E. Zimring, "Firearms, Violence and Public Policy," *Scientific American*, November 1991, p. 48.
3. Daniel D. Polsby, "The False Promise of Gun Control," *The Atlantic Monthly*, March 1994, p. 62.
4. Quoted in *The Washington Post*, March 31, 1994
5. Remarks on NBC TV's "Meet the Press," May 1, 1994
6. *USA Today* CNN Gallup Poll, published in *USA Today*, Dec. 30, 1993
7. Arthur L. Kellerman, et al., "Gun Ownership as a Risk Factor for Homicide in the Home," *The New England Journal of Medicine*, Oct. 1993 pp 1084–1091
8. *Ibid.*, p. 1087
9. For background, see "Suburban Crime," *The CQ Researcher*, Sept. 3, 1993, pp 769–792
10. In Surprising Turnaround House OKs Weapons Ban, *CQ Weekly Report*, May 7, 1994, p. 1122

The Importance of Your Research

Your job, like Worsnop's, is to help your reader understand the significance of your research. Worsnop has an advantage in that he has chosen a subject that has been under debate for many years in the United States. His strategy is to demonstrate that there are two sides to the issue with passionate views that must be heard. He also introduces statistics that ought to startle most readers into attention. However, you need not choose a subject of overwhelming importance or remarkable curiosity. Rather, you need only choose something that you have wanted to know about.

Worsnop's strategy begins with those in favor of gun control, then moves to its opponents, especially the NRA (National Rifle Association), which has been effective as a lobbying organization in Washington. The connection of guns and crimes is addressed in statistics: a rise of 21 percent from 1991 to 1992—almost 200,000 more crimes with guns. The Second Amendment to the Constitution is mentioned: the "right of the people to keep and bear Arms." And the central question is presented: how to reduce firearm violence while protecting the right of the individual to own a gun.

The subheads guide us through the rest of the article: "Do gun control laws curb violent crime?" The issue is clouded because no one can say how many crimes were not committed because a gun was not available. Opponents claim the criminals would have the guns and the law-abiding citizens would not if there were gun control. Neither side can prove its case because the argument rests on probability and supposition. The next subhead, "Does gun ownership afford protection against violent crime?" seems just as difficult to answer. Many people claim to have protected themselves with weapons; many people have been killed, sometimes with their own family guns. But, there, too, the evidence is not completely compelling on either side. The third subhead: "Is the gun lobby losing its clout?," is the only one of the three questions that can be answered readily: No. Since the National Rifle Association is the core of the gun lobby, and since it contributed $535,000 since the 1992 elections to House members, as opposed to $12,000 given by those favoring gun control, it is clear the lobby is still powerful. Moreover, the membership of the NRA has increased since 1992, to 3.3 million.

The research that went into the essay came from current newspaper reports, television interviews, and Department of Justice published statistics, as well as from important magazines such as *Atlantic Monthly, Scientific American*, and *The New England Journal of Medicine*. Some of the material came from *CQ*'s published reports. In every case, you can examine the source of the material and evaluate it as you like.

Formal Considerations

A major decision before beginning your essay concerns documentation. You may use a great deal or none, or you may adopt Worsnop's approach and use documentation sparingly. Naturally, if you are preparing an essay for a class, your instructor will give you the guidelines you will need.

In terms of form, generally you will be expected to present a typewritten paper of a specific length—usually between ten and twenty pages for a research essay. You will be expected to provide a list of works cited at the end of the essay, identifying the sources you quote or refer to. You will probably be asked to use endnotes for citations from authorities, but since the computer makes footnotes relatively easy to produce, you should check with your instructor about the proper way to prepare notes.

Handling Quotations

Quotations in a research essay show how other people, presumably experts in the field, have addressed your subject. Your own views will have evolved from your research, which usually consists of reading experts who have examined evidence at firsthand. When you wish to establish a key point, call on those experts by giving them a chance to speak for themselves in a quotation. Do the same should you wish to take issue with someone with whom you disagree: quote that person, then examine the quotation in order to question its merits. Using quotations may be very important for your essay. Some commonsense tips for quoting from sources are shown in the box.

TIPS THAT MAY HELP AS A GUIDE TO QUOTING FROM SOURCES

1. Be sparing in the number of quotations you use: you are aiming to support your argument, not to have it made by quotations.
2. Make certain that the context in which the quotation appears is accounted for in your essay: quoting out of context can completely distort the original meaning of the quotation.
3. Use quotation marks to indicate the quotation in the body of your text. If the quotation is more than forty words, indent the quotation

one tab mark from the left and one tab mark from the right of your margins: do not use quotation marks when indenting a quotation.

4. Do not quote a source without commenting on the quotation or without indicating the point of the quotation. You must always guide your reader so that the quotation will add up to something in the context in which you place it. Your own analysis of the quotation will be important to your reader.
5. Always aim to quote fairly, using the most important material from your sources. Do not set up your opponents as straw dogs by quoting the silly things they say. Argue with their strengths, not their weaknesses.

Not every quotation will need detailed analysis. Richard L. Worsnop lets those who favor gun control as well as those who oppose gun control speak for themselves without much commentary on his part. When, in his first paragraphs, he quotes Tanya Metaksa and Don Cahill, he chooses statements that clarify their position on the issues. The same is true about later quotations, which all go toward clarifying the opinions of the speakers on both sides of the issues. Worsnop does not analyze these quotations because he avoids taking a stand in the argument. His purposes are to lay out the issues and show us who holds what opinions on the key points. In other words, he provides information and it is up to us to analyze it and make up our mind as to where we stand. We need to believe that the quotations are fairly presented to us and that they accurately represent the speakers' views.

Sometimes, you will need to stitch together a quotation from several instances of a commentator's presentation. When you do so, you will have to provide the transitional phrases that make the links intelligible. Here is an example from near the end of Worsnop's essay:

> According to Polsby, "there's no doubt" that the NRA is losing influence, and that the House ban on assault weapons "is a great political victory for the gun control movement." But the NRA is only part of the story, he feels. "Democracy is working itself out, in the way that it will, bringing together a motley collection of potential allies who didn't previously know of one another's existence." Through this process, Polsby says, the gun control movement has emerged as "an effective counterweight to the NRA."

Worsnop's essential neutrality in presenting both sides of the issue helps us accept these quotations as being honestly recorded and honestly arranged. We need to feel we can trust the writer, which is one reason careful citation of sources is important. In this case we could read Polsby's article to check it out, since Worsnop's third endnote gives us the complete citation in the *Atlantic Monthly*.

Citations and Bibliography

Two sources for the proper style of citations and bibliography for research essays will help you in preparing your work. The first, for most work done in the humanities, is *MLA Handbook for Writers of Research Papers*, 4th ed. (New York: MLA, 1995). The other, for work in the social sciences and sciences, is *Publication Manual of the American Psychological Association*, 4th ed. (Washington, DC: American Psychological Association, 1994). The first of these is referred to as the MLA stylesheet, the second as the APA manual. The descriptions that follow offer some of the most essential kinds of citations in each of these formats, but you will need to refer to the publications themselves for more detail in certain cases. The reference room of your library will have both books. Be sure to ask your instructor which form of citations you should use.

MLA CITATIONS

The general rule in using the MLA style is to use as few footnotes or endnotes as possible. Citing your sources in the body of your essay is preferable to endnoting, and to make this possible you must prepare a works cited list to follow your essay. That list includes all the works, listed in alphabetical order by author, that you have occasion to quote from or refer to. Should you wish to include a list of works that you used but did not quote from or refer to, it should come after "Works Cited" and be titled "Works Consulted." These will constitute the bibliography for your essay and will guide interested readers to other works that will help them understand your topic.

When Worsnop quoted from Polsby, he provided a footnote to indicate the location of his source, but if he had a works cited list he would have used a parenthetical citation in this fashion: (Polsby 62). Generally, this is enough to point us to the source, and it avoids having the reader pause to look up an endnote. If there were two articles by Polsby in the works cited list, they would be identified by date or title in this fashion, (Polsby, "Fashion" 62). In any case, when you are in doubt try to use the simplest and clearest method of citation. When you read the essays that follow this discussion examine the ways in which the writers cite their sources, then adopt the method that seems most useful.

Your works cited list is always double-spaced and arranged alphabetically by the authors' last names. Works Cited comes at the top of the list in the manner shown below. If there is no author, then alphabetize by title within the same list. The first line of a citation is flush with the left margin, but second or third lines are indented five spaces. If you have two or more works by the same author, instead of repeating the author's name the second time, use five dashes: ——. with a period to indicate it is the same author. Here are some samples:

Works Cited

Book: single author

Ellmann, Richard. *James Joyce*. 2nd ed. New York: Oxford UP, 1982.

Book: two or more authors

Abrams, M. H., E. Talbot Donaldson, Hallett Smith, Robert M. Adams, Samuel Holt Monk, Lawrence Lipking, George H. Ford, David Daiches. *The Norton Anthology of English Literature*. 4th ed. New York: Norton, 1979.

A multivolume work

Blavatsky, H. P. *Isis Unveiled*. 2 vols. Pasadena: Theosophical UP, 1960 (orig. 1877). Vol. 2.

Essay in a collection

Parry, Benita. "*A Passage to India*: Epitaph or Manifesto?" *Critical Essays on E. M. Forster*. Ed. Alan Wilde. Boston: Hall, 1985.

Encyclopedia entry

Holman, C. Hugh. "Romanticism." *Encyclopedia Americana*. 1985 ed.

Article in a journal using continuous pagination in a volume

Marling, William. "James M. Cain's Tiger Woman." *LIT Literature Interpretation Theory* 4 (1993): 229–244.

Article in a journal that paginates each issue separately

Hecht, Anthony. "Paradise and Wilderness: The Brave New World of *The Tempest*. *The Yale Review* 81.2 (1993): 76–95.

Electronic Information Service

Fairbanks, A. Harris. "The Limits of Toulmin Logic." ERIC, 1991. ED 281 445.

Internet sources including E-mail

Lindsay, Robert K. "Electronic Journals of Proposed Research." *Ejournal* 1.1 (1991):n. Pag. Online. Internet. 10 Apr. 1991.

Angier, Natalie. "Chemists Learn Why Vegetables Are Good for You." *New York Times* 13 Apr. 1993, late ed.: C1. *New York Times Online*. Online. Nexis. 10 Feb. 1994.

Jacobus, Lee. <jacobus@uconnvm.uconn.edu> "Wit in Milton." May 1997. Personal email. (17 May 1997).

Interview

Boer, Charles. Telephone interview. 3 Dec. 1993.

APA Citations

The APA Manual uses many of the same techniques as the MLA, but with a few differences. At the end of the essay is a list of sources titled "References." All parenthetical citations are keyed to the list of references. The preferred method of citation is parenthetical in the body of your text. Place the author's name and year of publication in parentheses where you use the reference (Zygmont, 1988). If there is no author identified, use the first two or three words of the title and the year. Use quotation marks for an article or chapter title and use underlining (or italics) if it is a book.

The list of references uses the last name, first initials, date in parenthesis, the title, the place of publication, and the full name of the press. Article and book titles begin with a capital letter, but subsequent words do not begin with capitals unless they follow a colon or are a proper name. For journal names, capitalize the first letter of each word. Each item in the citation ends with a period.

References

Book: single author

Tuveson, E. L. (1982). *The avatars of thrice great hermes*. Lewisburg: Bucknell University Press.

Book: two or more authors or editors

Read, H. & Mountford, C. P. (Eds.) (1955). *Australia: Aboriginal painting from Arhnhemland.* UNESCO World Art Series. New York: Columbia University Press.

Essay in a collection

Spivak, C. E. & Albuquerque, E. X. (1982). Dynamic properties of the nicotinic and acetlycholine receptor ionic channel complex: Activation and blockade. In I. Hanin & A. M. Goldberg (Eds.), *Progress in cholinic biology: Model cholinergic synapses* (pp. 323–357). New York: Raven.

Encyclopedia entry

Lycurgus. (1910). *Encyclopedia Britannica.* (11th ed.).

Newspaper article

Barreca, G. (1993, December 14). Why husbands hate sundays. *Hartford Courant*, p. 1.

Journal article

Ong, A. (1990). State versus islam: Malay families, women's bodies and the body politic in Malaysia. *American Ethnologist, 17*, 253–276.

Article in a journal that paginates each issue separately

Anwar, Z. (1990). Veiled threats. *Far Eastern Economic Review, 147* (4), 32–33.

Report from Government Printing Office (GPO)

National Institute of Drug Abuse. (1979). *Perspectives on the history of psychoactive substance abuse.* (DHEW Publication No. ADM 79-810.) Washington, DC: U.S. Government Printing Office.

Article from an electronic information service

Rumelhart, D. E. & Norman, D. A. (1983). *Representation in memory.* (Report NO. ONR-8302; UCSD-CHIP 116). San Diego: University of California, Center for Human Information Processing. (ERIC Document Reproduction Service NO. ED 235 770.)

These sample citations, for both MLA and APA, will help you find the proper way to cite most of your research, but you must realize that unusual sources will demand that you go to the MLA Stylesheet or the APA Manual, both cited above, for more detail.

Putting Information in Order

The problems of citation are sometimes vexing, and they are at one and the same time both important and minor. Citations are important because they authenticate your research and help others follow your footsteps; they are minor because they serve only to point your reader to your sources. The sources themselves are significant because you can have no serious essay without good research. But it is also true that you can spoil an interesting essay by stumbling over methods of citation, by citing too much or too little, or by inaccurate quotation and citation. One good rule to follow is: Be consistent in your methods of citation. Keep in mind that you are serving your reader by citing accurately and well and you are serving yourself by providing all you would need for your own future work—whether it might be a revision of your current essay or a new essay on a related subject.

The most important value of research is its capacity to change your mind and expand your own vision. Some writers ask what they should do if their research contradicts the thesis they had established when they started writing. The answer is simple: Give thanks and change your thesis. The point is that good research *ought* to change your mind about things. You do not conduct research to prove what you already think is true. You conduct it to find out what really is true—whether the truth agrees with your early vision or not. Research should be conducted with a mind open to new possibilities. When that is the case, the potential for making discoveries will stimulate you and help make your work interesting to others.

Index